Navigating Ethnicity

HUMAN GEOGRAPHY IN THE TWENTY-FIRST CENTURY
ISSUES AND APPLICATIONS
Series Editor: Barney Warf, University of Kansas

Human geography is increasingly focused on real-world problems. Applying geographic concepts to current global concerns, this series focuses on the urgent issues confronting us as we move into the new century. Designed for university-level geography and related multidisciplinary courses such as area studies, global issues, and development, these textbooks are richly illustrated and include suggestions for linking to related Internet resources. The series aims to help students to better understand, integrate, and apply common themes and linkages in the social and physical sciences and in the humanities, and, by doing so, to become more effective problem solvers in the challenging world they will face.

Navigating Ethnicity

Segregation, Placemaking, and Difference

David H. Kaplan

ROWMAN & LITTLEFIELD
Lanham • Boulder • New York • London

Published by Rowman & Littlefield
A wholly owned subsidiary of The Rowman & Littlefield Publishing Group, Inc.
4501 Forbes Boulevard, Suite 200, Lanham, Maryland 20706
www.rowman.com

Unit A, Whitacre Mews, 26-34 Stannary Street, London SE11 4AB,
United Kingdom

British Library Cataloguing in Publication Information Available

Library of Congress Cataloging-in-Publication Data Available

ISBN 978-1-5381-0188-9 (cloth : alk. paper)
ISBN 978-1-5381-0189-6 (pbk. : alk. paper)
ISBN 978-1-5381-0190-2 (electronic)

∞™ The paper used in this publication meets the minimum requirements of
American National Standard for Information Sciences—Permanence of Paper
for Printed Library Materials, ANSI/NISO Z39.48-1992.

Printed in the United States of America

Dedicated to the Memory of
Susan Wiley Hardwick
An Extraordinary Ethnic Geographer

Contents

Preface

This book started out as a blur. All of my professional life has involved the study of ethnicity, and I had long wanted to write something definitive on ethnicity and how ethnic communities utilize space. When I was given a chance to write something, I jumped. Yet while the individual pieces were more or less coherent—various aspects related to the ethnic experience—I stumbled at the task of putting these together in a logical way. So the project lingered and lingered while I initiated and completed several other things. It turned out that waiting was a good thing. The idea of what I wanted to address in this book eventually resolved into focus, and the individual pieces found their appropriate place.

Perhaps the genesis of this book is telling, since ethnicity itself is something of a puzzle. It covers so many cases; it is described in so many different ways. There is no single academic literature to consult, but rather there are several—none of which cross-communicate. The ethnic literature in the United States stands separated from that of Canada, Australia, and the United Kingdom. This Anglophone literature is in turn distinct from the literature in the different European contexts and from scholarship that covers all the incredibly interesting situations in Asia, Africa, and South America. This is not to mention the multidisciplinarity of ethnic studies, particularly when considered along with race and national identity, which I likewise explore in these chapters.

This book differs from most other books on ethnicity. First of all, it is intentionally geographical. While abstract concepts of ethnicity can and should be explored, it all ends with how ethnicity plays out on the ground. The original notion was to write a book on segregation, a follow up to an earlier manuscript (Kaplan and Holloway 1998). But the more I thought about it, the more I realized that ethnic geography reveals multiple spatial arrangements. In fact, the majority of ethnic imprints do not involve segregation, strictly speaking, but rather variations of clustering.

Second, this book is intended to examine ethnicity and space systematically. Many books examine different cases—in fact, I have edited books just like that (Kaplan and Li 2006). Here I try to develop some of the most important aspects of ethnicity: from what the term means, to its historical changes, to its causes, its consequences, and how it is changing. In this, I use several examples. My own research has covered Montreal, Minnesota's Twin Cities, Northeast Ohio, Northern Italy, and Paris. I have also been fortunate to guide graduate students who have studied several other cases and places. As someone most interested in the universe of ethnicity, I introduce many other cases as well. Although I endeavor to present a broad spectrum of cases, the reader will notice that several world regions are underrepresented. As my knowledge base grows, I hope to rectify this in the future.

Third, I have long believed that ethnicity must be thought of contingently. The position, definitions, behaviors, and attitudes toward and by members of an ethnic group vary considerably, depending on the context. Ethnicity is also something that intersects with other identifiers: class, gender, age, residence. All these characteristics must be factored in when thinking about the role of ethnicity. That is why I have insisted on examining how group and context come together to create a particular condition.

Because this book represents a professional lifetime of learning, there are many people whom I must thank. At Johns Hopkins, where I received my undergraduate degree, two outstanding professors opened up the ideas behind ethnic geography. Andrew Cherlin, a sociologist, first introduced me to the ideas of the Chicago School and those who came afterward. Kathleen Verdery, an anthropologist, showed me what made ethnicity salient in some contexts and not so important in others. In graduate school, my interest in both ethnicity and nationalism was guided by my advisors in geography: Bob Sack and Martin Cadwallader. I would also like to credit Steve Holloway, with whom I worked on ethnicity and segregation for several years. My longtime editor at Rowman & Littlefield, Susan McEachern, has shown an incredible degree of patience as she waited year after year for this book to be finished. In preparing this work, I have received help and photos from my former students: Christabel Devadoss, Weronika Kusek, Dorris Scott,

Jim Smith, and Kathleen Woodhouse. Much of the line art in this book was rendered by Jennifer Mapes, who immeasurably improved many of the figures. Veronica Jurgena enhanced the language and syntax as she professionally prepared this manuscript for production. Veronica also helped in another way. As my wife, she had the dubious honor of living through its oh-so-long gestation and completion. But it is now completed, and I feel that it has been well worth the time.

1

⌇

Something about Ethnicity

Once in a while, a word comes along that can transform how we think about the places and people around us. The power of such a word lies less in its description of something new, and more in its ability to structure our perspective, promoting a shift in our understanding and even in our system of values. Such a word is *ethnicity*. Go back 70 or 80 years—this term did not exist. Examine the classic texts of the founders of the Chicago School of urban sociology, with their thick descriptions of human ecology, teeming immigrant neighborhoods, and now classic models of urban morphology; nobody discussed "ethnicity" or "ethnic groups." In fact, the word ethnicity did not make an appearance until 1933, in the Oxford English Dictionary (Glazer and Moynihan 1975). Instead scholars and lay people alike employed terms like "race" and "nationality" to carve out a specific population of people, characterized by certain cultural attributes, ancestry, and other factors that made them different from others. These terms, particularly race, nation, or tribe, were applied in order to separate groups of people.

Yet despite its ambiguity, ethnicity was a powerful idea. In a larger sense, it animated the notion of self-determination, the belief that every group of people had the right to establish a country of their own, and was a basis for the remaking of the world after World War I. In a smaller sense, the term ethnicity reaffirmed the distinctions between people within a society that cross-cut differences of social class. The "American dilemma," which Gunnar Myrdal (1944) eloquently depicted as the crevasse fracturing mid-century U.S. society, was the dilemma of race. Today, ethnicity

1

defines the world better than any other phenomenon. Of course, this can be awkwardly tethered to political economic ideas, but somehow ethnicity goes beyond economics. Look around the world as it exists today, and the vast majority of conflicts are ethnic in character. The conflicts in Iraq and Syria, where the Islamic State captures and enslaves people that they decry as heretics: these are ethnic. The conflicts within Europe, as refugees from the Middle East seeking a better life are met by people who see these newcomers as a threat: these are ethnic as well. The long-simmering tensions between police and residents within such inner cities and inner suburbs as Ferguson, Missouri: these are also ethnic. The rallying cries of many U.S. politicians: these are also ethnic. Run down the list of the hot-button issues that distress the world today, and these issues—whether they be deemed "racial," or "national," or "religious"—are in fact ethnic issues.

The importance of ethnicity arises first because of its role as a divider. If we consider how humanity may be classified, ethnicity and its variations are among the most critical for how people see one other. The creation of "others," a hallmark of self-definition, lies in defining groups of people distinct from one's own. The second reason is because of ethnicity's role as a uniter. It sorts individuals with other individuals, provides them with a sense of community, a variety of resources, and the cultural means of transcending the self. Third is ethnicity's position as a fundamentally geographical notion. The two dominant ideas in human geography—space and place—are reflected and reinforced by ethnicity. Ethnicity is not distributed randomly, but instead defines regions at all geographical scales. The geography of ethnicity has an important role to play in other aspects of life, and these spatial effects can determine the outcomes of members of that ethnicity. Ethnic groups also transform the places they occupy. The establishment of residential communities, the development of businesses and services, and the articulation of a network of institutions transform places to reflect a particular ethnicity and manifest how diversity is articulated geographically.

How, then, to think about ethnicity, especially in light of its many uses and the many contexts in which the term carries resonance? This chapter lays the groundwork by first considering the history and definitions of ethnicity as counterposed with other terms used to depict group difference. Just how ethnicity comes about relates to basic theoretical approaches regarding the nature of ethnic groups. This is followed by discussion of how the notion of ethnicity is deployed in several societies, and how different societies grapple with multiculturalism. Finally, I look at some of the basic tensions involved in a discussion of ethnic groups and ethnic group relations.

EXPLORATIONS OF ETHNICITY ONE HUNDRED YEARS BACK

At the beginning of the last century, scholars turned their attention to ethnicity. True, they did not invoke the exact term "ethnicity," but they were interested in particular groupings of people, whether they considered them nationalities or races. While ethnicity was a worldwide phenomenon, brutally manifest in colonial societies where divisions were stark and inequality intense, it was within the United States that the most sustained examination of this phenomenon came about, in a manner both reflective and groundbreaking.

The reasoning was bound up with a confluence of factors. The university system, one based around systematic research, was taking form in the United States. Universities, which had once imported their professors from continental Europe, now began to train graduate students rigorously in the development of new methodologies and new inquiries. The diversification of specialized bodies of knowledge, particularly in the social sciences, led to our present-day disciplines of sociology, psychology, anthropology, political science, economics, history, and geography. This in turn created strong incentives to investigate social phenomena in a sustained and systematic way. The United States at this time was experiencing two massive transformations. The flow of immigration, primarily from Europe but from some other places as well, was reaching a peak. Urbanization, fueled by the transformation of America as a modern industrial power, came to its own ascendance as the country grew to become a predominantly urban society. The great cities that developed along the Eastern Seaboard and in the Midwest attracted most of the new immigrant streams and rendered many of them socially and culturally unrecognizable, at least according to those who looked with alarm at these changes. Finally, there was the presence of race: that immovable and persistent color line that divided blacks from whites, to the overwhelming disadvantage of the former.

Scholars at the time—representing the new social sciences—could note the social divisions, and comment as well on what these all meant on the ground. From these divisions could be seen the inevitable tension of the insider versus the outsider. W. E. B. Du Bois was among the few African Americans who had gained not just an education, but was the first to obtain a doctorate. As the ultimate insider into America's racial quagmire, Du Bois was keenly aware of ethnicity and separation. He also understood the importance of context, as he had experienced some of the differences in the conditions of blacks within different parts of the country, growing up in Massachusetts, attending college in Tennessee, and teaching in Atlanta (Horne 2009). Du Bois wrote many books, but his first was *The Philadelphia Negro*, which was the first case study of a black community, infused with the type of empirical evidence that would become a common feature of sociology. For Du Bois, the stigmatization of blacks had a sociohistorical basis (and not a biological foundation, as so many at the time thought), and while he was clear-eyed about the present conditions of blacks, he was also quite optimistic about the future. To him, it was inevitable that many of the racial separations of his time would blur and disappear (Du Bois [1908] 1980). In a new world, based on economic linkages and globalization (just as much a factor then as a factor today), "if the United States expects to take her place among the new nations . . . then certainly she has got right here in her own land to find out how to live in peace and prosperity with her own black citizens" (Du Bois [1908] 1980, 32). These aspirations would render segregation all but impossible.

Following on the heels of Du Bois's study of a black community was the work of sociologists at the University of Chicago. This institution, founded in 1891 as Chicago had attained the status of the country's premier interior city and major destination for immigrants, became the premier center for the new study of sociology and a place where research on the local community was encouraged. From this vantage point, it is interesting to see the extent to which the study of race and ethnicity in the city dominated early research. The first academic luminary at Chicago was William I. Thomas, and it was through his massive study entitled *The Polish Peasant in Europe and America* that Thomas introduced many of the principles of rigorous empirical research based on study of letters, autobiographical data, and news clippings (but not interviews). Thomas's decision to study immigration reflected his view that "immigration was a burning question," and he wanted to determine "what relation their home mores and norms had to their adjustment and maladjustment in America" (quoted in Bulmer 1984, 46). This study examined the Polish cultural group in two distinct contexts (rural Poland and urban Chicago), and attempted to show the role of institutions in maintaining community. Thomas built up his analysis by looking at the community itself, as well as the supporting organizations such as the Polish press, voluntary associations, and different educational institutions (Bulmer 1984). This was a beginning departure from the biological notions of race—which were being applied to Poles as they were to other eastern and southern Europeans. Another aspect of this study was tremendously revealing in that it explicitly compared the role of context in shaping ethnicity. Poles, whose lives were shaped by tradition in their home country, came to the United States and behaved entirely differently in an urban setting. Of course, they were also perceived differently from the outside, and this shaped their experience as well.

The most outside perspective on early twentieth-century American urban ethnicity came from the renowned German social theorist, Max Weber. Weber is known best for foundational work on the costs of bureaucracy, the interplay between various sources of power, and the Protestant ethic. In 1904, he spent time in the American South and could not help noticing the manner by which race—especially as it applied to African Americans—was socially constructed. The fact that the slightest measure of African ancestry marked an individual as wholly black showed the extent to which race was a chimera, but one with tragic consequences. He was also confronted with ethnicity, particularly when visiting New York and Chicago, where he noticed that diversity was everywhere in a manner not seen in European cities (whose "immigrants" were more likely to come from the nearby countryside). To Weber, these distinctions were a product of social, economic, and political structures rather than some inherent aspect of biology. It was these processes that transformed incipient ethnic attributes into tangible communities (Stone 2003). It was also his observations that showed how ethnicity was situated within systems of power. The creation of racial categories allowed the poor whites of the South to feel superior, despite their low socioeconomic class, and displaced the hostility they may have expressed toward the wealthy landholding class and directed it toward the one group more miserable than themselves. Weber's other writing examined so-called pariah groups, of which the preeminent example came from the Jewish population in German and other European cities, but which Weber also generalized to other groups in other contexts, anticipating middleman minorities (Stone 2003).

So it is with these three scholars, representative of the emerging social science of one hundred or more years ago, that we can see the ideas of ethnicity take shape. The clearest idea was that ethnicity (and race) is constructed. It has no biological basis, running counter to the rhetoric of this era. This does not mean that it is less significant—in fact, the social construction of ethnicity makes it even more salient because it is implicated in systems of hierarchy and power. The second idea was that institutions above all had a tremendous impact on the nature and potency of ethnic ties. These are what helped to define ethnicity in a variety of different contexts. Not being geographers, none of these thinkers dwelled explicitly on the importance of space or location, but location was a background in all of these studies and observations. The final idea was the importance of context, and the structures embedded within each context, that shaped ethnicity in a particular place and rendered it into a contingent phenomenon. This crucial idea held that "ethnicity" varied considerably in contour and salience, depending on the situation at hand, and in the way an ethnic group's conditions intersected with other social categories.

CONTEMPORARY VIEWS OF ETHNICITY

By the 1960s, the term _ethnic_ began to gain some currency as a way to describe group differences. While new in usage, ethnic was an old term, stemming from the ancient Greek, which related to common descent. In the Middle Ages, ethnic came to mean "heathen" or "pagan"—in other words, neither Christian nor Jewish (Conversi 2004; Eriksen 1997; Royce 1982). But it was not a term that truly categorized groups until the late 1960s when, in well-known volumes like Frederick Barth's (1969) _Ethnic Groups and Boundaries_, the use of "ethnic" became popular in academic circles.

By the 1970s in the United States, the idea of ethnicity had completely taken hold outside of academia as well. Whereas race had been a category imposed and derided, ethnicity was something to celebrate. Ethnic studies departments opened up in universities. Ethnicity became more prominent in popular culture, especially on television. Ethnic jokes, ostensibly all in good fun, were made. Ethnic towns and neighborhoods—whatever their actual authenticity—fashioned themselves as places of interest, even as tourist destinations. The heightened importance of the ethnic categorization took hold as a third-generation phenomenon, at least in the United States, and was primarily used in reference to people who had descended from European immigrants. The first generation of immigrants, arriving from the 1880s until cut off by 1924's restrictive anti-immigrant legislation, had settled in cities, often creating for themselves "worlds within worlds" (Howe 1976). The second generation, those children of immigrants, sought to escape their ethnic identity and to wholeheartedly enter American society and culture (Gordon 1964). It was the third generation, seen as embracing their grandparents' immigrant past, who came to define themselves based on their national heritage (Novak 1972; Greeley 1974). We can argue over the authenticity in this search for ethnicity. After all, it occurred at a time when finding oneself was a national obsession, and a television miniseries like _Roots_, which dramatized the search of a black American for his African heritage, sparked an enormous interest in genealogical research. But rather than fading away as a major source of identity, ethnicity continued to be a prominent marker even as the ethnic heritage of subsequent generations becomes more and more complex. In many respects, it has even broadened as the United States has become increasingly diverse. The white ethnic groups of the 1970s have been joined by rapidly growing immigrant and second-generation groups from Asia, South and Central America, Africa, and even Europe.

Ethnicity also became a more important concept in other societies as well, although the terms and connotations differed quite a bit. In other settler societies such as Canada, Australia, New Zealand, and several South American countries, cultural divisions between the native populations and the European colonials were present from the start. As with the United States, slavery in many South American and Caribbean countries introduced an additional ethnic strain into the existing population milieu. And these settler societies also experienced waves of immigration that added even more complexity. Perhaps the more intriguing cases have come about in societies in which the dominant population has lived in a place for a much longer period of time—countries in Africa, Europe, and Asia. Most such societies developed with the intrinsic differences between separate populations who followed historical cultural practices, lived in distinct regions, and often spoke different languages. In some countries, the decline of empire and the building of nations has prompted more plural societies; in some instances, this has led to greater national uniformity. In other cases, most notably in Africa, completely separate groups were thrown together as arbitrarily drawn colonies later became countries. Perhaps most surprising is that many of these older non-settler societies—unaccustomed to immigration—have experienced recent flows of immigration, leading to more diversity than was the case before.

THE MANY FLAVORS OF "ETHNICITY"

In this book, I will be using the term *ethnicity* in a very broad sense. This makes sense because ethnicity categorizes peoples based on cultural difference (whether real or perceived). Like divisions of peoples by class, age, or gender, ethnicity is a fundamental mode of classification. Compared to other possible terms, ethnicity captures a wider spectrum of difference: it can include groups that are perceived as physically distinct—that is, racial groups—but also groups that are distinguished by a variety of other, non-physical measures such as differences in language, religion, or heritage. The notion of ethnicity also carries a great deal more flexibility, for it is quite possible to conceive of ethnic groups shifting over time, and for ethnic identification to change across generations (Nagel 1994).

Ethnicity emerged from several possible terms that share with it significant content, and yet offer inexact substitutes (Fenton 2003). When we are speaking about ethnicity, we are speaking about race; we are speaking about nation, tribe, and immigrant nationality; we are speaking about religious and language groups: and about all the other ways in which the essential meaning of ethnicity has been defined. However, the terminology that is used in describing ethnicity is an important indicator of how ethnicity is applied in various contexts. For example, a term like nation denotes a group of people who aspire to form an independent state, whereas a word like race connotes judgments about intelligence, character, and motivation.

Nation is among the oldest terms used to depict a culturally distinct group. Like ethnicity, it is defined ambiguously and has changed its meaning over time. In classical and medieval times, nations referred to peoples coming from somewhere else, and who were clearly distinct from the native populations. The Latin root word for nation (*nasci*) means "to be born," and so the idea of a nation was of a group of people having a separate ancestry (Connor 1978). As opposed to our usage of nation today, historical accounts might discuss the presence of separate nations within cities in much the same way that we would describe an immigrant group. The ideology of nationalism, which came about in the nineteenth century, added the belief of a distinct ancestry, and charged it with political meaning (Smith 1991). The term nation shares many common features with ethnicity, even deriving from similar linguistic roots, but it is now bound up with aspects of statecraft and is usually considered at a larger geographical scale. The idea of nation goes beyond simply cultural distinctiveness and group awareness, and veers into the political project of self-determination. Defined nations see themselves as a people in possession of or in search of their own political state (Kedourie 1993).

Terms like nationality, national minority, and a related use of ancestry have also been employed as designators of group difference, particularly in Eastern Europe and the former Soviet Union (Le Vine 1997). While sharing the same root as nation, *nationality* denotes a culturally distinct population, but does not necessarily include a political agenda. In fact, unlike nation, which is defined and bounded from within, nationality is often used by governments to designate certain populations. Morning (2008) showed that nationality was second only to ethnicity in use by government statistical agencies to enumerate cultural groups. The former Soviet Union described its cultural differences in terms of nationality—well over one hundred separate designations—and the practice persists. Soviet officials were certainly not interested in encouraging each of these separate nationality groups to form their own countries. A term related to nationality is *ancestry*. This is used most commonly in the United States, where the census designates ancestry as primarily a measure of descent. It does not mean more than an indicator of the country or continent that one's ancestors came from and, while a particular ancestry is clearly linked with an ethnic affiliation, it is a far more tenuous connection. A good example would be the ancestry of people originally from Vietnam, who might be either ethnically Vietnamese or ethnically Chinese.

Of course, *race* is the term that still makes the greatest claim to separate meaning. Race has continued to shape our vernacular, where the configurations of what constitute a race vary historically and by location. And though racism long ago ceased to be socially acceptable in its crudest forms, it festers to this day in many blatant and subtle ways. Ethnicity has often been used along with, but apart from, race. Ethnicity appears in our informal discussions, policy papers, and scholarly accounts. Perhaps the most prominent journal studying the phenomenon of ethnicity is titled *Ethnic and Racial Studies*. Why the terms are different is largely in how they have been used and what they are supposed to represent. The idea of racial distinction is an old one, though the use of the term race did not come into play until the eighteenth century in order to fashion a hierarchy of peoples based on physical characteristics (Smedley 1997). It was used primarily as a justification for a system of slavery based on a presumed biological inferiority, a break from prior societies in which slaves were not of any particular type. Race came to distinguish Africans, Indians, and Europeans—and was later extended to categorize other peoples. Prior to this, there was the idea of *color* as a signifier, with a "color line" separating whites from black or non-white peoples (Nightingale 2012).

Far more than any other designator of group difference, racial distinctions, varying widely by context, have been perceived as entirely natural, physically measurable, and unchangeable (Fenton 2003). The word race has always carried with it the idea of sharp biological difference. The notion of color was still significant here, with color wheels employed to assess precise skin tones. Late nineteenth-century anthropologists also measured facial features with calipers in their scientific search for human racial difference, leading to the establishment of racial hierarchies, a eugenics movement, marriage restrictions, justified discrimination, and even genocide. In this, they were following the notion that race fit within the overall "great chain of being" that ranked all organisms, terrestrial and celestial. Designated racial groups, defined by physiognomy, were placed within this overall ranking (Stepan 1982). Later maps would show how the world's "races" were distributed (see figure 1.1).

While we still use race as a means of distinguishing some social group, the application of this term has shifted widely. The United States persistently divided "white" and "black" populations, categories tarred by slavery and subjection. The idea of a racial hierarchy was so powerful that immigrants coming to the United States were forced to fit into the system somehow. They were not considered black, but they were not quite white either. Virulent racism against the Irish, for example, was often manifested in portrayals that equated them to the "negro race." Later groups that arrived—Italians, Slavs, and Jews—each represented a race as well. Late nineteenth- and early twentieth-century Europeans used race to distinguish populations from each other. Some even argued for racial purity or eugenics in order to improve the genetic stock. Such depictions carried a harsh edge. Pooling people into separate racial categories prompted racist attitudes, such as the intelligence testing that emerged to "prove" that some groups were simply inferior (Gould 1996). These

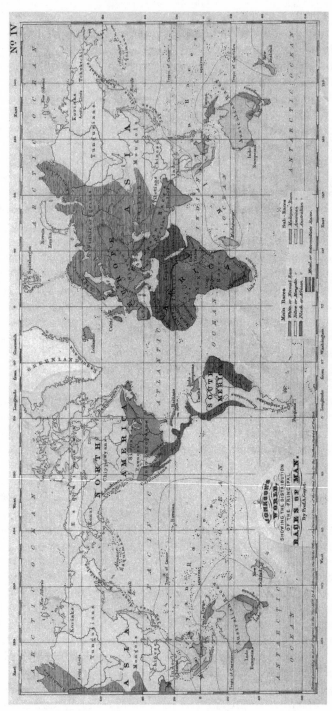

Figure 1.1.   One of several maps printed in the early to mid-twentieth century that looked at the distribution of "races" in the world.

divisions also implied impermeable biological boundaries between each group, as membership in a race could not be changed; it was transmitted from parent to child.

Race is no longer considered a serious biological concept. We look back at the racial designations of the past and the quest for racial purity with a mixture of contempt and revulsion. But race persists as a powerful social concept. Within the United States, the black-white template continues to hold sway, enough so that many individuals still feel compelled to put themselves on a particular racial "team," and a president with a Kenyan father and an English-ancestry mother is described as "black." Certainly, the idea of race exists within the census categories, which compel researchers and policymakers to utilize so-called racial categories. But it is slowly being replaced by a paradigm of multiple and hybrid "races" (Omi 2001).

Several other terms are used, and while these are popular in some contexts, they call up a variety of connotations. One such term is *tribe*, which has been traditionally used to designate a group of people, linked by common descent and by cultural and social bonds. Tribe could be seen as synonymous for ethnic group, and is in fact a preferred usage in several African countries, but because it has been much more commonly employed by Europeans to describe non-European groups—often in unflattering ways—the word has taken on a somewhat condescending connotation (Green 2006). *Community* is a softer term that is sometimes used to designate a group of culturally distinct people, but it tends to be far less fixed. The term *minority* most often describes a culture group. In this case, the term denotes that the group in question is numerically smaller than the major group in a society, although the term also suggests some degree of social or political disadvantage that accrues to the minority group.

All these terms share a common core of meaning, and can often be used as rough synonyms. However, they do differ at the margins, and carry distinct implications. A word like nation is quite appropriate and useful for dealing with peoples who make up a country, or who wish to form a country. But it does not carry the full spectrum of groups covered by ethnicity, and it adds a political objective to the group in question. A term like race, so commonly used several decades ago, has been used to describe all sorts of groups with the idea that the differences that separate this group are powerful and persist across generations. But race suffers from an inflexible definition, and a lot of unfortunate baggage. Other terms also seem less able to capture the full range of group identities, or project negative connotations. While I will also be using many of these other terms in this book as circumstances dictate, ethnicity is the word most used—the umbrella term that covers all the others.

WHAT ARE THE CRITERIA?

Coming up with a clear and consistent definition of ethnicity or an ethnic group is no easy task. Even the authoritative *Harvard Encyclopedia of
American Ethnic Groups* admitted that there is no agreement on a precise
definition of ethnicity, although there are certainly many contenders
(Peach 1983). One issue lies in who is doing the defining. As with any
group, an ethnic group can be defined internally by its own members,
or externally by outsiders. Royce (1982) describes the self-delineation
as an internal boundary drawn by members of a given group and the
criteria selected as to who is and who is not a member of this group.
How others delineate the group is an external boundary, made up of a
separate set of criteria. Even the larger dimensions of these criteria may
be at odds, and the external depictions in particular can be erroneous.
Efforts to describe individuals as "Muslims," for instance, may mistake region of origin for religion, as many people emigrating from the
Middle East have historically been Christian. A group's membership is
made up of this double boundary—internal plus external—but it is a
boundary that does not always align and, even if it does, it subjects the
group definition to different sets of standards (Royce 1982). Within the
internal boundary itself, the group's own definition may encompass
a fair amount of diversity, differences that are often obscured when a
group is defined from the outside.

Another aspect of definition entails the context within which any group
is defined. Nagel (1994) describes most ethnic identities as layered. There
are many distinct scales at which a given identity either diversifies—as
one moves down the scale—or consolidates. Scholars who speak of "panethnicity" (Espiritu 1992) are mostly talking about this process. As an
example, Mexican American identity at one level may amalgamate into
a Latino identity at a higher level of consideration. Likewise, a shift in
context can alter the salient level of ethnic identification, from Chinese
American in a small town to Taiwanese in a bigger city with many co-
ethnic residents. Students arriving from various countries in Africa to
study in the United States, some of whom later decide to remain in the
country, shift their self-identification as the context demands (Hume
2008). These scales of identification range from tribal, to "national," to
pan-African. In major cities with several African immigrant groups, students are able to utilize a "national" identity, though tribal identities are
often too specific. Many U.S. college towns, while diverse compared to
other American communities, have few people who hail from Africa, and
so a process of consolidation renders a tribal identity that is quite salient
at home into a more pan-ethnic "African" identity here. More problem-

atic for many people of African origin, and who appear as racially black, is how they navigate the persistent racial divide that marks life in the United States. For first-generation immigrants coming from African or Caribbean countries, it can be hard to avoid the racial divide; for the children of such immigrants, it may be nearly impossible, as members of the group are defined simply as "black" (Chacko 2003).

Next, we need to think about the kind of attributes that make up any ethnic definition. While ethnicity intersects with aspects of political ideology or social class, we know that this is an entirely different phenomenon. The basis of an ethnic group must be related to its cultural attributes (Peach 1983). In regard to what goes into an ethnic definition, Nagel (1994) has used the metaphor of a shopping cart. The construction of the ethnic boundary is the actual shape and size of the cart. What the cart contains determines the relevant contents or attributes of an ethnic identity. Most important is that the contents can change—as people throw things out and add things in—far more easily than the actual cart itself. This metaphor helps to inform how ethnicity is described. Among the myriad definitions—Isajiw (1974) considered a possible 27 meanings—come separate possible attributes that might go into the hypothetical shopping cart. One set of attributes includes "objective" criteria like common ancestry, religion, physical attributes (race), and language. Leaving aside the problem of how "pure" these characteristics are, they can mostly be measured through self-identification and are primarily cultural attributes.

Isajiw (1974) and others like Peach (1983) have also included items that would be much harder to pin down, yet could manifest a much deeper sense of ethnic attachment. These more subjective elements involve a feeling of peoplehood, common values, and a sense of close community with other co-ethnics (Royce 1982). These are critical to how ethnicity is defined internally, since ethnic groups cannot simply be sliced and diced according to some arbitrary definition and, most critically, the key salient attributes vary by group. Overall, members of an ethnic group need to feel that there is some level of commonality that keeps them together. Here again the double boundaries become significant. A relentless categorization of a group by the state or outside society—especially when combined with uneven power relations and patterns of discrimination—will undoubtedly engender internal feelings of solidarity, even if these ties were not terribly strong to begin with. As R. Jenkins (1994, 203) argues, the "experience of categorization may strengthen existing group identity through a process of resistance and reaction." Ethnic ties can also be buttressed from the inside via a myriad of formal and informal networks, institutions, and goals.

HOW DID ETHNIC GROUPS ORIGINATE?

How do ethnic groups emerge, and how are the boundaries that separate one group of people—one sociocultural community—from another formed? Ethnic groups exist somewhere between the self and all of humankind. But between these two poles lie much fluctuation and uncertainty. Much of this has to do with how boundaries change depending on context, as described above, but it also has much to do with how ethnic groups are formed in the first place. While the debate continues, most scholars have settled into three or, perhaps more accurately, two-and-a-half camps.

On one side are the primordialists, who argue that ethnic groups contain a common cultural kernel that has persisted for generations and that creates a far more essential basis of difference. While such a philosophy could verge into a belief in genetic, biological differences, as was popular among race theorists in the past, primordialists disavow the biological link and think in terms of cultural continuity. From a purely primordialist point of view, ethnicities and ethnic membership arise from a series of "givens." As described by Geertz (1973), these givens include kin connections, common language, common religion, and social practices, but beyond this, the sort of "ineffable congruities" of blood, speech, and custom as well (259). How far back such givens extend is never exactly stated, but the point that a child is born into a distinct cultural community that shapes her and that has persisted across several generations well wraps up the primordialist package. The issue has long been the extent to which ethnicity is a primary tie that persists in the face of changing social conditions. For Grosby (1995), members of an ethnic group perceive a sense of common kinship and culture, and this is not something easily swept away. Smith (1986) speaks of a core basis of ethnicity, attributes he terms "ethnies," that are manipulated by ethnic entrepreneurs into ethnic self-awareness.

Whether or not we agree with the primordialist perspective, it clearly animates members of an ethnic group (see Le Vine 1997). After all, ethnicity is based on meaningful and durable links. It speaks to primary ties that are long-term and stable, and not to ephemeral and situational social transactions, such as the sort of relationships one might have with colleagues in the workplace. But the scholarly community has often downplayed the value of primordialism. The well-noted critique by Eller and Coughlan (1993) takes issue with the a priori view of ethnicity propounded by primordialists. The authors argue that it makes no sense to delineate ethnic group attachments before there is any interaction with other elements of society. And while members of an ethnic group will feel that the ties existing between them and other members are ineffable, such views are not borne out by cases that exhibit how circumstances and situations effectuate these ties.

Two camps in particular offer perspectives separate from that of primordialists. The social constructivists see ethnicity as something created by the existing social environment. According to Nagel (1994), ethnic groups are constructed from several materials—religion, language, culture, ancestry—some of which may be important, and others less so. The contours of ethnic identity undergo continuous negotiation, based on internal interactions, interactions with outsiders, and the types of circumstances within which the ethnic group operates. A vital aspect of the social construction of ethnicity is found in ethnic group boundaries. To paraphrase Barth (1969), ethnic identity is created at the edge, because people identify themselves as members of an ethnic group in opposition to people they consider to be outsiders. There are a wide variety of contingencies under which these boundaries may be constructed. Barth's own work, focused on traditional tribal groups, demonstrated how boundaries were determined partly over resource allocations. But other contingencies, like immigration, can produce large alterations in ethnic identity formation. Populations coming from very different regions and sharing little in common with each other—in fact, even hostile groups—can dramatically change their membership boundaries and group identity after immigrating to a new land (Vecoli 1983).

The instrumentalists view ethnic identity as essentially a functional category. They do acknowledge some cultural commonality, but see ethnicity as primarily an instrument to achieve these goals. Glazer and Moynihan (1975) ushered in an appreciation of how ethnicity could continue to flourish in the United States, despite a "melting pot" ideology. They conceived of ethnicity operating as an interest group, as a powerful social category that commanded political power and made claims to certain resources. An instrumentalist perspective argues that people choose to adhere to an ethnic group, in part because of the types of benefits that membership provides. Any individual is going to assess the advantages and disadvantages of belonging to a group, and will actively belong to a group and will abide by the norms of the group only if he sees a net gain (Hechter 1986). Ethnic institutions are key players in this calculation because they allocate certain advantages to ethnic members, enforce sanctions against transgressors, and control the flow of information that ethnic members receive. This instrumentalist view comes closest to seeing ethnic ties as another form of social transaction, where such ties may be purposeful in one situation but less advantageous in another. For example, increasing contacts with outside groups and outside members can lessen the perceived advantages of ethnic members, and so ethnic adherence can diminish over time and across generations. Perhaps more than the social constructivist approach, the instrumentalist approach suggests a fair degree of fluidity in one's own ethnic identity.

SPATIAL AND PLACEMAKING
MANIFESTATION OF ETHNICITY

I would not be writing a book called *Navigating Ethnicity* if I did not plan to argue that ethnicity is quite geographical in nature. But this merits a bit of explanation as to how this can be spun out, because the geography of ethnicity means several things. First, and most basic, ethnicity creates tangible spaces at all spatial scales. At a geopolitical scale, countries are organized and arranged on the basis of ethnic difference. "Nation" is a cultural-political descriptor, but also a means of designating territory. This national territory may correspond or diverge from state territory— nations may be shut out of the geopolitical order, or be unhappy with the drawing of boundaries. At a smaller, urban scale, neighborhoods are organized and arranged on the basis of ethnic difference. Members of different ethnic groups—described in terms of nationality, race, or any of the various terms discussed above—often live in separate spaces. This is an urban phenomenon observed everywhere. The different living patterns are partially due to different income levels. But class explains only a bit, though it has a powerful role in outcomes and perceptions. Attitudes, part of which stem from class, explain a bit more, but these can be complicated as they involve the attitudes of several different groups toward each other.

The geography of ethnicity at scales both large and small shapes the nature of ethnic groups and the nature of the places they inhabit. The tendency for different ethnics to occupy distinct places means that ethnicity becomes territorial—a piece of land is associated with a particular group. The territory is a surrogate for how the ethnic group is perceived—and even how it perceives itself. The location of a group in relation to other groups is one of the criteria that help define it. The tangible boundaries between ethnic groups determine and reflect ethnic perception and interaction. These boundaries are hard at times. They may be enforced from the inside, as a group uses geography to keep itself together, or spatial limits may be externally enforced as a means of quarantining members of a particular population. This geographical feature has been termed *segregation*, and will be a large part of our discussion.

Yet boundaries between groups can be quite permeable, and this too is a feature of ethnic geography. Ethnic imprints do not necessarily have to involve higher levels of segregation, and ethnic groups can utilize space without necessarily sequestering themselves from others. Just because it is shared, spatial expressions are no less meaningful. In this regard, *concentration* defines some degree of physical proximity, which facilitates ethnic bonding. Social interaction, the ability to attend and profit from various institutions, opportunities to obtain ethnic products and services: these all depend to some extent on spatial propinquity (see Alba, Logan, and Crowder 1997 on the importance of these neighborhoods). Of course, the importance of spatial propinquity varies a great deal between groups, and this may not necessarily be directly related to the intensity of each group. Some groups, such as Indian Americans, may maintain strong ties but exhibit little clustering. More generally, we can argue about how contemporary technological trends—from a greater propensity to live, work, and shop in far-flung areas connected by long automobile commutes to the usage of social media and virtual technologies—have rendered physical distances less and less significant.

An important aspect of ethnic geography stems from the ways in which ethnic groups are able to transform and utilize the places they inhabit. A region or a neighborhood occupied by members of a particular group is not neutral ground where certain people just "happen" to live. It becomes a place imbued with the essence of that ethnic community. This essence is reflected in the development of a particular landscape—the network of signs, shops, housing styles, sounds, smells, public areas—that is unique to that place. This can be seen in communities around the world, as evident in this depiction of a Tyrolean village in Northern Italy (figure 1.2). Such ethnic placemaking is crucial, and occurs at all different scales. It helps to fix the impression of an ethnic group in people's minds, it rein-

Figure 1.2. Tyrolean village in northern Italy. This small village looks like it belongs in Austria, but is actually located within Italy's South Tyrol region. In these villages, German—not Italian—is the dominant language of communication. *Source:* David H. Kaplan.

forces the process of ethnic identification, and it promotes the development of a true ethnic community. It is this aspect as well—the localized, spatial outcomes of ethnicity—that will be discussed in this book.

ARTICULATING ETHNICITY: TOWARD A PLAN FOR THIS BOOK

The separation of people into cultural categories is widespread, and the ramifications are profound. Yet for such an important concept, ethnicity is awfully hard to pin down. We can see how several designations and labels shift over time and vary across regions. Equally thorny questions relate to how ethnicity itself is constituted, what are its boundaries, what is the salience of ethnic identity, and how such an identity is maintained. An enormous library of books and articles—of both the scholarly and popular varieties—tries to address these questions, yet the search for a simple response will likely be disappointing.

The frustrating richness of the ethnicity concept should not deter further exploration. We can still make a lot of headway, perhaps not in reaching definitive conclusions, but in arriving at a more solid understanding of the diversity of ethnic expressions. To be clear, there is no universal formula of causes, traits, or outcomes that characterize ethnic concentrations. However, there are certain processes involved that can be applied across contexts, and help to illuminate the nature of how ethnicity is constructed, the relationship between ethnic groups and others within the broader society, the expressions of ethnicity, and the variety of ways ethnicity is expressed on the landscape. The goal of this book is to untangle the causes of ethnic concentration and segregation, how these geographies are made manifest, and the consequences of such spatial separation.

This attention to process is what I believe makes this book distinct from other treatments of ethnicity. This is not a book that provides a series of cases—of several ethnic groups within a context, of a singular ethnic group across multiple contexts, or of different ethnic groups within many different contexts. It is not a book that examines ethnicity in relationship to other topics of interest: say the relationship between ethnicity and class, or the connection between ethnicity and the church. Rather, this book is informed by an analytical framework that tries to better understand both the causes and consequences of ethnic concentration. I stress the nature, rather than just the pattern, of ethnic spatial outcomes. For instance, if segregation occurs, is it permanent or transient? Is it a situation that lends itself to identity maintenance, or to eventual assimilation? Does it result in groups being victim to their own spatial entrapment, or in a position to be able to use their concentration to their advantage? Within this framework, there can be discussion of possible causes such as discrimination, voluntary placemaking, or chain migration. There can also be discussion of possible consequences such as ethnic economies, political activism, or social separation. Central to all of this, of course, will be the concept of ethnic identity, and the way it is manifested in cities across the world.

Many of the current treatments of ethnic concentration tend to articulate theory on the basis of the singular experiences of a particular group within a particular context. But group experiences diverge, and groups can be defined in various ways. The same holds true for context. Any understanding of ethnic concentration must explicitly recognize the array of contexts in which it occurs, such that an analysis of ethnicity in one setting may not be appropriate in another. Geographers are especially attuned to the importance of scale. Ethnic concentration often is perceived as occurring at the local scale of the neighborhood or the city, yet it is influenced by factors that operate over a wide range of scales—from the global to the local. This requires an explicit understanding of, say, geopolitical considerations operating at an international scale that heighten the salience of ethnic identity at the local context, or cross-national labor migration that responds to the needs of global capital and results in the possible stigmatization of neighborhood ethnic spaces. Through networks, locally situated ethnic groups can have major impacts on global-scale phenomena, such as international trade.

This framework develops a series of tensions/factors that cut across dimensions of group and context. The creation of spatially concentrated communities results from the choices and constraints that arise at global, national, and local scales. These forces produce a myriad of specific spatial outcomes. While this book will attempt to theorize about the relationship between ethnic identity and geography—whether in the guise of segregation, traces on the urban landscape, or in regard to the active usage of space—it is not intended only as a work of abstraction. Rather, this analytical framework will illustrate just how location, context, and place are shaped by ethnic identities, and how ethnicity helps to influence the character and form of modern cities.

Of course, it is impossible for a book of this size to present an encyclopedic overview of every ethnic situation as it exists in the world of today and the worlds of yesterday. This would be foolish to even attempt. Because the point is in analyzing the processes involved, the range of examples may appear uneven and tilted heavily toward areas with which I am familiar. However, an anthology of ethnicities or ethnic topics is not the point of this book, and examples can be found in several good edited volumes (see McKee 2000; Berry and Henderson 2002; Frazier and Tettey-Fio 2006; Airriess 2015; Teixeira, Kobayashi, and Li 2012). What this book accomplishes is to highlight the value of a geographical perspective, articulate the fundamental processes in shaping ethnicity, and show how ethnic differences can be applied around the world.

2

✌

Diversity in Urban History

People long ago began to differentiate themselves on the basis of ethnic attachment—though of course they would not have used that term. Much of this was associated with the rise of cities. Pre-urban villages were small, and composed of pretty much the same types of people. The factors binding them together were family, customs, limited occupational specialization and, most important of all—primary ties. Everybody knew everybody else for their entire lives. Once cities came about, with more people than any one individual could possibly know, then ethnic diversity began as well. This is probably because diversity of all sorts was present in cities. For the first time in history, thousands of people were living in the same constricted space. Households that had once stretched apart were now pushed together. Cities were most of all distinguished by class. Members of the elite, based primarily on religious standing, occupied hallowed sanctuaries forbidden to the common folk. Class distinctions extended beyond these elite compounds, however, as quarters just one step down from the elite were occupied by more privileged residents. Occupations followed a spatial logic in the earliest cities, especially for those jobs considered less appealing. Those poor wretches forced to do the dirty work shunned by others were themselves shunned, and banished toward the edges of the city.

From Mesopotamia to the Indus Valley, Northern China, and the Mediterranean, the earliest cities packed in thousands of people. The numbers themselves, perhaps 10,000–25,000 people, may not seem impressive. After all, they would barely qualify today as a small town. But at the time, and for the very first time in history, this meant that strangers were compelled to come together. Whole groups of people, following slightly different cultural principles and only dimly aware of one another, now converged in one place.

As cities developed through history, the nature and degree of urban diversity became more complex. The interactions between more cultures in different parts of the world led to once distinct peoples living among each other, whether voluntarily or by force. To minimize diversity, cities would have needed to close themselves off. The evidence is that, while few cities greeted foreigners as equals—at a bare minimum most cities withheld citizenship to outsiders—most cities allowed other groups entry. The more cosmopolitan the city and the more connections it had with the outside world, the more cultural diversity was likely to be found within.

Trying to categorize historical diversity is difficult. Each case is unique. However, it is possible to catalog a few basic processes that spurred greater diversity. This provides some clues as to how diversity was experienced within each society. As in all the discussions in this book, the key factors are the groups themselves: where they came from, how they got there, and the particular attributes that marked them. This must be considered in light of the context within which this diversity took place: the level of flexibility or tolerance, and the degree of social stratification.

THE INTRINSIC DIVERSITY OF URBAN LIFE

The earliest cities distinguished themselves from village society by embracing many more people. What is more, these new cities, likely only a few thousand in size, included a majority of people who were not directly engaged in agriculture and instead followed various specialized occupations. So cities included a far greater spectrum of occupations than did villages. Individuals involved in the same trades often lived together in the same neighborhoods, and these were defined by occupation. Metalworkers lived with metalworkers; tanners lived with tanners. What is more, there is evidence that certain artisan groups came to be associated with particular ethnic groups (Sjoberg 1960). What ethnicity means in this context is hard to say, as people from relatively nearby locations probably appeared different from the majority and so seemed "ethnic." In this sense, cities were intrinsically diverse, with new opportunities, and such places attracted people from the surrounding countryside.

The other important feature of early cities was that, as vanguards of civilization, they amplified the degrees of social stratification. Agricultural villages were certainly not egalitarian, but inequality was more personalized. Sexual and age differences were significant, to be sure, and skilled and charismatic villagers likely enjoyed a more prominent position. We might conjecture on whether status difference within villages extended beyond a generation—whether privilege was passed from parent to child. We do know for certain that such intergenerational inequality was integral to early and later cities. It became more institutionalized and also more categorical. Certain occupations were perceived to be of lower status; such would have also been true of particular ethnic groups for which occupation and ethnicity were linked together. And just as cities were set apart from the villages in the countryside, divided from the rural denizens by walls and gates, the expanding social differences ramified within the cities themselves (Kaplan, Holloway, and Wheeler 2014).

Where did the people who populated these cities come from? Big cities today pull migrants from all over the world, and the enormous cities of the ancient world, such as Rome and Chang'an, brought people in from very far afield. But in the earliest cities, most migrants likely came from near and middle distances and shared some cultural traits. In those years, even short distances were long, and village ties were strong. Village life was familial, and there would have been a large number of families or clans moving into the cities from the countryside (Vance 1990). Could these be considered ethnic groups? As we discussed in chapter 1, ethnic boundaries are flexible, and vary by the observer. What an outsider may have perceived as minute differences between these groups probably seemed quite consequential to these former villagers who banded together—both physically and affectively—against the more anonymous members of the city.

Describing cities in mid-twentieth-century America, Herbert Gans (1982) evoked the idea of "urban villagers." Cities were not undifferentiated mass societies—the gesellschaft, as Tönnies (1957) described it—but were composed of smaller spaces that operated as true communities. From ancient Greece onward, this concept applied to real villagers who migrated to cities. There were literally dozens of separate neighborhoods in ancient Athens, each occupied by former residents of the same community (Vance 1990). Transplanted village ties, bound up with family ties and secured by geographic proximity, may have lasted quite a long time and created significant urban diversity.

Likewise, the population in Mesoamerican cities was divided into groups defined by common blood. These separate identities—including more than 30 languages and cultures—were not based on ethnicity per se, but rather on "dynastic affiliation, class, and municipal location" (Grofe 2005, 1). The populations were geographically segmented, and enjoyed some degree of autonomy in the city (Adams 1966). However, urban location would have inevitably forced such disparate groups to come together, either sharpening their distinctions or fusing them into a greater pan-identity.

As cities grew larger and broadened their political, cultural, and economic influence, they came to attract people from farther afield. People entered the city in search of opportunity, but societies would make large distinctions between people who "belonged,"—who were native—and those
who were outsiders. Even within this distinction, "outsider" could involve
several gradations of difference. For example, each of the Greek city-states
was distinct from one another, and the residents of one polis were foreign
to the others. But they were all recognized as "Greek." Outside of this
realm were those considered "barbarians" (Kovacs 1998). Greek cities like
Athens came to include a lot of foreigners, maybe half as many as citizens,
and they were given a special designation that lay between freemen and
slaves. They were also excluded from political enfranchisement, ownership of land, and were subject to special taxes (Curtin 1984). With further
contacts, engendered by empire building and closer trade ties, all of these
populations would have come to live near one another.

THE FIRST IMPERIAL CITIES

Imperialism increased diversity in several ways. The growth of empires
brought more of the world together and led quite naturally to greater
cultural contact. The opportunities for trade between different regions of
the empire expanded. Imperial consolidation and control could rid the
waters of pirates and the roads of vandals, dangers that had long plagued
the exercise of trade. New infrastructural projects, such as Roman roads
or China's Grand Canal, were realized, bringing together a wider range
of lands and peoples. Great empires also traded with other great empires,
as witnessed by the Great Silk Road between Europe and East Asia, and
cultural contact ensued from this. Empires also had the resources necessary to construct great capitals and other major cosmopolitan cities; these
enticed many to migrate from distant lands.

The pinnacle of such cosmopolitan diversity in the ancient world was
found in the imperial city of Rome. As the seat of a vast territory spanning three continents and based around an internal sea, Rome attracted
people from all corners of its empire, and likely many from outside. Writ-
ers at the time remarked on Rome's incredible diversity and its ability to
attract representatives from all over the globe. One described Rome as
the "epitome of the whole earth" (from Piana 1927, 206). In fact, a Roman
crowd resembled a visual and auditory rainbow of different skin colors,
physiognomic features, accents, and languages, and the incredible density and organic disarray of the city itself allowed for many opportunities
for contact between different ethnic groups (De Souza Briggs 2004). In this
city, there is no record of enforced segregation, as would be seen in some

later medieval cities, but there were likely to be various quarters established, framed by the combination of ethnicity and occupation. The promise of citizenship was fulfilled more and more readily as the republic and then empire matured, and this likely weakened earlier ethnic ties as new citizens were encouraged to adopt Roman names, wear Roman dress, and enjoy the legal advantages of imperial status (Hope 2000).

Beyond the Roman Empire, diversity was found in each of the great civilizations. This was often a result of imperial expansion. Imperialism propagated cultural diversity because it brought together the conquerors—who themselves may have come from many backgrounds—and the conquered. The great Arab cities that rose up in North Africa and the Middle East made cultural diversity part and parcel of urban life. As the Arab/Islamic empires expanded in the seventh, eighth, and ninth centuries, the cities that emerged included a broad spectrum of peoples. The various Berber groups who lived in North Africa met up with the expanding Arab populations from further east. The sweep of Islam into the Iberian Peninsula brought together the Arab conquerors with a population that was at one time Roman, but long made miserable from previous conquests of Germanic invaders. In most cases, the existing populations of Jewish and various Christian denominations who had resided in these areas before the Arab expansion were allowed to retain their religion and to live among the Arab Muslims.

Cordoba, in what is now Spain, was at the center of the western Islamic caliphate and prospered between the eighth and tenth centuries (Menocal 2002; De Souza Briggs 2004). The city was ruled by Arab Muslims who had originally arrived in the area in the 700s and had established a government that was semi-autonomous from the central Abbasid Caliphate based far away in Baghdad (Menocal 2002). Upon arrival, the rulers took a decidedly different tack from other conquerors. While being Muslim conferred the greatest advantages, and many non-Muslims were enticed to convert, the rulers of Cordoba, like those of many other Islamic areas of this period, were fairly tolerant toward their Christian and Jewish subjects (Abu-Lughod 1987). There was a clear division between the Dhimmi or "people of the book" who practiced one of the monotheistic religions of Judaism, Christianity, or Zoroastrianism, and those who were still pagan in their beliefs. While residents who practiced the other monotheistic religions were prohibited from proselytizing and overtly displaying their religion—and expressly prohibited from any blaspheme regarding the Prophet Mohammed—they were allowed to co-exist and even prosper along with their Muslim neighbors.

The religious differences within Cordoba and other Arab cities generated a certain urban structure. Settlements were not officially segregated, but there was a fair degree of sequestration as groups sought some distance from and an ability to practice their religion without having to deal with outsiders. Hourani ([1991] 2013, 123) noted that

> most of the population lived outside the center, in residential quarters, each of them a mass of small streets and cul-de-sac opening off a main street; at some periods, the quarters had gates which were shut and guarded at night. A quarter might contain a few hundred or a few thousand inhabitants; it would have its mosque, church, or synagogue, its local subsidiary market (suwayqu) catering for its daily needs, and perhaps its public bath (hammam), an important meeting place. . . . There was a tendency for the inhabitants of a quarter to be linked by common origin, religious, ethnic, or regional, or by kinship or intermarriage; such links created a solidarity which might be strong.

So Jews and Christians lived separately from the Muslims and from each other. This appears to have been spurred more from convenience than from any animus toward outsiders. At the same time, we can talk about such neighborhoods as defended spaces. As Abu-Lughod (1987) points out, while segregation was not absolute—there was always some mingling, and the development of legal "ghettos" did not occur until much later—the divisions between neighborhoods were remarkably durable. Among poor Muslims, for example, the neighborhood became an extension of smaller dwellings that were not spacious enough to afford the necessary privacy, especially to women. Outsiders would have been restricted from this semi-private space. Segregation separated groups that were more likely to come into conflict because of their differences and had the potential for small misunderstandings that could blow up. In cases of civil turmoil or the threat of conquest, there were usually gates that could be shut—protecting the residents, at least temporarily.

What happened when members of one group were able to completely conquer an empire or kingdom previously controlled by another group? In these cases, rife throughout history, we find that the conquering group often established a whole new strata or layer for themselves, which they placed on top of the existing social order. Examples of this phenomenon abound, but perhaps one of the most consequential was the capture of China from Ming control by the Manchus to the northeast. The Manchus were a Mongolian people, long interwoven with Chinese culture but who separated themselves from the majority Han population. When they conquered China, the Manchus established a new dynasty and a new social/ethnic order. This was most clearly seen in Beijing, the capital of both the Ming Dynasty and the conquering Qing (Manchu) Dynasty (Sit 1995). Beijing had been demarcated during the Ming and Yuan Dynasties as a series of "cities" radiating from the most interior Palace City (now known as the

Forbidden City) where lived the emperor, surrounded by an Imperial City, and then surrounded again by an Inner City. The Outer City was beyond these walls and comprised the less valued members of the society. Upon the conquest of Beijing by the Manchus, nearly all Han peoples were evacuated from the Inner City to the Outer City, and Manchu peoples—about 240,000 of them—were effectively required to live within the Inner City. These very strict ethnic separations lasted for over three hundred years, until the end of the Qing Dynasty at the beginning of the twentieth century.

Imperialism also prompted the expansion of the dominant culture into new places—creating several points of contact with what would later be described as "indigenous" peoples but were then considered savages or barbarians. There were many approaches by which new territory could be secured. It could be accomplished with military garrisons placed in the middle of conquered territory, for example, but this still placed the empire at a numerical disadvantage. The most enduring way to extend imperial reach was through the recruitment of citizens to settle in the new lands. This had a few key advantages: It opened up new territory to citizens of the empire, providing them with compensation for their services and easing the pressures for land in the home territory. It provided new positions of authority—governorships and the like—to noblemen whose ambitions were thwarted at home. And it allowed the empire to create more demographic balance in conquered lands, balancing the indigenous majority with some of their own people. This often came at a horrific cost, as imperial incursions into new territories were nearly always accompanied by overwhelming violence and the intentional or unintentional destruction of whole populations and ways of life.

In Gaul, for example, the Romans established towns smack in the middle of a set of Celtic villages—much to the displeasure of the villagers themselves. These new Roman towns would have been connected to the rest of the empire by roads or sea lanes. Most were constructed along Roman town-planning principles, with a north-south Cardo and an east-west Decumanus anchoring a basic Roman grid pattern. Important Roman institutions—forums, baths, arenas—were established in these towns as well, projecting the grandeur of Roman society. These towns attracted Latin-speaking Romans as they quickly made their mark, and became meeting places for the new Roman residents and Gallic traders and others who sought to take advantage of the new order (Pounds 1990). The degree of cross-cultural contact grew more extensive as Gaul gradually Latinized. This was reflected in Roman towns and in the territories beyond. This contact was hardly without friction. Two thousand years later, the comic character Asterix continues to reflect the anger of the Gauls toward the Roman intruders (Missiou 2010).

HOW TRADING AFFECTED DIVERSITY

As long as human beings have produced items worthy of exchange, trade has been a significant factor in increasing cultural pluralism. Trading networks sent people to foreign cities in order to facilitate the sale and acquisition of particular goods. Often this was extended to include entire communities of ethnically distinct people and, in this regard, ethnicity and economy were linked together, a phenomenon we still see today. Many ancient cultures considered trade less respectable and best left to foreigners anyway, leaving their own citizens to pursue more noble pursuits. The city-states of ancient Anatolia included a number of Assyrian traders who came to trade commodities like tin and textiles in exchange for copper, gold, and silver. Assyrian merchants would take up residence in various Anatolian cities, many of them living there for long stretches of time as they negotiated with the local princes for the best terms of trade (Curtin 1984). The Phoenicians were well-known traders, moving across the Mediterranean to Carthage and Spain in search of trade and resources. In many cases, colonies developed out of these enterprises, linked to the homeland in the Levant, but also attuned to the circumstances of the territories they inhabited and the position of each within an interlinked trading network (Aubet 2001). The Greeks had a slightly different emphasis, as they established agricultural colonies that later on became somewhat oriented to trade. But the Greek expansion was likewise instrumental in forcing encounters between distinct cultures. In ancient Egypt in the town of Naukratis, the pharaoh established a distinct Greek quarter, with its own temples and some degree of autonomy (Curtin 1984).

Later cities in Europe's medieval period came to acquire considerable urban diversity as a result of their trading activities. The status of merchants in these medieval cities improved a great deal, and they often held the reins of political power. Few of these cities controlled large empires, but they had positioned themselves at the nexus of impressive commercial networks. As such they included many long-term "visitors," a category in medieval society. Foreigners in almost all of these medieval cities suffered from the disadvantage of not being citizens. Citizenship was held up as the principal status that allowed an individual to fully participate in the life of the community; in most cities, it was a status unavailable to foreigners, no matter their length of residence. As a result, while some foreigners were fairly well off, most were not and became marginalized by their status (Friedrichs 1981). In medieval Bruges, foreign traders replaced much of the native merchant class. Here and elsewhere, culturally distinct peoples were referred to as "nations." They resided in special districts, and operated trade associations, social

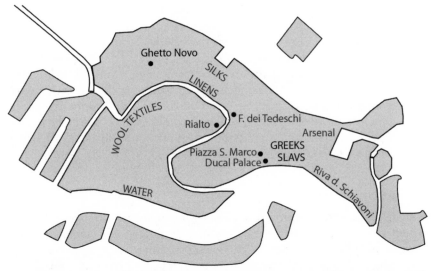

Figure 2.1. This diagram of Venice at its peak shows a city divided by industries, such as wool and silk, but also by ethnicity. Ghetto Novo was the name of the original Jewish ghetto. Greeks and Slavs likewise had their own quarters. *Source:* After Girouard (1985).

clubs, religious fraternities, and courts of appeal (Girouard 1985). Figure 2.1 shows how this operated within Venice.

While trading in medieval Europe expanded outside the corridors of political power, in China trade was centered in the important imperial capitals. As various dynasties consolidated power, they produced capital cities—and a series of secondary cities—with substantial areas and large populations. The city of Chang'an had been established by the Han dynasty as the capital, planned according to particular specifications. Two-thirds of the city was comprised of the palace compound, underlining the importance of administration and ritual functions. In the least propitious sector of the city was found the marketplace—and here, too, the location was emblematic of the very low position of the trading classes in Chinese culture. By the time of the T'ang Dynasty, a new Chang'an was built right next to the old Han capital. Again, the city was built on cosmological principles, with the palace and administrative compounds placed squarely in the north. There are more markets in this larger city, and a great deal of evidence for an impressive diversity, with several temples of different religions. These catered largely to foreigners, and in fact foreign traders from India and Persia were located near here (Sit 2010). Also included among the denizens would have been some Koreans, Japanese, Tibetans, Arabs, and other peoples that made their lives in the cities. Based on the location of the temples, there does not appear to be a rigid segregation.

HOW INEQUALITY CREATED ETHNICITY

Inequality was and is rampant in most societies, and was often layered onto ethnicity as members of a particular group were considered to be inherently inferior to other groups. This may have had something to do with the occupations that became associated with a group, jobs that were dirty or smelly or otherwise considered unclean. Or inequality was sometimes tied into groups of people who were pressed into slavery, creating a disparaged population that either began as ethnically distinct or became more so as a result of their low position.

Castes and Ethnicity

The development of untouchable castes in many cultures probably resulted from people who were charged with various undesirable chores, such as tanning and butchering, disliked by other members of the society. Over time, these jobs turned the people who performed them into a special group that was separated from the overall society and so resembled an ethnic group, "employing distinctive speech forms, personal mannerisms, and clothing" (Sjoberg 1960, 135). These castes were more than simple economic classes; in fact, their status was so wretched as to be considered outside the caste system altogether. As much as any ethnic group, and more than most, "untouchables" suffered a series of restrictions, brutalities, and insults that marked each day of their lives. Spatial restrictions were part and parcel of this.

The Japanese *burakumin*, for example, are clearly of Japanese descent, but have been marked as a distinct caste since about the tenth century (De Vos and Wagatsuma 2006). The perspective of this group being impure and unfit for association with other Japanese has also spurred a number of apocryphal histories, including the idea that burakumin descend from Korean prisoners (Hane 1982). The Japanese used these ideas to justify the ill-treatment of a group of people—treatment that they would not use on "real" Japanese. Due to discrimination, prejudice, and the nature of internal ties, this community "developed a distinct socioreligious identity and unity" that kept segregation intact (Donoghue 1957, 1006). In the past, all burakumin lived in specially designated districts on the outskirts of Japanese cities, creating a geographical basis to their separation as a group (Deliège 1999). Interactions with other Japanese were discouraged, and besides, these were often of such a humiliating nature—burakumin were expected to get on their hands and knees in these encounters—that most chose to avoid them (Hane 1982). Over the years, burakumin initiated several actions to ensure a fair degree of autonomy. This has included a set of religious rituals and a different dialect along with separate quarters.

At the same time, there has been a desire, particularly by middle-class burakumin, to conceal their lifestyle and to avoid interactions with ordinary Japanese. Even today, most burakumin face discrimination regarding employment, and the vast majority marry within the group (Hane 1982, De Vos and Wagatsuma 2006).

In China's Shanghai province, a similar situation occurred among the Subei people. Like the burakumin, Subei share most aspects of ethnicity with the Han Chinese, yet have been ostracized from Chinese society (Honig 1992). Coming from the less fertile, less densely populated northern section of Jiangsu province, Subei migrants to Shanghai were given a fictional place of origin (a place called "Subei") and over time endowed with a host of unsavory attributes often related to their relative poverty and their "offensive trades" like rag picking and pig raising (Honig 1992, 43). Their tendency to live apart from the others, in unregulated shack settlements, further aggravated their social distance. In essence, a stigmatized native place identity has produced a powerful socioethnic category.

The so-called untouchable caste in India is the best-known example of a derived stigmatized identity. Where members of this caste came from is still a bit murky, but they appear to have descended from aboriginal peoples on the Indian subcontinent that could not be incorporated into the conquering Indo-Aryan/Hindu culture (Hiro 1975). They continue to be a part of Indian society, but always on the outside and always subjected to horrible humiliations by higher level castes. Access to temples, municipal facilities, cafes, tea shops, barbers, shops, roads, and even water was (and is) severely restricted (Hiro 1975, Deliège 1999). Relationships with upper-caste members were strictly taboo, and punishable by torture and death. Untouchability continued as a major element of Indian society, and the untouchable population itself (sometimes termed "scheduled castes") today constitutes about one of every seven Indians. As was the case with the Japanese burakumin, the untouchable populations (and this comprises several groups) are often consigned to a location outside the cities and villages. In fact, every aspect of their lives was and is spatially constrained. Their residential quarters are placed as far as possible from the high-caste Brahmin quarters and temples (Deliège 1999).

Slavery and Ethnicity

Another way in which ethnicity was suffused with inequality came through the abhorrent act of slavery. Slaves could come from anywhere, and many originated within the home society. One might become a slave based on having committed certain crimes, or being unable to pay one's debts. Some parents sold their children into slavery because they had nothing to feed them and this was one way to avoid starvation (Davis

2006). But slavery was linked to foreign ancestry in many instances. The identification of slavery with foreignness, exoticism, or race has varied. Greek cities actually required that slaves be outsiders—even though that included other Greek city-states (Thomas 1981). Initially most Roman slaves were foreign, barely conversant in Latin. Several came from the imperial periphery. According to Balsdon (1979), three-fifths of all Roman slaves came from Asia Minor. In the Hausa city-states in what is now modern-day Nigeria, slaves were taken from non-Hausa populations during raiding parties (Griffeth 1981).

Within cities, slaves were brought in for household labor and were incorporated in the residences and the lives of their owners. In the countryside, slaves maintained separate quarters from the non-slave population. While most slaves within the Roman Empire worked in households, there were also several examples of slave-driven agriculture. The regions of Sicily and the southern Italian peninsula were transformed into vast farmlands of olives, grapes, and grain, owned by wealthy Romans and powered by the labor of slaves—many of them captive people from conquered lands (Davis 2006).

In many societies, slaves had the opportunity to gain their freedom or their children's freedom. This created a status of people that was quite ambiguous. Within Roman society, where the role of freedmen and freedwomen is probably best known, these ex-slaves constituted a vital part of Roman society even as they functioned awkwardly within it (Veyne 1987). Freedmen continued to be bound to their former masters and, though they were granted Roman citizenship, they could not immediately exercise the same rights as full citizens. Higher offices were closed to ex-slaves, for instance. At the same time, many freedmen and especially those who had served the rich and powerful could become quite wealthy themselves. What is more, the children of freed men and women could assume full citizenship; while a slave ancestry was by no means honorable, it was a status shared by many Romans.

In many of these instances, the relationship of slavery with ethnicity was a mutable one. Most slaves were likely of foreign descent, and would have appeared as clearly ethnic at first. There was a desire, in fact, to show the physical distinction between free citizens and slaves. While dark skin sometimes played a role—indicative of hard work out in the sun—often the physical features associated with slaves derived from the characteristics of recently conquered populations (Davis 2006). Actors playing slaves in the Roman theater would don red wigs, since many real slaves at the time were red-haired Thracians. Over time, the acquisition of language and culture led slaves to appear more and more Roman. There does not seem to have been any particular markings that Roman slaves were required to wear, though some were branded and later on wore collars around their necks

(Hope 2000, Davis 2006). This lack of distinctiveness was considered a means to prevent uprisings; according to the Roman senator Seneca, slaves could not recognize one another and band together in conspiracy and rebellion. With freedom, any ethnic aspect of slavery was washed away, such that people were often unsure of the presence of slaves in their ancestry.

This is a different case when speaking about slavery in more recent history—particularly as found within North and South America. More than any type of slavery that existed beforehand, American slavery was tightly bound to the idea of race. Since most slaves were of African descent, those who shared particular physical traits were considered suspect even when free. As Elkins (1963, 61) wrote in his landmark analysis, the South had so twisted the conflation of race and bondage that in the mind of the Southerner, "All slaves are black; slaves are degraded and contemptible; therefore all blacks are degraded and contemptible and should be kept in a state of slavery." To be sure, some slaves did gain their freedom through escape, self-purchase, or manumission (Cole 2005), and this population of freedmen and women lived among the majority population. Yet the situation of American freedmen was far more tenuous than had been the case in earlier historical periods, or even in other contexts during the same time. The color of freedmen made most blacks ineligible to vote in many states. They were easily pursued or kidnapped, with little recourse to the law. And the "free" black population was truly marginalized geographically, a situation that would persist well past slavery's end. The levels of spatial separation varied though, as freed slaves in the countryside often inhabited the worst land. Within small towns and cities, with not as much space, there is evidence showing where ex-slaves and their children congregated. Free blacks were effectively denied entry into a whole host of facilities—restaurants, hotels, public parks, churches, and schools—and kept as separated as possible in all realms of life. Many retreated to the more ramshackle districts at the periphery of the cities. They were not completely segregated in these areas, since these were still interspersed with the residences of the poor white population, but they were certainly concentrated (Wade 1964).

EUROPEAN COLONIZATION AND DIVERSITY

With the wave of colonization that began in the 1500s, European colonizers attempted to settle their new possessions. This was a way to maintain control, and was a mode of colonial governance, resource extraction, plantation agriculture, and a safety valve for their own land-hungry residents. In the process, the Spanish, French, British, Dutch, and Portuguese colonizers established overseas settlements that effectively superimposed their culture on top of existing indigenous cultures. Like the Romans 1,500 years earlier, these new colonists inevitably occupied a privileged place that was reflected in the structure of their cities.

The colonial cities mirrored the spatial interactions between the European colonists and the indigenous peoples whose spaces they usurped. Figure 2.2 schematizes how these changes could occur. In some cases (a), cities were established on top of existing settlements. The native peoples who had lived within the settlements were occasionally allowed to remain within the remodeled cities. In other cases (b), the cities became restricted spaces intended for European use only, and the native population was forced out. In yet other cases (c), Europeans created wholly new settlements, with the natives often excluded from the city itself but occupying settlements outside the city and beyond its walls. Finally, some cases (d) saw the indigenous population reduced considerably, becoming a diminished presence within this new society. It would be a mistake to consider these to be discrete types, since each historical situation could capture different elements of each.

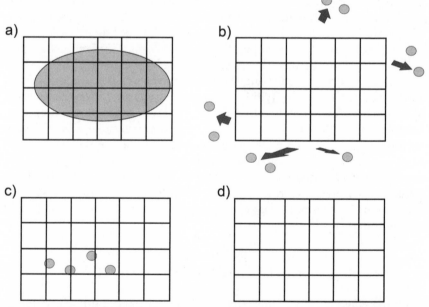

Figure 2.2. A schematic of colonial settlement changes. In (a), colonial cities are established on top of existing settlements, with indigenous peoples often remaining within the new cities. In (b), the established colonial cities are restricted to Europeans, and the indigenous population expelled. In (c), completely new colonial cities are created, with the indigenous population consigned to the periphery of the city. The nearby indigenous population is eliminated or considerably reduced in (d). *Source:* David H. Kaplan.

As an example of the first tendency, imperial powers often took over existing settlements in Asian and African ports and restructured them for their own purposes. The economy that had existed beforehand was remade to service the export of materials for industry. The Europeans who established themselves in these cities—British, Portuguese, and Dutch—built exclusive neighborhoods abutting the original urban layout. European colonists also imported labor from other lands under their control, adding significantly to the cultural mélange. Throughout Southeast Asia, for instance, Chinese and Indian workers flooded into great colonial outposts like Singapore, Manila, Djakarta, and others.

Take the case of Rangoon. Rangoon's original layout was used by the British to orient the colonial port they laid on top of the indigenous city. Many of the original Burmese remained, but they were joined by some British overseers and a massive influx of Indians who were quickly becoming the largest group in the city (McGee 1967). The European compound was located on the most desirable land, with airy houses and clubs. The majority Indian population was divided into several sectors, from slums occupied by washermen to prosperous neighborhoods settled by the mixed Anglo-Indian population. The original Burmese population was located along the river's floodplain, creating a landscape that looked in many respects like a traditional Burmese village replete with traditional industries such as boat building and umbrella making (McGee 1967).

The Spanish experience in South and Central America was similar in some respects. The development of cities was critical to Spanish control in its South and Central American colonies. Many of these colonies supplanted indigenous kingdoms, and cities were often plopped right on the existing capitals of the conquered peoples. At the beginning, there would have been a fairly small Spanish population, clustered in the midst of a larger native population, but the Spanish made certain that all newly established colonial cities were formed in their own image. One of the first acts of the conquistadors—under the codes laid out in the Law of the Indies—was to force the natives to demolish their temples. The cities then followed a pattern in which the center of each town was marked by a large plaza bearing the major spiritual and political emblems of Spanish authority, and the surrounding blocks were assigned to the Spanish provincial elite. In this case, natives were forced out of the "official" space of the city, as only Spaniards could be considered sanctioned residents, but the Indians were still very much needed as a source of labor. To get around this, the Indians were placed in the outskirts, and referred to as *extramuros* (outside the walls) (Markman 1978).

Interestingly, the accounts of colonial Brazilian cities showed a different tendency. To be sure, there were extreme racial inequalities that intersected the social structure. But the cities were organized differently.

Many clung to the coast, and were shaped with a lower city along the waterfront, which included the marketplaces, and an upper city where were found most government buildings and residences (Godfrey 1991). Within a city like Salvador, Bahia, there was a profusion of separate social and cultural groups, but little segregation. Prosperous white families often occupied upper-story apartments, while poor brown and black residents would be found in basements (Kraay 2001).

The advent of large-scale trading companies, chartered by European countries in the 1500s and 1600s and eager to expand their commercial scope into new territories in Asia, Africa, and the Americas, brought with them a host of new merchants and support staff who ventured into several far-flung places with the permission of the local ruler. In many cases, this expansion of trade would soon mutate into imperialism, but it brought together disparate groups while it lasted.

Imperialistic trade expansion led to instances where English, French, Dutch, or other European colonizers took over existing cities or created their own settlements in a colonial territory. To take one case, the British established a series of Presidency Towns from which they ruled the South Asian subcontinent: Madras, Bombay, Calcutta, and later Delhi. Among a sea of Indians, the British presence was a minuscule 100,000 people. But in each city they constructed a wedge of European residences that began near the center of the city and stretched into the more spacious surroundings in the suburbs (Kosambi and Brush 1988). Figure 2.3 shows the plan for Madras, on the southeastern coast of India, where the racial separation between native Indians and Europeans was most acute.

The largest of these Presidency Towns was Calcutta. It was the site of the British Fort William in 1696 and became a major Indian city in the eighteenth and nineteenth centuries—in fact, the second largest city in the British Empire after London (Dutt, D'Sa, and Monroe 1989; Nightingale 2012). As a city designed for commerce, it attracted British East India Company merchants who traded in textiles, salt, and opium, as well as other functionaries. Company nabobs gained fabulous fortunes, and felt themselves increasingly at home in this new city, with all manner of resources and native labor at their disposal. Among the first measures was separation of "white" towns for the British and "black" towns for the native Indians (Dutt and Pomeroy 1993). The British areas were laid out in regular fashion with plenty of space between structures, and officials lived within large colonnaded bungalows, erected in marble, festooned with imported and lavish satins, crystal, vases, and other furnishings, and surrounded by parkland or formal gardens. This fortified "White Town," home to company officials, was soon joined by a "Black Town" made up of ambitious Bengalis eager to enjoy the economic benefits of proximity. While a few Indians were quite wealthy—and in fact, a few of the wealthi-

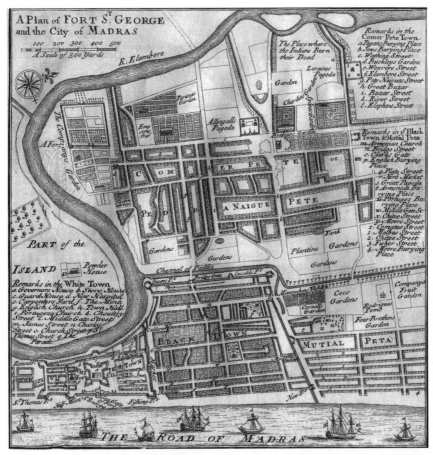

Figure 2.3. As a Presidency Town, Madras was separated clearly between the "Black Town" of the native Tamil population and the "White" Town where the British colonialists resided.

est themselves lived in White Town—much of Black Town was characterized by densities approaching 700 people per acre in 1941 (Brush 1962). The two "towns" were clearly distinct, but interdependent. And between the two of them, Calcutta grew to be an enormous city for the time, with some 400,000 people.

This division lasted throughout Calcutta's colonial history. The White Town of the East India Company formed a pleasant and central portion of the city (Dutt and Pomeroy 1993). The contrasts between this and the Black Town districts were quite marked. The British areas were laid out in regular fashion. Most British officials lived within large colonnaded bungalows surrounded by parkland or formal gardens (Brush 1962). The

Black Town districts, though home to a number of wealthy merchants, had a completely different look and feel. Most neighborhoods were marked by extreme congestion that persisted and increased (Brush 1962). The separation brought about by the early development of British and Native districts also lingered, with further separation later on between Hindus and Muslims and according to caste (Bose 1965).

The colonial cities established in North America were brand new, as the indigenous population did not have a history of town building. Initially, they would have been inhabited by colonists close to the indigenous villages, in a manner similar to the Roman cities. As these cities became more influential, the native population might settle just outside the perimeter of these foreign towns. Urbanization was introduced by the new conquerors, but quickly became part of the economic lives of the indigenous peoples too. Yet, natives were allowed only restricted access inside the new cities, if access was to be granted at all. Especially within the English colonies, North American Indians were mostly outcasts and largely ignored (Meinig 1986).

Meinig (1986) also points out how the degree of contact between the indigenous population and the European colonists varied by location. In the frontier lands, European traders—often French—relied on the Indian tribes for their knowledge of fur and other commodities. French traders often ventured far afield, along the Great Lakes and the riverways, in search of fur. The knowledge of the tribesmen was invaluable, and the traders gradually integrated into the tribal society itself (Kaplan 1990). Many married Indian women, and their offspring developed a distinct ethnic identity, termed Metis.

Along the more settled regions of the East Coast, the contact between Indians and Europeans—mostly English settlers—was disastrous from the Indian point of view (Cronon 1983). As with the interaction between the Spanish and the indigenous peoples of Mesoamerica and Peru, Indians along the eastern shores of North America had no immunity to Old World diseases. Exposure to smallpox could devastate 80 percent or more of the Indian population, causing the wholesale destruction and necessary reorganization of Indian society. The rapid annihilation of the Indian population then opened up land for European colonists.

A few Indian survivors remained within this newly created European society. Some occupied land that they no longer controlled, and had been reorganized to serve the purposes of others. According to Meinig (1986, 208):

> Some of these remnants lived in designated reserves, tiny enclaves demonstrating the coercive power of the Europeans, their policies of cultural separation, and their legal concepts of exact territorial demarcation and jurisdiction; a good many Indians simply found informal refuge in tracts of forest,

swamp, or shore, while others lived adjacent to towns in close dependence upon Europeans.

The Indian survivors were relegated to the edge of the colonists' towns and villages. They were compelled to adopt European tools, dwellings, clothing, and language. Yet they never assimilated into the Anglo societies, and the colonizers' views of them were increasingly tinged with contempt. Unlike the immigrant groups who came to find their way into the North American cities, the indigenous Indian population for the most part remained outside. Over time, a few were corralled into small reservations, but the majority of Indian survivors were forced away, beginning a sad chapter that would continue for many years. The Indian Removal Act of 1830, which forced all Native Americans—even those well assimilated into white society—west to Oklahoma, eradicated nearly all the Indian presence on the U.S. East Coast.

INDUSTRIALIZATION AND DIVERSITY

It was not until 1800 that any one city could be reliably considered to contain one million people. Of course, populations of a million have been bandied about to describe cities like ancient Rome, Baghdad, Chang'an, and Constantinople. But these are likely exaggerations. The massive infrastructural, agricultural, and territorial needs of such premodern cities would have been daunting. But we have reliable evidence for this degree of urban growth beginning in the nineteenth century. London achieved the million mark about 1800. Paris followed; and then likely New York. Moreover, a lot of other cities also increased in size. In fact, the overall urban population of Europe—where most urbanization activity took place—increased sixfold during the 1800s, even as the overall population doubled.

What single factor drove this urban expansion? It was all bound up with industrialization. The development and expansion of an industrial economy enabled mass production, which required mass consumption. While the new factories produced, a rapidly expanding urban population consumed. Urban logic fundamentally changed. Up until this point, the economy was effectively rural. Cities were important because they positioned themselves as the fulcrums around which this economy turned—they set the rules; they siphoned the surplus. But cities were constrained in that they could only service rural products, and so the vast majority of people needed to be located outside the city. With industrialization, the economy effectively turned urban. Even if the new factories were located in villages, these villages would grow into cities. And existing cities just grew larger.

The growth of great cities and the proliferation of medium-sized cities pushed together hundreds of thousands, and then millions of people, eager to work in the new factories. These people came mostly from elsewhere. Some would be taken from surrounding villages, but cities extended their reach far beyond to distant regions and especially to other countries. The search for opportunity precipitated waves of in-migration, and so cities grew at the countryside's expense. Industrial cities captured more and more of a country's rural population. Crossing national borders depended on how much opportunity was perceived, and how easy was the entry. The United States had plenty of land, and had long welcomed immigrants—at least European immigrants—to its cities and farms. When the available farmland closed up, the cities continued to attract an enormous tide of immigration. It was the industrial cities in the Northeast and Midwest that were key, as the smaller, less industrial Southern cities held little appeal. By the turn of the century, immigrants and their children constituted over half of the population in America's industrial cities (Ward 1971). These numbers would continue to rise until the U.S. Congress cut off overseas immigration in 1924.

There were other settler societies that also picked up substantial immigration. In many cases it was the availability of land that attracted the earlier waves, but it was the industrial opportunities that kept more immigrants coming. After World War II, Canada provided a welcome destination for many immigrants. While the United States continued to be restrictive into the 1940s and the 1950s, Canada became far less so—at least for European settlers—and immigrant groups were attracted to the large cities of Montreal, Toronto, and Vancouver (Herberg 1989). Formal discrimination against non-Europeans was finally eliminated in 1967, and a points system was introduced. In the case of Australia and New Zealand, both countries adhered to policies that favored British national origins well into the mid-twentieth century. Australia later eased up by allowing more Europeans to settle, and then finally abandoned its "White Australia" policy in 1973, replacing it also with a points system. New Zealand finally moved away from a national origin–based system in 1986, allowing for substantial Asian immigration for the first time (Ongley and Pearson 1995).

At the same time, the many European cities—principally in Britain, Belgium, Germany, and France—that were rapidly industrializing did not necessarily attract overseas immigrants, as this would come later in the twentieth century. However, industrialization did lead to greater immigration and diversity. Newcomers from around the British Isles flocked to the new opportunities in the British industrial cities. Another interesting case was Paris, where the volume of immigration from other European countries was so robust that it helped France become among the most ethnically diverse societies of the 1920s. Migrants from Belgium,

Germany, Italy, Poland, and Spain arrived looking for employment in construction, seasonal agriculture, and other menial jobs. France, with birthrates far below that of most other countries, had more opportunities and also had a citizenry that was less willing to take on some of these jobs (Ogden 1989). Most French immigrants settled in border areas and in the Paris region. The result was that immigration helped to shape European cities as well, just not yet at the scale that was occurring in North America, and certainly not anything close to the levels of perceived diversity that impact European cities today.

WHAT HISTORY TEACHES US ABOUT ETHNICITY

Ethnicity is a new term, but the concept of ethnicity dates back to the beginning of history. What a short survey like this chapter can offer is a sense of the many ways in which ethnicity has been fashioned, how ethnic groups have interacted with one another, and how ethnicity transformed the city. One important idea presented has been that ethnicity is observed whenever two or more cultural groups come together. The most common way that people of a particular culture describe themselves is as "people," with others being "barbarians," "savages," or worse. Urbanization and globalization—two processes so dominant in the twenty-first century— are what brought people together and forced some form of accommodation, though normally under unequal terms.

This brings out the second idea, that ethnicity and inequality tend to go together. In several instances, the origins of severe inequality itself has effectively created ethnicity, or forced the slight cultural differences between people to calcify and become impermeable. In nearly all instances, ethnic groups form a sort of ladder—hierarchical pluralism—with a top group, a bottom group (or groups), and possibly several groups in between. One can view this through the lens of intersectionality, which examines how social categories such as ethnicity, gender, and class interact to propagate and amplify disadvantages, resulting in persistent inequality (Tasan-Kok et al. 2013). The relative status of a group affects the life chances of its members in any number of ways, to be detailed later.

Third, the ways in which ethnics are defined and their relative status as compared to other groups is manifest both in the spatial arrangements of the city and in the landscape marked by each ethnic group. One could not go into a "European town" of a colonial city and not be impressed by the spaciousness, the graciousness, and the continued signaling that this was a group that ruled on the backs of all other peoples. A shabby settlement on the outskirts of town more often than not marks a group that is itself socially, politically, and economically marginalized. There are not always such stark spatial expressions, but they happen frequently enough, and continue to exert their hold on modern cities today. The ways in which ethnic groups are incorporated into different societies, and the spatial expressions of this incorporation, are the themes of the next chapter.

3

℘

Contextualizing Ethnicity

Every society has its own way of navigating ethnic differences. While it is not possible to account for all the variations in how ethnic groups are constructed, how they interact, and their relative positions, knowing how the broader society constructs its national identity and how it handles the cultural diversity within informs the nature of ethnic relationships. As discussed in chapter 2, societies have managed their diversity in different ways. So it is useful to consider a few basic related themes as they apply in different contexts. From this, we can begin to identify several themes in how ethnic groups are incorporated into societies. This goes along with the fundamental motif of this book—that ethnic identification cannot be essentialized. The nature and boundaries of an ethnic group depend on the broader society and the other ethnicities present.

Who decides how ethnic groups can and should incorporate? In this respect, the national culture as it has evolved over time is key. Each country has a different conception of itself and how it looks at others. These different conceptions can be seen in policies such as the approach to immigration, the ability of foreigners to acquire citizenship, or even in the usage or non-usage of words like "diversity" or "ethnicity." It is also important to note that these national views change over time, often spurred by forces nudging this change along. Several countries, for example, have moved from countries of emigration to countries of immigration. Many of these same countries have also gotten significantly older. Taking a larger view helps us escape the trap of many ethnic studies, which examine such a vital phenomenon through only a single lens.

THEMES IN ETHNIC INCORPORATION

The first theme has to do with how ethnicity fits into the way a society sees itself. For instance, the "melting pot" is more than a well-used metaphor; it is also an ideology that promotes a particular matter of cultural and political incorporation. In the case of the United States, this ideology promoted the notion of each immigrant group eventually assimilating into a fairly undifferentiated group of "Americans," though it did offer an additional aspect: that newcomers had the capacity to change what an "American" means. The truth is that the melting pot scenario worked for many immigrants, as people that would have been considered quite different eventually did blend. Among immigrants coming to the United States, the Irish were initially considered an inferior race; by 1950, they had attained true "whiteness" (Roediger 2005). A different form of assimilation entails the idea that culturally different groups are expected to blend in and conform to the dominant culture. Countries like France view all members of society as Frenchmen and Frenchwomen first and only (Brubaker 1992, 2001). Of course, this official orthodoxy can fly in the face of very real prejudices that exist among many French residents, but it helps to explain why ethnicity in France is often played down. In the early nineteenth century, there was still a large majority of people within France who did not speak French and, hailing as they did from Brittany or Provence, would not have considered themselves French. French policy worked to erase that difference in accordance with what "French" culture was supposed to be (Weber 1976).

While varieties of assimilation have clearly occurred in some cases, there have been many instances where assimilation either does not get started, or does not have a chance to complete. Even among the various European descendants in the United States, the resurgence of "white" ethnicity in the 1970s provoked views that the United States was more of a lumpy stew or a salad bowl than a melting pot. The new notion of diversity, of hybrid nationalities, can be described as "differentialism," and it exists today in many societies, especially settler societies like the United States, Canada, or Australia. Poised against this would be those societies where hybrid identities or even the value of an independent ethnicity is shunned. In such cases, the expectation is that all members of the nation adhere only to the nation, without developing an additional "ethnic" identity. How this occurs can vary by society. Contrasting this would be the Japanese sense of nationhood, which is airtight to the extent that it is virtually impossible for outsiders to become Japanese in any manner: "There is aversion to extending citizenship toward those of non-Japanese origins and toward a segment of its population that bears the stigma of past premodern outcaste status" (De Vos and Wagatsuma 2006, 128).

The second related theme involves the classification of a country's residents. Categorizing a population in the census by some sort of ethnicity (whether or not it is termed such) is two centuries old, and it is an activity which has always been contentious. The main issues involve the belief that one can objectively measure subjective identities. Beyond this, counts resulting from a census provide a snapshot of the numerical power of an ethnic group, and so have political ramifications as groups attempt to maximize their size, or may decide to boycott the census for fear of revealing minority status (Kertzer and Arel 2002). For other societies, the act of counting itself is considered divisive. Given the French state's view of its citizenry, it has logically resisted most forms of classification because such an activity contravenes the unity of the French nation (Blum 2002). The act of designating categories can shape how groups perceive themselves and other groups nearby—helping to fuse together formerly disparate identities (Kertzer and Arel 2002). Morning's (2008) work on how ethnicity is officially classified is instructive in this instance. She found that out of the census documents she collected, 63 percent used an ethnic classification of some sort. But the terms varied. Ethnicity was the most common term, followed by nationality, tribe, and then race. In general, the study found that ethnic enumeration is less common in Europe and Africa, perhaps signaling a greater concern with national unity (Morning 2012). Nationality was a common designator in Eastern Europe and the former Soviet Union. Tribe was more popular in South America, whereas race was a term used mostly in North America (which included Central America and the Caribbean). It is quite a political statement in and of itself for a society to enumerate its ethnic diversity; even more telling is how a society chooses to categorize it (Simon and Piché 2012).

The third theme is the relationship between ethnic groups and status. This is mostly expressed socioeconomically, but can be political as well. In nearly every society ethnic differences map on to status differences, whether as a legacy of past injustices such as slavery, current discrimination, occupational segregation, or uneven levels of economic or human capital. In fact, a system of ranked ethnicity has been by far the normal situation in all plural situations (Horowitz 2000). But the ranking changes based on who is in power. Ranked ethnicity applied to all more articulated states, kingdoms, and empires throughout the world. When European countries began to assemble empires, they often scrambled the existing arrangements by imposing their colonists as the dominant group among indigenous peoples, replicating a system of ethnic stratification and often doing so in a way that was consciously racialized—denying the original people any rights whatsoever. Many settler societies developed from this territorial imperialism, allowing colonists to acquire land that had belonged to native tribes. The indigenous populations would be pushed out, separated from the new society that had been imposed on them. Or they might be confined to playing a subjugated role in this society. Complicating matters even further was the introduction by the imperial overlords of new populations. As we discussed in chapter 2, slavery had long been a part of most empires, and many slaves were unlucky enough to be war captives or other unfortunates brought in as spoils of conquest. The new European empires, especially in the Americas, went further. All European imperialists participated eagerly in the Atlantic slave trade, bringing individuals from the African continent to each of the American colonies. These groups immediately became part of the multicultural mix under conditions of drastic oppression. New populations were also introduced as labor migrants, filling a niche distinct from colonizer, colonized, and slave. Unlike slavery, this migration was not forced, but these populations would be enticed by the prospect of a much better life. Different groups were brought in to different regions. In the case of Southeast Asia, controlled by the English, Dutch, Spanish, and French, Chinese immigrants entered as tradespeople and merchants. In the case of East Africa, South Asian immigrants assumed the mercantile role. These groups have been described as "middleman minorities," held at a remove from other groups in society and placed in a stratum between the high-status group that ran the society and the low-status people that they ruled (Bonacich 1973). For the most part, members of these middleman minorities came over with the full expectation of returning home after they had made some money. And while some did, many others remained, and have continued to play a role in society after colonialism's end.

However formed, such distinctions in status help to sharpen ethnic divisions, rendering them quite salient. At times, the same group dominates in both the political and socioeconomic realms and, as such, can press its advantages. Other times, political power differs from socioeconomic clout. When this occurs, political elites from one ethnic group use their power to curb the economic advantages of other ethnic groups. For example, minority English speakers in Quebec used to enjoy major social status advantages and tremendous economic clout (Porter 1965). Once Quebec's French-speaking majority acted on its political advantages, it set policies to reduce the social and economic advantages of the English language and, by extension, of the English-speaking group. A more heavy-handed policy was established in Malaysia, where the government initiated procedures seeking to curb the economic power of the Chinese minority (Cartier 2003). The point is that ethnicity is framed in large part by such inequalities. It determines the way the group sees itself and is seen by others, and it figures into the group's position in society.

The fourth theme concerns the relationship between a particular ethnic group and other important ethnic groups within the society. This is merely to emphasize that no ethnic group exists in a vacuum; its definition, salience, and opportunities for action are determined by what and who surrounds it. This is especially true under immigration. A new population entering a society will find itself compared and contrasted with existing ethnicities. Such perceptions play a powerful role in where the ethnic group is placed. One effect might come from the extent to which an ethnic group is seen as similar to existing groups within the society, and can find itself categorized alongside them. For example, the children of African and Caribbean immigrants to the United States cannot help but be incorporated within the existing racial dynamic of American society (Kasinitz 2004). They must negotiate their place within this dynamic and try to separate themselves out further, create a variety of pan-ethnic associations, or gradually incorporate "black" society. The choices that are required are far different if the same group of immigrants finds themselves in a country such as Sweden, where no indigenous black population exists. Another effect can result from how a particular population is given a special niche vis-à-vis the existing groups. The so-called middlemen minorities describe groups that have been brought between the large, indigenous and, in most cases, colonized population, and the smaller population of colonizers. Such groups, whether they are Indians in East Africa or Chinese in Indonesia, often prosper from the economic opportunities in this situation, but also find themselves the objects of antagonism and political discrimination.

Diversity is a popular term that itself carries a diversity of meanings. Much of it has to do with what type of diversity we are discussing. While cultural/ethnic diversity is the focus of this book, and often a shorthand for what "diversity" refers to, there are many other forms of diversity: class, gender, sexual orientation, political views, age, ability, geography, and more. Another aspect stems from the scale at which diversity may be considered. Wright and Ellis (2000) make the point that often we consider diversity at the neighborhood level, when in fact much of the action occurs at the scale of the region. We also need to consider the salience of these different groups. A self-described "hyphenated" identity can indicate assimilation into the broader population, and less and less meaningful ethnic distinctions. Someone who traces his or her existence or ancestry back to Germans, Italians, Slovaks, and a number of other different populations does not really belong to any one of these groups; this ethnic identity is more or less symbolic (Gans 1979). In another context, ethnic distinctions, however construed, are important to people's attitudes and behaviors. The significance of ethnicity may be tied into how it fits within the broader society, and how it intersects with a range of other identities with which people define themselves. The combination of these cross-cutting and reinforcing identities—for instance the correlation between ethnicity and economic disadvantage—can play a powerful role in determining how a particular ethnic identity is construed.

MODES OF INCORPORATION

Incorporation describes how groups within a society relate to each other and to the broader polity. This became a more pressing issue with the rise of nationalism (Herb and Kaplan 1999). National identity and nationalism as we know it did not truly exist prior to the eighteenth century. People might be ruled by the same king or emperor, many felt kinship on the basis of a common language, and certainly there was a strong sense of religious identification. Yet, kings often did not speak the same language as their subjects, languages varied tremendously across small regions, and religious identities were too widespread to truly constitute what we would consider a nation. People held a loyalty—or were compelled to hold a loyalty—to those people who protected them or to whom they owed filial obligations. Citizenship was mostly a feature of cities and conferred upon a select few. Most people—in places around the world—were considered subjects. Nationalism changed all that: people were defined in relationship to each other, and this relationship was based primarily on an idea of cultural affinity.

How well ethnic groups incorporate into a society must be viewed in conjunction with the national ideal that defines that society. Definitions of modes of incorporation today include the kind of mixing that occurs at the ground level—where people interact and define themselves as part of one group or another—and at the level of the state, which promulgates and propagandizes a particular ideology. Sometimes these levels are in alignment, but sometimes they are not. The state may consider itself to be a fairly homogeneous place at the same time as it encounters a great deal of diversity on the ground. What is more, both the reality and the ideology of incorporation can change quite rapidly. During periods of intense ethnic civil war, such as characterized the Balkan states during the 1990s, it was considered astonishing that groups that had been living in such relative harmony could turn so viciously on one another at a moment's notice. How this comes about is a mystery of human nature, although often the signs can be foretold.

Figure 3.1 is intended to outline some of the different modes of incorporation for cultural groups within a society (after Ashworth 2011). The x axis runs from what would be considered a more singular or homogeneous society, to one where there are several different groups and a great deal of diversity. The y axis distinguishes between situations with a fair degree of interaction between groups on a daily basis, and situ-

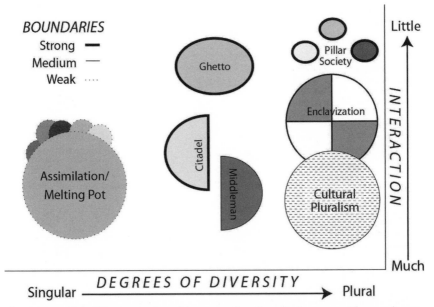

Figure 3.1. The different modes of incorporation for ethnic groups. The *x* axis runs from what would be considered a more singular or homogeneous society to one where there are several different groups and a great deal of diversity. The *y* axis distinguishes between situations with a fair degree of interaction between groups on a daily basis, and situations with very little interaction. *Source:* After Ashworth (2011).

ations with very little interaction. Interactions between groups are not necessarily friendly or even cordial, but interaction of some sort should take place in these cases.

Table 3.1 shows how different modes of incorporation reflect perceived differences between a group and the society, the quality of cultural identity, the societal and group view of group rights, the power relations between the groups, levels of interaction, the succession of group distinctions across time and generations, and the types of changes that can occur in regard to the cultural attributes of the group. Of course, all sorts of contingencies may present themselves, but this seems to cover much of what matters when looking at how groups' incorporation reflects the preexisting conditions and how it shapes social and spatial outcomes.

One of the objectives of this book is to relate the social structures of ethnicity to some sort of spatial patterns. However, there are no simple direct relationships in how these modes manifest themselves in spatial terms. Spatial patterns are exceptionally significant to the lives and opportunities of groups, but cannot be predicted as well as they might. They are instead contingent on a host of different factors, which influence exactly how groups may express themselves geographically.

Table 3.1. Different Modes of Incorporation and Their Effects on Ethnic Communities

	Cultural Differences	Cultural Identity	Group Rights/ Political Autonomy	Power Relations
Assimilation/ Melting Pot **Integration**	Declining	Either conformity to one group or blended	None	Even
Persistent Minorities	Persistent minority distinctions	Minority identity/ identities often defined externally		Hierarchical Structure
Citadel			Rights supersede those of the majority	Minority Domination
Middleman Minority			Group rights restricted	Economic power; little political power
Ghetto			Few rights	Little/no power, perhaps some self-efficacy
Multiculturalism	Yes	Strong	Varies	Equivalent with some differentials
Pillared Society/ Divided Cities	Yes, often enhanced	Fixed and ossified internally and externally	Operate as independent societies	Hierarchies within pillars
Enclavization/ Encapsulation	Yes	Identity at the group level	Some group rights—may be contested. Institutional completeness	Some groups disadvantaged; others may acquire some power
Cultural Pluralism	Yes	Identity at the individual level	Diversity, but defined more individually	Dynamic and shifting

Interaction	Succession	Temporal Changes	Examples
Complete	Merging of differences, retention of some symbolic aspects	Movement toward blending	White American immigrants
			French national integration
	Most cultural identities merge, but particular identities remain salient		
Control but little social interaction	Rarely breached	Often temporary, especially postcolonial	Indian hill stations; Europeans in Dar es Salaam
Economic interaction	Fixed	Can remain a long time	Chinese in Jakarta
Some interaction at bottom of economy → no interaction	Fixed	Can remain a long time	Soweto, South Africa
			Classic African American ghetto
Varies		Identities retained	
Limited interaction ranges from cordial/distant to actively hostile	Hardened distinctions less likely to change across groups	Change requires major events; e.g., civil war	Catholics/Protestants in Belfast; Muslims/Christians in Beirut
Not as much	Groups retain cultural distinctiveness, but often with alterations. New immigration refreshes identities	Shifting and dynamic	Minorities in the Netherlands; ethnic groups in Kenya
Considerable	Cultural distinctiveness retained, but fewer ways to anchor it. New immigration refreshes identities	Shifting and dynamic	Toronto ethnic groups

However, some tendencies can be drawn out, and their geographies and significance can be divined, by some of the attributes listed in table 3.1. These are more fully explained below.

Assimilation and the Melting Pot

The far left of figure 3.1 describes either an assimilationist or a melting pot mode of incorporation. This is where a society sees itself as eventually becoming practically uniform. This does not mean that all cultural distinctions are wiped away—in many cases that would be impossible—but it signifies that blending is the ultimate goal. While both assimilation and melting pot achieve the same rough outcome, there is a distinction between the two terms. Assimilation implies that new groups will come and blend into a cultural framework established by the dominant group. A melting pot suggests a transformation of the entire society as it blends together attributes of different entering groups with the dominant group. In some ways, the American ideal has shifted from one of assimilation, in which new groups were expected to adopt the Anglo Protestant mentality of the founders, to one of the melting pot, in which the society considers itself in a state of evolution—albeit with varying degrees of enthusiasm toward this goal. Other settler societies have also evolved in that direction as they begin to embrace new groups and changes to the overall culture. Clearly the successful completion of an assimilation/melting pot will result in complete interaction between groups, because viable group distinctions will no longer exist.

The first mode of incorporation, assimilation (which includes a melting pot scenario), is relatively straightforward. The expectation is that all manner of distinctiveness tends to vanish over time, and this would certainly include any sort of spatial distinctiveness. While few societies are truly uniform, all societies have experienced the assimilation of once-distinctive groups. These groups have gradually become indistinguishable from the rest of the society, even though they once were distinct subpopulations. They may or may not have been spatially distinct. The closest examples would be those of many white European immigrants to the United States, who largely followed in the path of the two-three generation model of assimilation (Alba and Nee 2014). In these instances, the goals of improving economic circumstances, providing even better opportunities, and finding a nice place to live resulted in greater contact. More and deeper interactions, culminating in marriage across ethnic lines, meant that so many groups once looked down upon—notably Italian and Polish immigrants—became better accepted over time (Roediger 2005). The boundary of "white" Americans expanded to embrace this group—

often over two and perhaps three generations—until there was virtually no specific geography attached to them as a group.

Assimilation describes more of an aspirational goal than something that occurs in reality. In many cases, newcomers arrive in a society structured by ethnic/racial divisions, and find themselves categorized into one of these larger groups. In the post–World War II era, Herberg (1983) invoked a "triple melting pot" within which white ethnics assimilated into a Protestant, a Catholic, or a Jewish tradition. While this categorization left out African Americans and completely ignored Asian Americans or Latinos, it held some utility at a time when religious distinctions were powerful and marrying across these faith lines was a big deal. Most significantly, it revealed that social context was not monolithic, but could be split into multiple contexts. This idea foregrounded the notion of "segmented assimilation," which describes where groups are channeled into distinct populations by virtue of their ethnicity or race. Portes and Zhou (1993) use the example of the United States, where the extant racial divide between whites and blacks causes immigrants from the West Indies or Sub-Saharan Africa to assimilate into the African American community. This has little to do with any group preference, but follows from conditions encountered in the receiving society. European and some Latino immigrants, by contrast, may more easily assimilate into the white population. Other societies have different sociopolitical structures that make a big difference in the assimilation pathways of immigrants. The French model, which I discuss above, still aspires to a thorough integration of each individual without acknowledgment of any special group status. Political attachment to the French state and the values of the French nation is encouraged. The children of immigrants, especially, are brought into the French nation through the schools and the workplace (Schnapper 2003).

Citadels

The ranking that occurs among ethnicities within nearly all societies achieves an extreme version when one ethnic group assumes complete dominance over others. The distinction is further heightened when this overlord group does not constitute anything close to a numerical majority, but instead operates as a conquering minority. The ruling class is aligned with a particular ethnic group—normally people who have conquered a territory and have moved in to administer it. This group distorts and overlays the existing social structure to create a society where they are clearly on top. What is more, they normally take steps to sequester themselves from the rest of the population (Marcuse 1997). The spatial expression of such sequestration is easy to see. Members of the overlord group secure for themselves the most attractive parts of the city, while limiting access to the "natives." From these lofty redoubts, they rule the society and all other ethnic groups. These neighborhoods are termed citadels, reserved for society's elite to mirror their position and exclusivity.

The creation of citadels was common within colonies. We have already discussed the development of segregated neighborhoods in colonial Indian cities such as Calcutta. But these cities could be miserable during some seasons of the year. During the nineteenth century, many British colonists—uncomfortable with the urban heat and humidity and seeking to avoid unhealthful, "miasmatic" conditions—established special cantonments in the hills and mountains. Here the status differentials and the segregation between colonizer and colonized was perpetuated: "the Elysian hills not only offered a break from the weather—and a chance to play house in a make-believe English country getaway—they also provided the most monumental of segregated perches for a condescending ruling race" (Nightingale 2012, 121).

In these hill stations, mansions, oversized "cottages," and Swiss-style chalets were strung across the slopes and ridges, whereas "hutment" allocations were provided downhill for the necessary native labor and merchants (Nightingale 2012). Throughout, as with most such segregated situations in which ethnicity and class are interlinked, Indian servants were requisite residents of the white neighborhoods, although they could never belong to these areas. Rookie officers were expected to retain a couple dozen servants alone!

After former colonies became independent countries, the citadels continued on. Even though there were no specifically race-conscious residential requirements, Smiley (2009) describes the situation in Dar es Salaam, Tanzania, where established housing plans effectively segregated the Europeans (at first Germans and then British) from the Asian and the African populations. The impact was the same, however. Enclaves like this thrive when there is a direct power basis. Once that power basis is gone, it becomes more difficult to maintain that level of segregation, though remnants of this former spatial arrangement are likely to remain if members of the privileged minority remain in the country. If and when the colonialist minority moves out, wealthier members of the indigenous group occupy these neighborhoods. By the 1960s, much of the residents of the European section in Calcutta were succeeded by prosperous non-Bengali-speaking Indians (Berry and Rees 1969).

Middleman Minorities

Another consequence of imperialism was the introduction of new ethnic groups to new lands, under the auspices of the colonial power. Usually, these groups were brought in to fill an economic niche, as traders, artisans, or laborers. Such newcomers were effectively slipped into a stratified system with a small number of colonialists and a large population of native peoples (who were themselves often divided culturally). The members of this middle ethnic group would be set apart, either voluntarily or justified by their fear of living too close to the indigenous population, and so operated as middleman minorities (Bonacich 1973) because they were located at the social and economic intersections between colonizer and colonized.

South Asian migrants assumed this middleman role in much of East and South Africa. Many South Asians initially ventured from the Indian British colony to the colonies on the western littoral of the Indian Ocean. These folks were mainly involved in long-distance trade but, by the turn of the twentieth century and especially the 1910s, were being encouraged by the British government to settle in their East African colonies. British favoritism and advantages in human capital benefitted this group, especially in comparison to the indigenous population. To be sure, there were considerable ethnic and socioeconomic differences within the broad group of "South Asians," but by and large they held a middle position between Europeans and Africans. Eventually, they came to own many of the more prosperous wholesale and retail firms, and were disproportionately active in higher-paid professions (Van Hear 1998). Even though many Asian Indians lived in quite modest circumstances, these prosperous individuals became the face of the middleman minority, stoking the resentments of native peoples.

Within Southeast Asia, Chinese migrants entered a variety of colonies, including Spanish Philippines, French Indochina, British Malaya, and the Dutch East Indies. These newcomers came to occupy a special place within these societies. On one hand, they were given a fair degree of autonomy and encouraged to make money as merchants who often provided their services to the indigenous population. Imperial powers granted these new migrants more freedom than was allowed the indigenous groups— and for the Chinese, there was far more economic opportunity than they could possibly find in their homelands. While many Chinese considered themselves sojourners, and many likely returned home, many more put down roots, eventually establishing a cultural presence for generations.

The contexts also differed from society to society, depending on the ruling powers. The British were more controlling than the Dutch, and the Spanish even more so than the British. Dutch authorities were more likely to control the Chinese community indirectly. In what is now Indonesia, colonial Dutch authorities used a system of indirect rule over the Chinese community (Freedman 2000). Many Chinese in cities like Batavia (now Jakarta) grew rich through their business dealings but, on the flip side, ended up being distrusted by both colonists and colonized. The Chinese population was spatially constrained from the start. They were required to live within a specific neighborhood just outside the town wall. During the Dutch period of control, Chinese settlers were told to live in particular quarters, and even dress in a "Chinese way" (Leisch 2002a). These regulations were relaxed in the later stages of Dutch rule, and then no longer applied after independence. But the Chinese continued to prefer their own neighborhoods for living, and chose Chinese areas for the rest of their activities. Nowadays, many Chinese even live within gated communities (Leisch 2002b). These same neighborhoods persist today as a distinct Chinese settlement. After Indonesian independence, the Chinese population has always been treated as distinct, despite their long tenure. Anti-Chinese policies and popular riots as recently as 1998 have only exacerbated segregation, both from compulsion and by their own choice (Leisch 2002b).

Ghettoization

Ethnicity can be mutable. Ethnic composition and interrelations can change quite a bit from one generation to the next. Ethnicity can also be quite persistent. In such a case an ethnic group continues to draw its boundaries from one generation to the next, or have a boundary drawn around it. When this persistence is coupled with extreme levels of alienation between members of that group and the larger society, we often see a ghetto take form.

The Italian term *ghetto* refers to a Jewish neighborhood established in Venice (Calimani 1987), but such ghettos were found in other Italian cities and throughout Europe. The ghetto was conceived as a permanent quarter, ringed by buildings, high walls, and canals. Entrance was restricted, and required the payment of a toll (Hutchison and Haynes 2012). The Venetian authorities required that there be police patrols restricting entrance and exit, paid for by the ghetto inhabitants. Jews had to wear special stars and garments identifying themselves. Inside the ghetto were the pawnshops and a mix of people hailing from many regions as far flung as the Atlantic to the Middle East—many of them having fled to Venice as victims of the Spanish Inquisition. The concept of the ghetto was that it would contain a population that had to be cut off from the mainstream population, as contact with the ghetto residents could be distasteful and harmful. But in addition to the negative aspects, ghetto habitation could safeguard residents, as it provided them with protection from Christian mobs. In the case of Venice, the ghetto served as the primary Jewish quarter until 1797.

The establishment of the Venetian ghetto and other quarantined spaces for Jews found within medieval European cities was created by economic necessity colliding with canonical law. The Catholic Church prohibited the faithful from charging interest to lend money. Yet the development of trade, manufacturing, and all aspects of a robust economy demanded the opportunity to borrow funds. Since Jews were outside of the system, they provided this service, and since they were prohibited from owning land and pursuing many other occupations, they came to occupy this economic niche, necessary but reviled. For Jews to be allowed in the city, they needed to be placed at a distance from the main population. Initially this was on an island off Venice itself, but in the early 1500s, Venice established the Ghetto Novo or New Ghetto, and next to this was established the Ghetto Vecchio or Old Ghetto. About seven hundred households lived within this space (Hutchison and Haynes 2012).

Since these early instances, a ghetto has come to mean a neighborhood where close to absolute segregation exists. All individuals in the neighborhood belong to a particular ethnic group, and they are not allowed residence outside of this neighborhood. Of course, the first references were to so-called de jure ghettos: sequestered neighborhoods established by law or dictate. In the twentieth century, the Nazis brought back medieval persecution with a sadistic twist as part of their Final Solution. The notorious Group Areas Act legislated in apartheid-era South Africa first resettled African residents of areas deemed "white" into special townships. Soweto, outside of Johannesburg, was established in 1955 as a repository for those blacks evicted from their prior neighborhood inside the city. After this, all "natives" were required to carry special reference books that listed previous movements, employment history, and legal issues. People were arrested for failure to produce this book on demand, and the penalties for traveling into a "white" area without cause were quite severe (Nightingale 2012).

The more common form of ghettoization today is de facto, where extreme segregation is encouraged by government policy. In the American context, there have been two persistent cases of this phenomenon. One is among the African American population, who were forced into highly segregated neighborhoods and allowed much less opportunity to interact except under authorized circumstances. The other situation occurred among the Native American population, kept in separate reservations as a result of government policy. These groups were not allowed to blend into society. It is ironic that just when American assimilation was heralded, up through the 1960s, those groups were denied and ignored. Outside of the United States, we could probably place many outcaste groups in this category. The burakumin in Japan historically lived in outlying villages that resembled ghettos, and were so marginalized as to not even appear on official maps. The European Roma are also an interesting example, that somewhat fit into this categorization. Highly reviled in many societies, they rarely mix with others and maintain their separate communities, often found on the outskirts of cities on property that they do not own.

The sense is that Roma decisions to cluster are made somewhat volun-tarily, but because of their illegal squatting, they are frequently compelled to move (Greenberg 2010; Sim 2016).

The circumstances under which ghettos are formed are quite different from other ethnic neighborhoods that emerge among other new arrivals to the city. For one thing, they are more permanent. For another, the segre-gated neighborhood is more likely to include just a single group—unlike the more pluralistic environments often found within ethnic enclaves. The boundaries of the ghetto may change and even soften with time and generations. But the walls of segregation are very slow to dissolve.

Pillared Societies

There are several variations among societies that consist of several dif-ferent populations who consider themselves distinct and are considered distinct by others. The idea of having groups exist side by side, often with a fair degree of autonomy, was a feature of many past societies. Many suc-cessful empires accommodated diversity; some of them institutionalized it. So the Ottoman Empire, which played a leading role for six centuries, developed what is known as the millet system, in which members of non-Islamic faiths were organized as communities with their own system of laws. In a more modern state, the Dutch initially followed the path of providing each of its constituent populations all the necessary resources to become institutionally complete (Prins and Saharso 2010, Breton 1964). The policy motto was "integration with preservation of identity." This pil-lared society allowed for the founding of different schools, equal support for religions, and other cultural supports. Ultimately, though, the Dutch were not happy to have the sort of true division that could go alongside the presence of these differences, and so began to amend this policy in the 1980s and seek a more integrative policy instead.

A more extreme form of a pillared society is to consider a truly divided society, leading to the presence of divided cities. These situations involve two or more ethnic groups that have distinct national identities. Within these groups exists a fair degree of enforcement and also a fair degree of autonomy, whether granted by the larger national government or carved out by the forces of the group itself. A pillared society includes groups that cohabit the same country and often the same cities, but separate out in ways that impede cross-ethnic interactions except of the most scripted sort.

An excellent example of a pillared society would be the city of Beirut (Calame and Charlesworth 2009). Beirut, as the primary city in Lebanon, has long walked uneasily between its Maronite Christian, Sunni Mus-lim, and Shi'ite Muslim populations. The politics of Lebanon explicitly acknowledged this separation with powers clearly demarcated between confessional groups. In terms of resident lives, before the 1970s some residents did live in multiethnic spaces, but for the most part the groups were divided socially and spatially. In the wake of the civil war, which began in 1975, a "Green Line" was established, dividing Christian and Muslim communities (see figure 3.2). This line physically expressed the

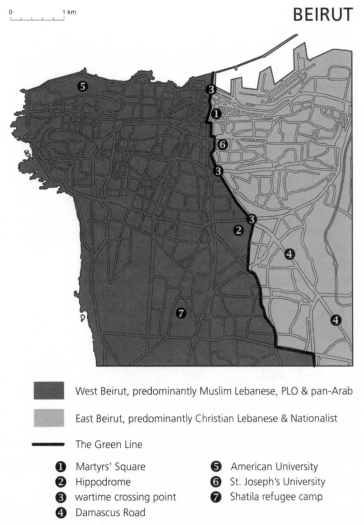

West Beirut, predominantly Muslim Lebanese, PLO & pan-Arab

East Beirut, predominantly Christian Lebanese & Nationalist

The Green Line

❶ Martyrs' Square   ❺ American University
❷ Hippodrome   ❻ St. Joseph's University
❸ wartime crossing point   ❼ Shatila refugee camp
❹ Damascus Road

Figure 3.2. During peak hostilities in the 1980s, there was a strong and clear division in Beirut between the Muslim and Christian halves of the city. These two districts were separated by a Green Line, so designated because of the vegetation that grew where buildings and streets were abandoned. *Source:* From Calame and Charlesworth (2009). Used with permission from the University of Pennsylvania Press.

lack of interaction, save for outbreaks of extreme violence. The partition itself was dismantled in 1990, but its ghost remains, and Beirut continued as a pillared society. Only recently have there been signs of new life along this once-abandoned strip.

Other examples include distinctions between the Catholics and Protestants in Northern Ireland, where separate paragovernmental enclaves have been established with near uniformity within and extreme separation without. Jerusalem has long struggled with its division between Muslims and Jews, and the extent to which it must duplicate every function: roads, schools, hospitals, economies, and identities (Calame and Charlesworth 2009). For a less violent example, Brussels also operates within the pillared context of Belgium, where the division between Walloons and Flemish is fairly stark. Yet within the capital region itself, the two linguistic groups are clearly concentrated but the spatial divisions are not as stark. This spatial arrangement, along with a larger sense of belonging to the capital region, helps to attenuate some of the disunion (Murphy 2002).

Incorporation within a pillared society, especially a hostile one, means that multiculturalism is manifest at a very coarse scale. There may be a common city government, or a common state at some level, but members of each community live separate existences and have little opportunity for interaction. There are variations on this theme as the threat of overt hostility goes down. And it is possible to conceive of a pillared society that functions to the benefit of everyone. But unfortunately, most seem to emerge from some degree of conflict.

The Pluralist Model

While a pillared society suggests a polity in which different groups choose not to get along in any meaningful way, a multicultural or plural society allows for interaction between groups. Of all the modes of incorporation described here, this is perhaps the hardest to capture and includes the greatest number of variations (it is also the subject of chapter 10). This is because multicultural societies experience different trajectories and outcomes, their governments will promulgate different policies, and the economic situations will vary a great deal as well.

Many societies subscribe to an ideology that recognizes persistent differences and tends to view group membership as a significant intermediary between the individual and the state. The pluralist model of ethnic incorporation allows for the retention of separate ethnic enclaves, and very often a different way of managing political and economic activity. We can describe this as an "enclavization" or "encapsulation" model, in that group boundaries are unofficially and officially used to designate people and can be the basis of political, cultural, and economic rights. It is a model that is sought by some ethnic groups as a way of protecting their identity and maximizing their political power (Qadeer 2016). It is even seen as a possible explanation for the stubborn differences found among many ethnic groups within the United States. Pluralism often means that ethnic members relate less as individuals and more as part of a group. Each group is given an opportunity to represent itself among all the groups in society, maintaining some internal cohesion even as certain levels of separation between that group and other groups is inevitable. The Dutch case is instructive in that the Dutch have long sought to accommodate separate immigrant groups by granting them a large degree of group rights. In a policy introduced in the 1980s and since altered, designated minorities managed their own institutions, paid for by the government, and were represented as groups within a corporate whole (Uitermark, Rossi, and Van Houtum 2005). The policy was abandoned under concerns that it was causing too much government-subsidized separation (Prins and Saharso 2010).

Pluralism as practiced can have a dark side, as the most openly racist societies, from Nazi Germany to apartheid-era South Africa to the pre–civil rights U.S. South enforced a system of identity cards, separation, and inevitable persecution. The political situation in Kenya, for example, reflects a case in which ethnicity forms the basis for realizing political goals. Ethnic groups are mobilized as a way to compete electorally, and political parties are styled as way to develop pan-ethnic coalitions (Ajulu 2002). The bad news is that this leads to situations where the ethnic victors can deny others access to various resources, such as education and government employment.

Truth be told, many circumstances probably lie between assimilationism and pluralism. It depends upon the group and on the context. Even in the United States, where an assimilationist ethos prevails, there is a great deal of lip service paid to ethnic identity: Columbus Day parades for Italian Americans, St. Patrick's Day events for Irish Americans, and other ethnic festivals that highlight the tapestry of the United States. By the 1960s, social scientists were arguing that the American melting pot was more of a "lumpy stew" or a "salad bowl" (Zelinsky 2001). Books entitled *Beyond the Melting Pot* (Glazer and Moynihan 1963) or *The Rise of the Unmeltable Ethnics* (Novak 1972) pointed to the endurance of these ties. However, despite the clear longing of many Americans for a hyphenated identity, social distances continued to close for many. Rates of intermarriage, often considered the last stage in assimilation, increased between ethnic groups (Gans 1979). This led to diminishing rates of spatial difference between particular groups, though the major social and spatial differences between whites, African Americans, and Latinos continue.

Pluralism is also a feature of societies in which different ethnic groups have traditionally played distinct social and economic roles. Far from benign, these roles are often emblematic of socioethnic stratification, in which ethnic groups are arrayed from bottom to top, and such pluralism may breed a fair degree of resentment. The buffering of ethnic groups between a colonizing people and the peoples they colonize is common to many societies.

NATIONAL IDENTITY, ETHNIC IDENTITY, AND ETHNONATIONALISM

Ethnicity can only develop in the presence of others, and within a specific context. The contours and experiences of every ethnic population are determined by several factors, including the level of economic development, the history of ethnic relations, the economic configuration, and the historical legacy. Among the most significant is the nature of the political system.

For much of world history, a successful civilization would be bound within a political empire. From the Roman, Han, Islamic, Mughal, Incan, Aztec, Ottoman, and many, many more, empires represented the highest military and political achievement. They also united broad swaths of territory and many communities of people. In an empire, nationalism does not really exist, and many empires were diverse on the basis of their circumstances. In fact, it was quite common for an empire to be ruled by a dominant minority. This was the case with the Manchus (Qing dynasty), who swept in from Manchuria and proceeded to carve out their zones of power and control. It was the case among the Mughal emperors of northern India, who likewise controlled groups that were culturally and religiously alien. Other Islamic empires were likewise "tolerant" of diversity—allowing its expression, though always making sure that clear lines of stratification were kept in place.

Today ethnic relations are set within a national context. The idea of a nation, of national identity, is the key basis in determining the ways different ethnic groups relate to each other within a society, and how ethnic groups are defined (Herb and Kaplan 2008). The advent of a nation-state ideal led to many different outcomes when it came to ethnic incorporation. While the ideal was in place, few countries managed to form a territory where the national group occupied exclusively the boundaries of the state and nowhere further. In fact, the geography of national groups was, and continues to be, messy.

There are many distinctions in how the nation is defined, and this is vital to modes of incorporation and how minority populations are accommodated. The national ideal may be "civic" (Breton 1988). The principle behind this is that a national community can admit peoples from culturally different backgrounds. Upon entrance into the society, they are given the opportunity to enter the nation as well. This ideal would perhaps fit best under the heading of cultural pluralism, where significant diversity exists but identity is still constructed at a personal level. Often a civic nationalism is based on a shared ideology or aspirations. Often, but not always, new members are expected to acculturate—to learn the cultural attributes of the nation, with language being the most prominent. The United States is often held out as the foremost example of a civic nation, as it has incorporated many different cultural groups over time (and excluded several others from full membership). France in many ways has also practiced aspects of civic nationalism—admitting many separate groups into the French nation, but demanding that each lose its (public) cultural distinctiveness to fully embrace the French nation.

The ideal of an ethnic nation is one in which the criteria for belonging are based on cultural similarity and, often, lines of descent. For the Japanese, for example, national identity is based on longtime ties to the Japanese islands and to the distinct language and religious traditions that the denizens of these islands share. These distinctions have even been framed biologically—leading to a racialized sense of what the Japanese nation means (Murphy-Shigematsu 2000). Yet there are several peoples living in the Japanese islands who do not share "Japanese" traits. The Ainu population found in Hokkaido is indigenous, distinct from the Japanese in appearance, and possessed of a separate language (which is spoken less and less). The Japanese attempted to fold the Ainu into their ethnicity through intermarriage—a strategy rejected by Ainu activists (Siddle 2009). The burakumin and Korean minority, discussed earlier, are excluded from this national conception as well (Weiner and Chapman 2009; Neary 2009). And the Japanese who live outside the main islands, in Okinawa and to the south, are also only tenuously linked to the Japanese nation.

The binding of a particular ethnic identity to the nation has become much more prominent in recent years. Many countries have spawned what are described as ethnonationalist movements. Connor (1993) defined ethnonationalism as simply the loyalty to one's own ethnic group as it represents a prospective nation. Ethnonationalism has been the hallmark of many nationalist movements and is the basis for the ethnic nationalism described above. It has long been a strategy to mobilize self-determination for minority groups who wish for their own country.

Since Connor's piece, ethnonationalism has devolved from an affirmative identity toward an explicit rejection of both civic nationalism and pluralism. From being aligned with minority aspirations, it has become more associated with majorities who worry about the dilution of their cultural and political influence. Ethnonationalist movements—often under the guise of populist parties that skew left or right economically— have crept out of the fringes and into the mainstream in European countries and, now, the United States. The greatest fear of their proponents is that the character of the nation is being irretrievably transformed by changes wrought by diversity. An empirical study by Inglehart and Norris (2016, 4) shows that support for populist parties "was strengthened by anti-immigrant attitudes, mistrust of global and national governance, support for authoritarian values, and left-right ideological self-placement." These traits fit into what the authors describe as a cultural backlash against a changing nation.

Recent years have seen several examples of this trend. The advent of "white nationalism" in the United States seeks to retain the American nation as a preserve of "whites," however this may be defined (Taub 2016). Other groups, while allowed to remain, are considered to make much more secondary contributions that must be sublimated to the national character of white America. The 2016 election of Donald Trump, while not explicitly self-defined as a white nationalist movement, was supported by many proponents of this philosophy. The election of the Law and Order party in Poland, while economically liberal, stems from a resentment of European liberalism and culturally alien newcomers (Traub 2016). The Brexit vote in the United Kingdom, which abrogated British membership in the European Union, was fueled by people who felt anxious about immigration and European encroachment on British values and control over their own borders (Kaufmann 2016). In addition, the strongest anti-immigrant sentiments occurred in those towns and villages that remained relatively homogeneous, but where diversity was close by. The voting for ethnonationalist parties was highest *near* high immigrant areas, but not within these areas, and can be described as the "halo effect" (Rydgren and Ruth 2013).

One takeaway from this chapter should be that the nature of ethnic identity depends in large part on the nature of national identity. How do people in the country see themselves? National identity can be constructed in a number of ways. It can be exclusive or open. It can be more rigid or more malleable. Each of these has implications for the mode of incorporation open to different cultural groups that enter the society.

4

❦

Fashioning Spatial Concentration

Any observer of the social landscape will tell you that different groups
cluster together. People who are similar in certain ways tend to be
more comfortable associating with each other. In an essay for the *Atlantic
Monthly*, columnist and pundit David Brooks (2003) spoke about how
people self-segregate as much as possible. Upscale Democrats live next to
other upscale Democrats. Church-going pro-lifers are often found in the
same community as other Church-going pro-lifers. Within professions,
within social networks, and within neighborhoods, Brooks argues that
diversity is more of a mirage that applies less to daily life than we want
to admit. These arguments do have an element of truth; after all, people
seek comfort by associating with similar people.

This shows why ethnic and racial segregation is such an important topic.
In this book, I prefer to speak more broadly of clustering because it can
encompass a variety of outcomes, of which true segregation is only one.
Groups may live together but in mixed environments, or they may concentrate in terms of activity spaces like retail shops instead of residences.

The purpose of this chapter is to try to sort out the factors involved in
generating different patterns of group clustering. The factors involved can
be categorized, but the operation of these factors will vary from case to case.
Different countries have different views of what diversity means, they have
different configurations of the groups involved, and they have different parameters for what the government is capable of doing. Some societies have
long been accustomed to the impact of new peoples coming in and settling,
whereas other societies have only recently had their national homogeneity
disturbed by a new and sometimes unwelcome diversity.

SOCIAL DISTANCE AND SPATIAL DISTANCE

Ethnic concentration at whatever level does not occur simply by chance. Distinct forces set into motion patterns of geographical behavior among members of the ethnic group, and among those groups with which it interacts. The context matters a great deal, too. An ethnic group residing in one city may display sharply different spatial tendencies from the same group in another city, largely because the circumstances vary.

One key dynamic in conditioning spatial configuration stems from the different relations between groups. Back in the 1920s, a sociologist named Emory Bogardus (1925) compared what he called the social distance between groups and their spatial distance. The more a group felt and was perceived as distinct from other groups, the more likely this group was to be spatially segregated. Social distance is usually asymmetrical. Members of the group could decide they wanted as little as possible to do with other people, and so they sequester themselves. This is found among certain populations, such as the Amish or Hasidic Jews, who feel they can better preserve their culture through isolation. More common is the situation in which an ethnic group is stigmatized by the majority group who want as little as possible to do with them. Late nineteenth-century discrimination against Chinese immigrants in the United States and Canada exemplifies this circumstance, where members of the minority are encouraged and even forced to occupy separate spheres. All contact between members of the stigmatized group and members of the majority are tightly controlled and circumscribed.

Assimilation theory suggests a gradual closing of social distance. Milton Gordon's (1964) hugely influential book, *Assimilation in American Life*, considers this relationship explicitly. As a minority group remains within society, and begins to participate fully in its economic, political, and social life, it functions more and more like members of the mainstream group. The first stage occurs when and if members of the minority group take on occupations similar to those of the mainstream. This may be followed by greater political involvement, as identity politics give way to membership in mainstream political organizations and voting patterns that mirror the majority. Complete social integration—wherein members of a group are no longer perceived as being different, or the differences are so minor as to not preclude social entanglements with members of the majority— follows from this. Intermarriage between members of the ethnic group and of the majority group (or the group that it is assimilating into) also increases dramatically to a point where it ceases to be surprising or even notable. The children of these unions are then of mixed ethnicity, and so assimilation is complete.

This well describes the experience of a number of different ethnic groups who came to the United States, at one time pilloried and even considered to be members of a different race or even different species, but now fairly indistinguishable from the mainstream society. Individuals who trace their ancestry to Ireland, Italy, Greece, or a number of other European countries have followed the assimilation process. Whether this particular process works for other minority groups is hard to say, and certainly it is questionable whether this applies to members of minority groups outside the United States, where the national contexts are so wildly different. Certainly, most settler societies have seen a decline in social distance among key groups. Non-settler societies are more complicated, but here too we can consider populations that at one time would have been kept at arm's length, but are now indistinguishable from the dominant group.

Social distance has big geographical implications because it is so bound up with spatial distance. Social separation is more easily achieved through spatial separation. For those groups who wish to sequester themselves as a means of preserving their way of life, the drawing of territorial boundaries is among the most straightforward strategies they can use. Rather than having to discourage contact with one's neighbors, it is easier if all the neighbors belong to the same church, speak the same language, and follow the same traditions. For groups who are discouraged from interacting with the dominant population, their relegation into particular spaces saves the majority the trouble of having to come across them in their everyday life. Group access to majority spaces is severely circumscribed by specific duties and customs.

The relationship between social distance and spatial distance has been shown to be applicable in studies that asked members to rank other groups by their desirability and then compared these rankings to segregation indices, discussed in chapter 5 (Pineo 1977; White, Kim, and Glick 2005). These measures also apply declines in spatial distance to declines in social distance. When members of an ethnic group are spatially intermixed among all other people in the society, then that suggests that assimilation may be afoot.

Some more recent views have argued that social and spatial distance are not inextricably linked and, in fact, may be decoupled. Zelinsky and Lee (1998) argue that in a modern mobile society, ethnic groups maintain their own identity without being required to live in close proximity to each other. There are instead other venues that allow for frequent get-togethers, all accessible by car. While members of ethnic groups are spatially dispersed, mobility allows them to maintain ethnic community ties. In this situation, what Zelinsky and Lee term *heterolo-*

calism, the flows across space and between ethnic groups become more significant than the patterns created by the residential concentration of these groups. Since this article was written, opportunities for members of an ethnic community to maintain ties across wider spaces have only expanded with the emergence of the Internet, and the accompanying opportunities for social media and virtual face-to-face contact. I discuss these further in chapter 11.

This heterolocal pattern can apply to a number of American ethnic groups, who continue to forge close ties while at the same time living in a more dispersed manner. This can often be found among wealthier ethnic populations. The Asian Indian population in the United States rarely settles in clustered neighborhoods, but instead scatters across the metropolitan area (Skop 2012). Asian Indians prefer to live near work, and often intermingle with the majority white population. Many Indians in the United States are well off and can afford housing in affluent suburbs, nor are they victimized by too much prejudice (though some examples do occur). The result is that the settlement pattern is heterolocal, with no distinct Asian Indian residential landscape but instead a suite of institutions, festivals, and associations helping to anchor this community. Of course, countervailing examples can also be found. The Jewish population in the United States has been fairly inclined to concentrate residentially, even though it has become among the more affluent ethnic groups (Glazer and Moynihan 1963; Goldstein 1969). So heterolocalism is a useful perspective, but it depends on the group. What is more, it reproves a view of clustering that only considers residences at a fairly tight scale, when in fact ethnic clustering can encompass many more experiences, and often occurs at larger geographical scales.

IMPOSING SEGREGATION

Perhaps the key issue to consider is whether ethnic clustering is imposed or voluntary. Do ethnic groups (and by definition, this includes so-called racial groups) live together, separate from other members of society because they have to, or do they concentrate in like neighborhoods because they want to? When we speak of *constraint*, we are referring to a situation in which members of a group are forced to inhabit specific spaces.

The degree of constraint varies. The historical ghetto demonstrates absolute constraint, in which members of a group were systematically quarantined into a space. Of course, within these spaces life circumstances varied, as the medieval Jewish ghettos were not nearly as awful as the Nazi-era interpretation. The most notorious recent example came from South Africa, where the policy of apartheid was propounded at the local scale as well. The Group Areas Act mandated that "coloureds," "Indians," and "Africans" live in specified neighborhoods distinct from the dominant "white" population (see figure 4.1). Traveling outside these areas—essential for work or shopping—required a pass (Western 1981). Today such quarantined spaces still exist, often found in labor colonies. The development of a two-tracked system of legal protection is endemic

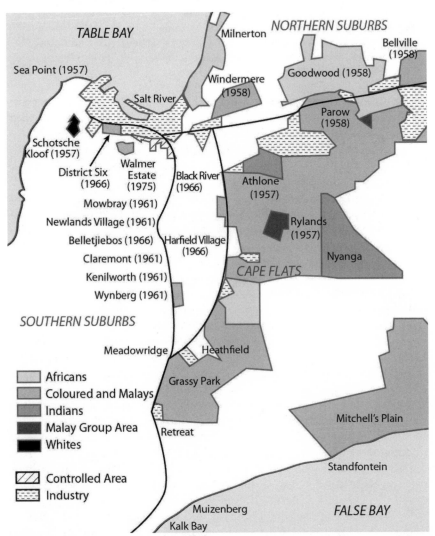

Figure 4.1. Designated segregated districts in Cape Town, South Africa, as of 1977, with the dates representing when a particular area was "declared" for a specific racial population. *Source:* **Map produced by Jennifer Mapes, based on material in Bickford-Smith et al. (1999).**

to the states of the Persian Gulf, which require a massive number of non-nationals to keep their economy going and their construction rising (Fargues 2011, 278):

> *De jure* separation is embodied in all the legal provisions that differentiate between nationals' and foreign nationals' rights and duties, the obligation of every foreign national to have a national sponsor (the kafala system), the prohibition of intermarriage (with only very few exceptions), and foreign nationals' lack of access to a number of fundamental rights (such as family reunion and access to public education for their children) and labor rights. *De facto* separation is reflected in the lack of or in the severely limited interaction between nationals and non-nationals.

For instance, the workers brought over to build the lavish hotels, shopping malls, and office buildings in Dubai live in special zones, far from city residents (Elsheshtawy 2008).

The African American ghettos of the United States were not overtly forced in the same way, but arose from a variety of mechanisms at a variety of scales that made severe segregation inevitable. Beginning with the early migration of black Americans from the rural South to the urban North, the segregation patterns established were always far more durable than was the case for European immigrants (Lieberson 1980). In the years before the 1968 Fair Housing Act was passed, restrictive property covenants stated that property could be bought and sold only under the stipulation that it not be sold to blacks. Other groups—such as Jews or Chinese—were also targeted by such covenants as well. This language prohibited owners from selling to minority individuals, limiting their ability to occupy particular neighborhoods. Even without such written stipulations, landlords or real estate agents were free to refuse housing to blacks without fear of prosecution. In addition, a dual housing market, in which blacks were forced into particular neighborhoods, developed. There was no opportunity for African Americans to live where they chose, and the increasing numbers of blacks who migrated to northern cities (where the jobs were) only forced a larger number of people into a limited set of spaces. In cities across the north, the "black belts" broadened slowly, but retained their sharp boundaries (Morrill 1965; Rose 1969).

The construction of public housing after World War II might have been an opportunity to ease the segregation patterns that had begun to deepen in U.S. cities. After all, this has been the strategy of Dutch and Swedish cities that use social housing as a way to promote more diverse living arrangements, at least in regard to social equity which can then open the door to greater integration (Van Kempen and Van Weesep 1998; Murdie and Borgegard 1998). This was not the case in the United States, however, as all steps were taken to preserve racial separation. The construction and management of public housing devolved to local housing authorities, who were given broad discretion. Neighborhoods were demolished and residents were moved to high-rise apartments that were normally segregated by both race and class (Kotlowitz 1991). In Chicago, efforts to place returning black veterans in public housing after World War II were met with angry white mobs. Rather than push on, the Chicago City Council forced public housing projects overwhelmingly occupied by African Americans into a narrow set of sites in existing African American neighborhoods, replacing the old, horizontal ghetto with a new, vertical ghetto (Hirsch 2009).

These sorts of mechanisms are often referred to as *institutional discrimination*, because they use agencies, regulations, and other bureaucratic means to steer members of an ethnic group into particular areas. One example of how institutional discrimination perpetuates segregation shows up in the establishment of the mortgage market in twentieth-century American cities; this effectively promoted existing spatial arrangements and made it much more difficult for blacks to own housing and to share spaces with whites. Lenders categorized neighborhoods in cities on the basis of credit risk, and much of this "risk" was tied to racial composition. As is shown in figure 4.2, the residential security maps produced by the Home Owner's Loan Corporation were color-coded by risk grade (Jackson 1985). The worst grade, colored red on maps, was considered unworthy of credit, and this low grade derived from the presence of just a few black families. In many ways, these maps represented the tip of an iceberg of wholesale housing discrimination. Myriad private lenders, abetted by the actions of the Federal Housing Administration, made thousands of decisions, all arriving at the same conclusion: African Americans and the neighborhoods they lived in did not qualify for housing mortgages (Hillier 2003).

The passage of antidiscrimination laws has removed the most blatant forms of discrimination, but it continues in more subtle forms. Studies conducted by auditors—usually involving matched pairs of white and black couples looking for housing—demonstrate that many landlords still discriminate. Real estate agents still often steer blacks into "black" areas and whites into "white" areas. And numerous examinations of the mortgage lending market show that, while redlining is illegal, banks have continued to discriminate against minorities and minority neighborhoods in making mortgage loans. Perversely, in the last 15 years the banks have steered many of these same folks toward subprime and sometimes predatory loans (see chapter 9). And in South Africa, where formal ghettoization enforced by the Group Areas Act has been abolished, discriminatory practices continue to impede the integration of the black, white, and "coloured" populations (Asmal, 2000; Christopher 2001).

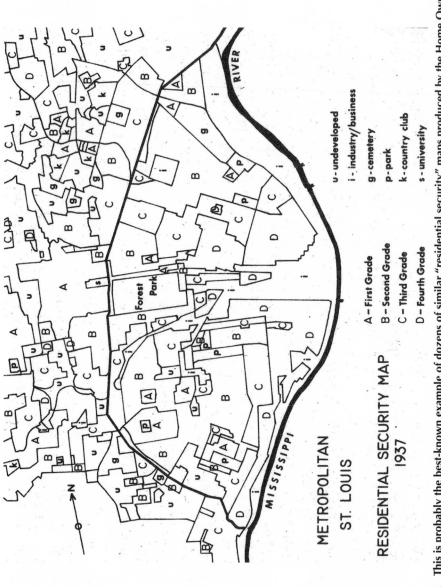

METROPOLITAN
ST. LOUIS

RESIDENTIAL SECURITY MAP
1937

A – First Grade
B – Second Grade
C – Third Grade
D – Fourth Grade

u - undeveloped
i - industry/business
g - cemetery
p - park
k - country club
s - university

Figure 4.2. This is probably the best-known example of dozens of similar "residential security" maps produced by the Home Owner's Loan Corporation for American cities. The maps were color-coded by risk grade, providing a guide to lenders, with the lowest grade of "D" used for neighborhoods with African American residents.

Even without formal mechanisms that restrict housing, socioeconomic disparities have a huge effect on ethnic segregation. Neighborhoods in most cities are distinguished on the basis of class, and wealthy, poor, and middle-class neighborhoods are kept separate. Most ethnic groups are arrayed along economic lines, particularly those groups that are new or subject to discrimination. Inasmuch as separate ethnic groups enter the housing market with significant income disparities, they are likely to occupy different spaces. In most European cities there is little evidence of outright discrimination against particular ethnic groups, but the housing choices of many ethnic and immigrant groups have been circumscribed by relative poverty. Malheiros (2002) showed how immigrants in Southern Europe occupy much of the self-constructed slum housing on the urban fringes of cities. And ethnics in Dutch cities experience much the same dynamic, as their own poverty forces them into lower-quality neighborhoods avoided by the majority (Bolt, Van Kempen, and Van Ham 2008).

CHOOSING SEGREGATION

Choice is the flip side of constraint when applied to the decision of where to live. As anybody who has looked for an apartment or a house to rent or own realizes, there are myriad aspects of the decision. How much does the place cost? Is it close to work? Is it in a nice neighborhood? How are the schools? These are also decisions guided by available information, since it is difficult to know all the options (and even more so in the past). House hunters need to obtain what they see as the best place within the budget that they can afford, given what they know.

When these parameters in the choice of housing are considered, it is understandable why members of a particular ethnic group might decide to live together. For new immigrants, their field of knowledge is going to be quite limited, and their budgets will be extremely tight. Receiving assistance from a relative or a fellow co-ethnic through churches or other institutions makes a great deal of sense. It is a mutual project, as very often members of the existing ethnic community cannot wait to help new arrivals. As one respondent in Ley's (2008) study of Korean and Chinese immigrant churches stated, "[My father] used to go to the airport whenever he had time, and would just wait for a plane to arrive from Korea, and would see if someone might need a place to stay or help in getting places" (Ley 2008, 2064).

Sometimes apartments can be sublet, or there can be some particular knowledge that might be useful. With a bit more money, or if one wants to buy a house, there may be a desire to use a co-ethnic realtor, who then can also help steer the client to specific areas. This is true in the Toronto suburbs, where Portuguese realtors help to structure the information available to home buyers and tend to favor Portuguese neighborhoods (Teixeira and Murdie 1997). In all of these calculations, living in a neighborhood populated by co-ethnics makes a lot of sense, but it also stems from true economic constraints. All else being equal, people live where they do in order to maximize their satisfaction and minimize discomfort or conflict. But people who have less money also require more in the way of community resources (Hickman 2013)—someone to watch over their children for a couple of hours while they do a job, for instance, or vital public spaces where folks can interact—and so living among friendly and familiar people becomes an essential attribute in a way that it would not be for the affluent. What is more, those folks who have less money often go without personal transportation, and so are even more inclined to seek out this spatial closeness.

This might be part and parcel of *resurgent ethnicity*, the notion that groups are attracted socially and spatially to other co-ethnics due to a natural favoritism for one's own people (Logan, Zhang, and Alba 2002; Wen, Lauderdale, and Kandula 2009). In discussing how concentration can have positive as well as negative impacts, Peach (1996) argues that segregation is "one of the key methods of accommodating difference" (379). According to him, the good kind of segregation is voluntary, based on choices, and can confer all manner of benefits. To be clear, since these are generally the benefits of being close to one's co-ethnic community as opposed to being separated from other communities, these positive impacts do not necessarily require strict segregation, but they do encourage clustering.

Indeed, the spatial concentration of a group enhances what Fischer (1975) calls *subcultural affiliations*. Within a large community, the opportunities for interaction increase. Groups more easily maintain their ties to each other and preserve certain aspects of culture. Members of the same group are much more likely to bump into each other on the street, while shopping, and in a variety of environments. Clustering also provides a critical threshold by which more institutions, businesses, and organizations that especially cater to the needs of the ethnic group can survive. In turn, their establishment solidifies and valorizes the ethnic community itself. This is the cornerstone of *institutional completeness* (Breton 1964), by which groups maintain churches, news organs, welfare societies, clubs, and other institutions that keep them together. More institutional completeness strengthens intra-ethnic relations, leads to a greater sense of community, and reinforces the internal boundaries that define the ethnic group. It is a question of *bonding social capital* (Portes 1998), in which institutions encourage interaction by putting ethnic members in regular contact with one another, promote a common perspective and message through shared media outlets, and instill a set of goals to which every member subscribes.

To be sure, this is all possible within a large, dispersed space—but it requires more time and effort. The clustering of people within a small space minimizes these investments and facilitates contact. It enables community members to maintain a city within a city. In some of the larger ethnic spaces, most of the services provided in mainstream society are replicated within the ethnic neighborhood itself.

The combination of a substantial ethnic population and ethnic institutions confers a degree of familiarity and comfort (Boal 1976; Kaplan 1992). An ethnic neighborhood is often emotionally charged because it provides succor to its residents and a type of psychological defense against outsiders. This can be seen within cities where distinct ethnic neighborhoods are found. The island of Montreal has long been divided between English Canadian municipalities and neighborhoods in the west side and French Canadian neighborhoods in the east side. Within Montreal, for instance, the resident of one of the many English Canadian neighborhoods feels quite unperturbed strolling the streets where others speak the same language, practice the same faith, and share similar attitudes. That same person may feel significantly less content when walking through a French Canadian neighborhood (Kaplan 1992). A lot depends on context. In peaceful situations, the difference in feelings may not be extreme, but where feelings of hostility persist, one's own ethnic neighborhood bestows an emotional and physical sanctuary.

Ethnicity can imbue the neighborhood with symbolic value as well, a point I will discuss further in chapter 6. The very name of the neighborhood takes on cultural connotations. A neighborhood such as "Harlem" becomes internationally known shorthand for a place that manifests the black experience. Other neighborhoods may not be as well-known as such iconic ethnic spaces, but they carry local significance. Such neighborhood symbols are historically useful as well, because they reinforce past events and sentiments. This increases their influence on present-day ethnic attachments. In fact, sometimes these place brandings might be important enough that community leaders actively seek out an ethnic designation, even if the population composition does not warrant it. In a city near Los Angeles, ethnic entrepreneurs tried to label a business district "Little India," despite the fact that Indian Americans comprised less than 5 percent of the population and many residents were opposed (Sheth 2010). But many businesses will gladly take on the mantle of an ethnic community if there is money to be made. Many residents also appreciate the added clarity of a known neighborhood designation.

CONSTRAINING CHOICE

The distinction between constraint and choice is often less clear-cut than it appears. We tend to think of choice as a positive thing, but what seem like "choices" can be based on factors that are not optional at all: fear, internalized prejudice, or a reaction to the choices of other groups. In fact, many of the observed choices are set within a limiting set of parameters based on structural constraints, and resulting in a segregated environment (Brown 1983).

One such constrained choice stems from the sense that an ethnic community, either as individuals or as a whole, is threatened. This obliges the community to go into a kind of defensive crouch, exemplified by the geographical patterns it exhibits. These defensive aspects have been demonstrated in studies of ethnic neighborhoods in contexts of ethnic strife. The neighborhood resembles a fortress—or a walled city—reminiscent of ancient and medieval cities whose boundaries were used to cordon one group off from the other.

Belfast and Londonderry are well-known and well-studied cases in our era. Since before the onset of the "Troubles" in 1970, Protestants and Catholics felt safer locating in their respective neighborhoods. While the high levels of segregation may have had other determinants, fear itself was a great motivator. Boal (1969) uncovered separate residential and activity patterns in Belfast as a result of this effort to preserve one's physical safety. Later studies show that Catholics and Protestants tend toward particular spots (McPeake 2000). In Londonderry, Kuusisto-Arponen (2002) mapped out numerous areas where members of one or the other group feared to travel. Markers such as graffiti and other cues can provide residents with the insights they need to delineate the more contemporary "walls" that divide some cities.

Such concerns constrain choice, often under the banner of self-segregation. Many groups enter a context in which they are clearly not wanted, at least by some segments of the native population. Leaving aside the wealthy expatriates, most newcomers cannot afford to live in the more affluent districts and must find their home within the more populated parts of the city. Threats of personal violence bubble at the surface, and a "minority" person is more likely to encounter an unpleasant and even dangerous situation if he wanders onto the wrong street. Avoiding certain neighborhoods and concentrating on others can be a valuable defense mechanism. Writing about the Muslim South Asian population in British cities, Phillips (2006) observed the avoidance of spaces in Bradford. These off-limit areas are seen as unwelcome to South Asians engendering fears of racial harassment. Much of the same could have been said about African American newcomers to northern cities after World War II. Beyond the fact that discrimination effectively prohibited their residential choices in large swaths of Chicago, Cleveland, or Milwaukee, there was the sure knowledge that venturing into white neighborhoods might be grounds for a beating, or worse (Wiese 2004).

Constrained choice also derives from the activities of another group, usually the majority group. Their decisions force a particular segregated outcome. The process known as *tipping* begins with members of a minority ethnic group moving into a neighborhood occupied by the majority. This is not welcomed by the resident majority, who may rationalize their objections from simple racism, to a fear of expanded crime, to a drop in property values (Farley and Frey 1994). The process is aggravated by the reactions of initial leavers, who worry over a relatively small minority percentage. These departures then render the neighborhood composition intolerable to the much larger proportion of later leavers, whose fears can be stoked by unscrupulous real estate brokers seeking to cheaply purchase vacated properties so as to resell them at a much higher price. Whatever the reasoning, the accumulation of these individual decisions turns a neighborhood around very quickly, flipping its ethnic composition in just a few years.

Again, the African American movement into white neighborhoods in northern U.S. cities best exemplifies this process. The initial response to this migration was a battalion of restrictions and discriminatory treatment in the housing market. Yet even in the absence of outright housing discrimination—or perhaps more accurately, in addition to this discrimination—many whites reacted to the black newcomers by leaving these neighborhoods. Research has shown that whereas blacks preferred more integrated neighborhoods, whites preferred to live in predominantly white neighborhoods. For whites, this decision to leave corresponds to a "tipping point" (see Schelling 1971; Clark 1991). When a neighborhood crosses a certain black percentage, it soon becomes all black as existing white residents move out.

The phenomenon of tipping is found in other contexts as well. European countries have experienced a strong upsurge in immigration over the last 50 years, and new arrivals come from farther and farther afield. This is true of former colonial powers, like Britain, France, and the Netherlands, who tend to attract a disproportionate share of immigrants from erstwhile colonies. Yet other wealthy countries with little recent history of colonialism have been implicated as well. Sweden had only a 1 percent foreign-born population in 1940, but now has an immigrant population of 14 percent. What is more, the composition of immigration has changed, with increasing proportions coming from non-European countries. And while Swedish cities, like European cities in general, do not have nearly as potent a level of segregation as the United States, there is still a threshold at which members of the majority are no longer comfortable and seek to move out. Andersson, Hammarstedt, and Neuman (2012) discovered that tipping points are reached in each of Sweden's cities: as a neighborhood contains more immigrants, fewer native-born Swedes move in, and more of the existing native residents move out. The tipping point is fairly modest; for the years between 2000 and 2007, it ranged from 3 to 40 percent immigrant, with an average of 9.5 percent. The authors found a fairly equal proportion of native Swedes who avoided immigrant neighborhoods, and existing residents who moved out.

WHY SEGREGATION?

Human geographers base many of their insights on the relationship between attitudes and spatial behavior. Just as an individual may move from her hometown to the big city in search of excitement and opportunity, so may she decide to live in a neighborhood because it feels "right," has a nice mix of amenities, and puts her more at ease. The decisions are driven by difference—often, in fact, a desire to avoid difference. No matter how righteous a person might be, we all make decisions to avoid strangeness and discord every single day as we seek to navigate a world that is more familiar. This is true of society, where a sense of alienation from certain groups translates into a desire to keep away from those groups. Likewise, camaraderie begets closeness—for all the birds who share the same display of feathers.

However, while the aggregation of these individual decisions is powerful, it would be naïve to consider these aspects alone. There are powerful forces that sway individual decisions, which compel people to live within certain areas, and which make what may seem like choices into clear constraints. Authoritarian governments can compel members of certain groups to live sequestered away from everyone else. More subtly, government may promulgate the sorts of restrictions that do not directly target members of a group, but carry the same restrictive effect. Other societal institutions, unless specifically barred from discriminatory practices, block free residential choice as well. Even when such constraints are not apparent, or after they have been identified and dealt with, the impact lingers. Segregation brought about by institutional discrimination can carry long-term effects. Often, what appears as a choice may be a product of implicit biases and economic disadvantages—channeling the selections that people make.

We cannot view the geography of ethnicity benignly. Certainly, it can carry many benefits for group cohesion and cultural expression. But once achieved, this geography also operates as an additional constraint. These processes shaping the geography of ethnicity ultimately shape the lives and opportunities of ethnic members themselves.

5

ᴔ

Measuring and Modeling Spatial Segregation

The concentration of members of a specific group is a significant sociological and geographical fact. The causes behind these patterns are complex, and the consequences can be quite meaningful. To better understand concentration, it helps to be able to measure it, or even model it if possible. This allows us to trace one group's experience over time, or to make comparisons between different groups, or between the same group in different contexts.

The terminology employed in discussing any sort of spatial sorting allows for some qualitative distinctions. Clustering could be considered any sort of concentration of the population group. It does not indicate that members of the group have exclusive possession of the space, but that they have a degree of spatial proximity that is not random. The clustering can be fairly loose, more apparent at the county level for example, or tight, where the clustering can be seen at the scale of a neighborhood block. The degree of clustering is important in and of itself, but it does not say anything about whether the space is shared with members of another group. If a group is clustered in such a way that it is completely separated out, then we begin to talk about actual segregation, which indicates that group members reside in a distinct area. Ghettoization occurs when all members of a single group are exclusively placed in a single space. This has been a common feature among stigmatized groups in the past.

There has been a fair amount of scholarship seeking to measure these different patterns quantitatively, to create a sort of typology, and to attempt to understand all the causal factors behind this clustering. To clarify, while conceptually segregation is a subset of clustering, often the term "segregation" is used to refer to both phenomena.

Segregation measures differ, from a universal index to local measures that can vary from neighborhood to neighborhood. Universal measures will take a large area—perhaps a city or a metropolitan area—and assign a single number to it based on how segregation operates within all of its many districts. It is analogous to taking the median income of a region. While the number tells you a lot, clearly there will be a great deal of variation between different parts of that region. This is where local measures of segregation can be valuable.

UNIVERSAL MEASURES OF SEGREGATION

Many universal measures of segregation have been developed over the years (see White 1986). The most famous of these are the index of dissimilarity and the index of segregation (identified by the letter D or S, respectively). These are functionally equivalent measures. The index of dissimilarity (D) compares the residential location of two groups, whereas the index of segregation considers a group vis-à-vis the rest of the population. The index of dissimilarity was popularized by sociologists seeking to capture what was happening in a city in a single number (Duncan and Duncan 1955; Taeuber and Taeuber 1969). This measurement has effectively dominated other indicators of segregation ever since researchers began using it. Success had bred more success; today, the dissimilarity index is often employed just so that it can be compared with other published cases using the same index.

The index of dissimilarity is calculated by dividing a region into several units. Commonly, a city can be divided into wards or census tracts. The distribution of a group in each of these subunits is then compared with the distribution of another group in each subunit. All of these individual distributions are then aggregated to form an index. If two groups' distributions are similar—say, they each have about the same percentage of the population in every ward as they have in the city—this will result in a small D value. If the groups' distributions are dissimilar—if members of one group are more concentrated in a few wards, whereas members of another group live in other wards—then the distributions will yield a large D value. D ranges from 0 to 1, or sometimes from 0 to 100 as a percentage. People often describe the resulting number as an indication of what proportion of a group would have to move to achieve complete evenness. A D score of 0.5 or 50 indicates that 50 percent of individuals would need to be relocated to other subareas for no segregation to occur at all.

The index of dissimilarity is easy to calculate, is intuitive, and is comparable with much existing research. It is not affected by the relative size of a group. Even a minuscule population could demonstrate a high index of dissimilarity. But this is part of its problem as well. No matter how unevenly distributed, small groups will never be really isolated, and will have to regularly encounter members of the majority.

Another popular measure was developed to account for the probability of bumping into others. The index of exposure, represented as a P^* index, was popularized mostly by Stanley Lieberson (1980). The exposure index measures the chance that people belonging to one group (x) will encounter members of another group (y) within their neighborhood, so it is a function of location and group size as well. Like the D index, it is measured from 0 to 1. A large minority who lives in a classic ghetto, for example, will occupy a lot of space and have very little exposure to members of the majority. They will have a low xP^*y score, which means the probability of members of group x being exposed to group y is also low. A group that is small in size may be unevenly distributed—with a high dissimilarity score—but still end up with substantial exposure to other groups, and will have a high xP^*y score.

The isolation index is conceptually the inverse of the exposure index, and measures the probability that members of one group will be exposed to members of that same group—in notational terms, xP^*x. This is also measured from 0 to 1. High isolation indicates that the members of a group are only encountering members of their same group. In some ways, this is the classic notion of segregation. African Americans in a city made up of several black neighborhoods will experience high isolation.

Of course, the reporting of these statistics depends completely on a statistical infrastructure that provides the necessary small-area data. Several countries do not have this, perhaps because they do not desire to broadcast that type of information. Other countries, like the United Kingdom and Canada, provide information on religion so that indices can be applied to the distribution of Catholics, Protestants, Muslims, and Jews—something that would not be possible in the United States. Changes in statistical acquisitions and reporting can completely change the ability to compile these indices. The U.S. Census recently abandoned the long-form census in favor of annual surveys, which provide more up-to-date information, but make it harder to study small areas such as those addressed by segregation indices. Under the Conservative administration, Canada decided to dispense with many aspects of its census collection, making it nearly impossible to obtain any information on racial and ethnic distribution. This policy has since been reversed with the change in Canada's government (Jackson 2016).

ENHANCING SEGREGATION MEASURES

The problem with these segregation measures is that they are effectively aspatial; they do not consider the relative geographical location of the units they measure. So imagine 5 census tracts, each with a high Latino proportion, in a city of 30 tracts. These tracts could be clustered together in the northeast part of the city, or each tract could be dispersed to separate quadrants of the city. Either way, the dissimilarity and isolation indices would be the same, but the actual segregation experiences would be quite different.

Spatial relationships can be incorporated into these indices by adding a measure of adjacency. An adjusted dissimilarity index that accounted for the length of shared boundaries between tracts was first introduced by Morrill (1991) and elaborated by Wong (2003). Similar D scores can reflect markedly different spatial patterns, as shown in figure 5.1. Essentially, adding a second element reduces the dissimilarity index, depending on whether adjacent units have similar or differing ethnic proportions. When adjacent units differ greatly from each other in ethnic composition, this reduces the segregation of the target group, and so the adjusted D score is much lower than the unadjusted score. If the ethnic composition is the same, then the adjusted D score is close to the unadjusted D score.

This adjusted index helps to account for the idea that a concentrated population is going to have a distinct experience from a dispersed population. Ways of modifying the index by distance between tracts can also be added to the calculation of the isolation index (see Massey and Denton 1988).

There are a few other, less commonly used universal measures, including centralization and concentration. All of these universal indices provide metrics for each city and, now more often, each metropolitan area. A report by Iceland, Weinberg, and Steinmetz (2002) utilizes such indices to demonstrate changes between 1980 and 2000 for each U.S. metropolitan area. These types of tables provide important comparisons across a wide range of groups and contexts, showing separate aspects of segregation.

One problem with universal segregation measures is that they may be insensitive to the presence of multiple groups and the proportions of these groups within specific neighborhoods. This is an issue of increasing importance as cities throughout the world become more diversified. For instance, Wong (2003) has created dissimilarity indices to account for multiple groups. But more specific measures can look at each neighborhood or area. For example, Allen and Turner (1989) employed an entropy index, which measures the extent to which different groups were mixed in each urban "place" ranging from some of the smallest to the largest (New York City). Maly (2000) proposed a neighborhood diversity in-

			D	D(adj)
a) 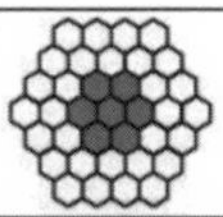		Large centralized racial/ethnic cluster in the core	1	0.80
b) 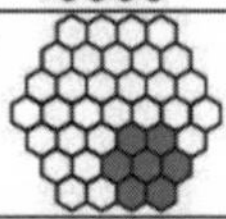		Large de-centralized racial/ethnic cluster on the edge	1	0.88
c) 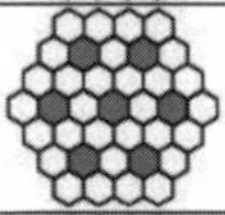		Uniform pattern of racial/ethnic enclaves with one in the core	1	0.53
d) 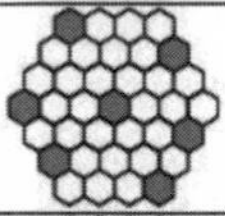		Scattered, or random pattern, racial/ethnic enclaves with one in the core	1	0.72
e) 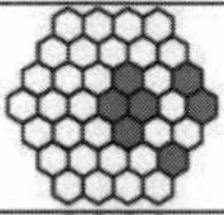		Relatively large racial/ethnic cluster in the core; small clusters at the edge	1	0.74
f) 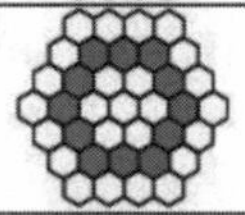		Contiguous racial/ethnic enclaves in the middle ring	1	0.47
g) 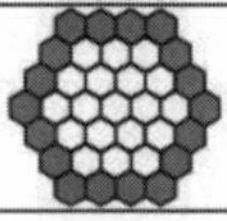		Contiguous racial/ethnic enclaves in the outer ring	1	0.67
h) 		Contiguous racial/ethnic enclaves in the outer ring with small city boundary	1	0.57

⬡ 100% Black ⬡ 100 % White

Figure 5.1. The same dissimilarity index can suggest quite different spatial configurations. This diagram demonstrates how an index more sensitive to spatial proximity better reflects these differences. *Source:* Brown and Chung (2006). Used with permission from Wiley.

dex that calculates the proportion of each group within each subarea as this compares to the proportion of the group within the city as a whole. Highly segregated tracts exhibit high values, compared to low values for integrated tracts. In an interesting twist, Holloway et al. (2005) developed an index of exposure to neighborhood diversity to determine whether mixed-race households encountered more or less diversity in their neighborhoods. They discovered that such households clearly lived in more diverse neighborhoods.

LOCALLY SENSITIVE MEASURES OF SEGREGATION

The advantage of universal measures of segregation is that they can take a large area, like a city or a metropolitan area, and assign a single number. This helps researchers comprehend the level of segregation and also compare city to city, and metropolis to metropolis, as well as compare the experience of different groups. This heuristic simplicity comes at the cost of missing the significant variations that are found across the metropolitan landscape.

Scale is an essential feature of segregation measures. Group concentration and separation are perceptible at different scales of resolution; it depends on the size of the subunits employed. A census tract, found in one form or another in many countries, includes thousands of people and a fairly large areal extent. While such a tract may be mixed as a whole, there can be internal divisions only captured at a more granular level. Segregation may be found in the housing estates of one neighborhood, between neighborhoods, or even between cities and their environs (Firman 2004).

Reardon et al. (2008) explicitly addressed this issue by developing a segregation profile to show how segregation may shift based on the size of the unit being considered. In many urban contexts, segregation tends to drop as one considers larger and larger units. An individual may live on a very segregated block, but within a larger precinct that is more racially mixed. Ever more integration may be observed at the scale of a ward, and even more so for the city as a whole. Yet within this general profile are numerous variations. Fowler (2015) classifies some profiles as standard, which conforms to the regular decline in segregation at larger scales; flat, where the same levels of segregation persist across scales; steep, with high levels of microsegregation expanding out to relative integration; or rising, where the larger scales of resolution bring out higher levels of segregation. Some groups are only segregated at a small scale, meaning that they experience clustering and proximity to fellow ethnics but are still exposed to other ethnics in the course of their daily lives. Other groups are segregated at scales both small and large, limiting their exposure. It is even possible for one's immediate neighborhood to be fairly integrated, but be sited within a fairly segregated city. Districts experiencing gentrification (which is often accompanied by racial change) can display patterns of super-localized high segregation, broadening out to greater integration, and then scoping out again to a predominantly segregated pattern.

Figure 5.2 shows how this might be perceived spatially; a high level of segregation at an extremely localized scale (say a cluster of buildings as part of social housing) may show up as less segregated and more diverse

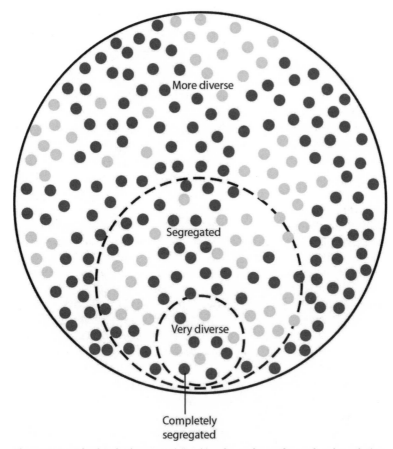

Figure 5.2. The level of segregation often depends on the scale of resolution; high levels of segregation at a highly localized scale can give way to greater diversity at the larger scale of the neighborhood. Segregation may again rise at the municipality level, only to fall at the county or metropolitan level. *Source:* David H. Kaplan and Jennifer Mapes.

at the larger scale of the neighborhood. Increase the size of the units to the scale of a municipality and the segregation level may increase again, only to decrease at the level of the county.

In Delhi, India, for example, larger districts are more mixed, but segregation is quite definite at lower spatial scales of blocks or groups of buildings (Dupont 2004). Similar results are found in Rome, where the segregation of immigrant groups is masked by the larger urban districts, but is apparent at the smaller scale of the urban zone (Cristaldi 2002). Even within relatively homogeneous Japanese cities, segregation is visible at finer spatial scales (Fielding 2004). These sorts of statistical considerations affect any measurement and make it difficult to compare across national contexts, since the size of units where data are available can vary considerably.

Geographic information systems (GIS) have greatly facilitated the calculation and display of locally varying measures of segregation. One of the most popular techniques is called the local indicators of spatial autocorrelation, or LISA for short. Spatial autocorrelation refers to the fact that variables in adjacent areas often share similar values by virtue of proximity. This can be a statistical issue if attempts are made to regress variables of spatial units, but when it comes to measuring and visualizing patterns, measures can be drawn up to show where segregation is most pronounced.

Moran's I is a coefficient measuring how likely units with a concentration of a particular ethnic group are to be surrounded by other units with concentrations of the same ethnicity. Groups that evidence a high level of spatial autocorrelation correspond to a positive Moran's I. Alternatively, groups that are not clustered correspond to a value close to 0. Groups that are negatively associated will report negative values. The measurement is affected by how far the units are allowed to extend, as weighting closer units more heavily will often result in a stronger association (Maré et al. 2012). Cross-Moran coefficients can demonstrate how likely ethnic groups are to be surrounded by groups of another ethnicity. A positive value shows that two groups are more likely to live near each other, whereas a negative index shows that groups are spatially avoiding one another. Pacific Islanders in Auckland, New Zealand, spatially correlate with Maoris but negatively correlate with Europeans (Maré et al. 2012). Moran's I can also be used to point out local areas of autocorrelation, often depicted on maps that show clusters with high associations and clusters with low associations. A study of Mexican cities yielded information on a variety of social characteristics; for example, significant clusters of indigenous peoples, low income, and participation in the informal economy were found on the periphery of Merida, Yucatan (Monkkonen 2010).

The use of the Getis-Ord G* index is an increasingly popular way to depict neighborhoods where segregation occurs (Getis and Ord 1992). Like many local area statistics, the "bandwidth" is critical, as it determines the distance by which neighbors are measured. The G* statistics is often portrayed as a z-score, where values above 1.96 indicate that the concentration is statistically significant. The G* allows observers to show local hotspots of ethnic clustering; higher z-scores correspond to more extreme cases. Pockets of intensity can be easily identified.

THRESHOLD ANALYSIS

A trio of geographers have revealed another way to depict segregation, not through a specific index, but through a categorization scheme (Johnston, Poulsen, and Forrest 2009). They argue that this threshold analysis represents a major advantage over single-number indices by allowing a measurement of neighborhood composition. This is particularly relevant within plural cities, where neighborhoods may contain more than two ethnic groups. In so doing, these researchers consider the charter group (or what we might otherwise refer to as the dominant group), the largest minority group, and then other minority groups.

In this case, neighborhoods are classified according to the proportions of people who live in the area (see figure 5.3). Let's assume that whites are the charter group, while blacks and Latinos are the two minority groups. Type I neighborhoods house nearly all whites—at least 80 percent. Type II neighborhoods would be considered integrated, with substantial proportions of black and/or Latino residents. Type III neighborhoods are also integrated, but in this case black and/or Latino residents form a majority.

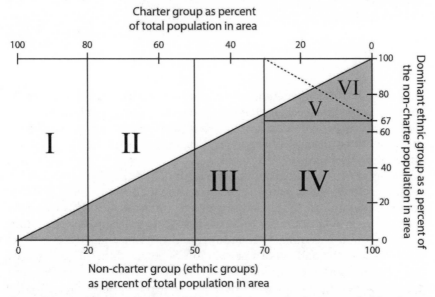

Figure 5.3. In this schema, type I neighborhoods are nearly all composed of the charter group. Type II neighborhoods are integrated with members of minority groups. Minority groups form most of the population in type III neighborhoods. Type IV neighborhoods are composed nearly exclusively of mixed minority populations with few members of the charter group. Type V and VI neighborhoods are confined to a single ethnic group, with type VI neighborhoods displaying the highest level of segregation. *Source:* After Johnston, Poulsen, and Forrest (2009).

Type IV neighborhoods are minority neighborhoods, but mixed between blacks and Latinos. In Type V and VI neighborhoods, either blacks or Latinos clearly form the lion's share of the population. The difference is that type VI neighborhoods include a large proportion of blacks or Latinos who live in the city as a whole. This describes a highly segregated, ghetto-like situation, and is rarely found outside the United States (Johnston, Poulsen, and Forrest 2010).

An analysis of London shows how this can be applied. Whites (the charter group), Indians, Pakistanis, Bangladeshis, Africans, and Caribbeans were used to categorize neighborhood types and compared between 2001 and 2011 (Johnston, Poulsen, and Forrest 2015). There were no type VI neighborhoods, but the geographers did note the change in the relative proportion of the neighborhood types. The number of neighborhoods that were exclusively white (type I) dropped in half, whereas the more mixed type III neighborhoods, where whites share the neighborhood with members of a non-white group, effectively doubled. The mixed neighborhoods with a negligible white population (type IV) more than tripled. Overall, this exercise showed a tremendous increase in London's multiethnicity, a diminution of white-only spaces, and more and more neighborhoods that were shared between different racial and ethnic groups.

URBAN AND FACTORIAL ECOLOGY

Measurements of segregation may capture how members of a group experience their spatial environment, but these are quite singular and do not necessarily provide a deeper understanding of the range of experiences encountered by groups. This has resulted in the search for typologies of different types of group clustering.

Among these measures are the contributions of the Chicago School of human ecology, which examined the settlement and movement of immigrants and ethnic groups in early twentieth-century cities. This was a period, before immigrant restrictions were put into place, when the volume of immigration was quite high and many immigrants hailed from places quite exotic to the native-born population. Scholars at that time observed these immigrants moving into poorer, more dilapidated quarters near the city center. In the process, these ethnic groups came to occupy the neighborhood, and then took over the neighborhood from the group who had lived there beforehand. This mobility was called human "ecology" for a reason, because this form of clustering was seen as analogous to a species invading and succeeding a particular niche. It was less focused on individuals than on cultural groups who were making these moves en masse. The original population that was displaced by the new group ended up moving to another neighborhood farther from the city center. Upward and outward social and spatial mobility allowed members of this original group to move into neighborhoods with more spacious housing. They then occupied this particular urban niche, succeeding yet another group who then moved farther out to occupy a neighborhood of even higher status.

This view of a city—and it was determinedly based on the American city—was informed by the twin notions that 1) group segregation was a natural phenomenon, and one of the key drivers of urban form; and 2) that as immigrant groups assimilated and grew wealthier, they would end up moving outward from the urban core as they moved up the socioeconomic hierarchy. Monographs were produced, especially in the 1920s and 1930s, describing some of these neighborhoods (Bulmer 1984). Here again, the perspective of the analysts was far from neutral. The Chicago School included a heavy reliance on urban determinism, which posited how location in the city could have powerful effects on its residents. As Wirth (1927, 71) concluded, these segregated spaces need to be "viewed as a socio-psychological, as well as an ecological, phenomenon."

This idea that ethnic groups cluster naturally in sections of a city was formalized with the advent of social area analysis in the 1950s, a deliberate attempt to map patterns of social difference. Social area analysis posited that the city was divided into several dimensions (Shevky and Williams 1949; Shevky and Bell 1955). In the U.S. context, these dimensions might be socioeconomic status, family status, and ethnicity. Each dimension described a distinct pattern, as shown in figure 5.4. Groups based on socioeconomic status were often arranged in wedges surrounding the city center. Family status (single, married, married with children, empty nesters) were represented as concentric zones radiating from the city center. Ethnicity—sometimes described as segregation in these models—appeared as patches that overlay these other dimensions.

Factorial ecology later employed statistical techniques to quantify these dimensions (Murdie and Texeira 2000). The contexts and groups were different, but metropolitan areas yielded consistent factors related to socioeconomic status, family status, and ethnicity, with other factors also emerging. Moreover, "ethnicity" as a generalized factor can shift, depending on which city is being measured. For instance, Driedger (1999) used factorial ecology to characterize some of the differences among Canadian cities, and these show some important contextual variations. Montreal exhibits segregation patterns based on language group and immigrant status, which makes sense considering that the city lies at the interface between Canada's two charter groups. Toronto is marked by the segregation of "visible minority" immigrants, appropriate given its status as a city with an exceptionally high percentage of immigrants from many parts of

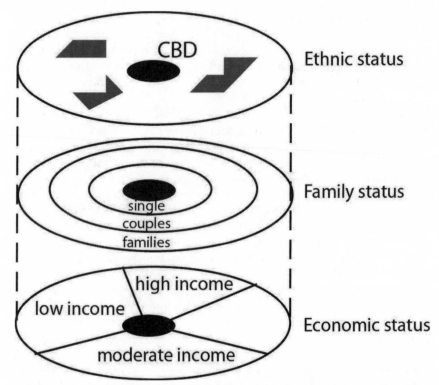

Figure 5.4. This schema displays the patterns revealed by three social dimensions. Socioeconomic status shows up as wedges surrounding the city center. Family status is displayed as concentric zones radiating from the city center. Ethnic status overlays these other dimensions. *Source:* After Shevky and Bell (1955).

the world. Vancouver, with its position as a Pacific Rim gateway, shows the divide between immigrants and native-born Canadians of mostly European stock. The smaller cities in the Canadian prairies tended to follow either the Vancouver or Toronto type of segregation.

A factorial ecological study by Berry and Rees (1969) confirmed the influence of segregation in non-Western contexts. In this case study, measuring cultural segregation was not directly possible, since none of the variables available in the Indian census explicitly measured religion, nationality, or caste. Yet the authors were able to interpret many of the factors ethno-religiously, based on using some factors as proxies for others. Within Calcutta (Kolkata), factorial ecology evinced clear markers of segregation between Hindus and Muslims, and between castes. Later analyses of Kolkata also suggested significant segregation by religion (Dutt, D'Sa, and Monroe 1989).

HOW TO CALCULATE AND MODEL SEGREGATION

An understanding of ethnic concentration and segregation demands reasonable methods of measurement. The index of dissimilarity has been most widely used because it is the easiest to calculate, the easiest to interpret, and had a long track record of usage in the published literature. But the D index only captures one aspect of segregation, does not work very well in multiethnic environments, and does not capture spatial relationships. As a result, many other methods have come about, and the advent of geographic information systems has allowed for some fairly sophisticated measurements to be developed.

The modeling of segregation is another issue. The lessons from the Chicago School applied to a particular trajectory, in which immigrants moved to certain parts of the city, only to move upward and outward over generations. Of course, this process left behind African Americans, for whom any upward progress was blocked by personal and institutional racism. Other ethnic groups have since entered the American scene, and their pathways have diverged considerably. And once ethnic concentrations are considered around the world, it is clear that no model can really apply. Rather, it is best to consider categorizations, such as threshold analysis, that help to capture the generally contingent nature of ethnic habitation in cities.

It is also worth considering those indicators of segregation that are less reliant on official data sources. This is particularly important in those societies where such small-area sources are lacking, but these indicators can also be useful in capturing other ways in which segregation is apparent. Simply observing the people within a neighborhood, their patterns of activity, and the shops and institutions they frequent often affords a truer understanding of the small-scale geographies of ethnicity than do the official records. Indicators showing how groups separate from one another may be expressed by such items as graffiti, written in such a way as to mark off group territory. Or these may be represented by barriers, both permanent and temporary, that keep groups from mingling. For those navigating urban spaces, it is vital to interpret all of these subtle and explicit cues showing group boundaries and territory. And, while not easy to model quantitatively, these are also helpful to the researcher striving to understand group difference.

6

⤜

Ethnic Culture Regions and Placemaking

Ethnic groups work to stamp their identities on the landscape in multiple ways. As a neighborhood becomes associated with an ethnic group, this creates meaning, and this meaning varies between members of the group (insiders) and members of the broader society (outsiders). While these activities occur as a result of a variety of structural forces, and the relationships between the ethnic group and other groups within society, they are still clearly proactive. Whether arising organically or intentionally, such ethnic spaces are places that have been developed and nurtured by the ethnicity involved.

Another reason why ethnic landscapes are significant is that they emphasize the role of agency. The role of structure continues to be quite significant, but must be considered as a counterpart to the affirmative actions taken by the members of ethnic groups. To take one important case, the development of an ethnic business is a means by which one ethnic family, often with assistance from a larger number of people in the group, decides to build something on the landscape and create an enterprise that will serve fellow ethnics, and at the same time improve the family's welfare. It is a mark of aspiration. Multiply these steps by dozens of ethnic entrepreneurs and the impact can be profound, generating a set of spaces that are concrete and recognized.

The spaces created by ethnic populations may be quite obvious, heralded by ethnics and others seeking to establish ownership of a space. They can also be controversial in their own way. This chapter looks at how different groups take the spaces that they occupy and make them into something meaningful, beneficial, and remarkable. In order to drill down to the more local scale, we begin with the geographical concept of a culture region, followed by a discussion of how ethnic groups succeed in "making" the places they live in by inscribing their cultural features onto the landscape and imbuing a neighborhood with their own particular identity.

DEFINING CULTURE REGIONS

Generally speaking, the ability of a group to shape its space relies on it having some form of dominion over the space. The depiction of so-called culture regions has long been key to the study of geography. Nearly one hundred years ago, Paul Vidal de la Blache spoke about how cultural, along with environmental and physical attributes, could shape various landscapes, each unique in its own way (Vidal de la Blache 1913; Martin and James 1993). All aspects were incorporated into a dense regional geography that promoted the specificity of places. He called this *genre de vie*, and it included the language, religion, cultural traditions, and foodways that co-existed within a fairly small area. In many respects, this philosophy was taken up and amplified by Richard Hartshorne, who saw place synthesis as the essential sauce blending together the various flavors of geography. The *Nature of Geography* was first and foremost a call for regional knowledge (Hartshorne 1939). It followed the Vidalian school, which promoted the notion that place was an essential reflector of identity and that, by studying places, one would get to know the people who inhabited them.

Vidal de la Blache's core relationship was between the environment and the people who lived within and exploited this environment. While he assembled all elements in deriving unique regions, these regions can also be delineated based on cultural attributes alone, forming *culture regions*. At the most basic level, a culture region is where a particular culture—and the group that carries this culture—is represented at some meaningful level.

There are two basic issues to consider about a culture region. The first issue is that the level at which a culture has a meaningful presence can be difficult to determine. If one group comprises nearly 100 percent of the population of a region, it is quite easy to describe this as a culture region defined by members of the prevailing culture group. We have little doubt that the country of Iceland is also a culture region defined by its Icelandic population. With immigrants making up only about 6 percent of the population, Iceland is clearly a land for, by, and of Icelanders (Central Intelligence Agency 2017). Multinational states at times have been set up such that their ethnic populations are separated by region. The former

Soviet Union even made this a clear aspect of territorial policy, with many of the Soviet republics ethnically defined.

In a diverse country, culture regions based on uniformity can be hard to come by. Most areas are more mixed, where one group may dominate in some way but not come close to uniform saturation. In these cases, what percentage of the population suffices to designate a culture region? Any group that represents a majority of a region's population is likely to have a significant presence. As a rule, a region can be defined by even a slight majority. Miami is considered a Cuban culture region, though Cuban Americans constitute just a little over half the city's population, and that proportion is declining. It is the same with the Mormons in Utah, where a majority of some 60 percent defines the cultural/religious nature of this state. Sometimes, even a majority is not necessary, especially at smaller geographical scales. Allen and Turner's (1997) examination of Southern California's "ethnic quilt" designated those ancestral groups that held a plurality of the population as having the most significant presence.

Other factors help to define the nature of a region beyond simple proportionality. Wilbur Zelinsky coined the "doctrine of first effective settlement" to aver that the group that arrives first in a land is going to have a disproportionate influence—one that is hard to dislodge (Zelinsky 1992). A look at American ancestral roots provides a good example of this doctrine. The plurality of people in the United States is of German ancestry, yet we do not speak German because English had the incontestable advantage of arriving here first. The first group gets to lay down the structures of the society, and frames the dominant culture. This can be quite difficult to dislodge. This is the point that Conzen (1993) makes when he discusses so-called ethnic substrates. Groups such as the English, Germans, Irish, and Hispanics have a population presence across large swaths of the United States, and these are going to have an influence on the culture of the region even without a majority. The layering of these substrates also makes it difficult for any one group to command a majority.

Ethnic groups with a long-standing occupance will have the time to infuse a region with markers of their culture. In attempting to delineate the Mormon culture region, Donald Meinig (1964) developed a tripartite categorization based on occupance and proportions. This is shown in figure 6.1. The "core" of the Mormon region is not necessarily those places with the highest proportion of Mormons—with a more diverse Salt Lake City being a case in point—but the places constituting the center of the Mormon religious-cultural complex. Beyond these lie a Mormon "domain," which comprises a contiguous space where members of the LDS Church dominate—with a long history of settlement, and always a healthy

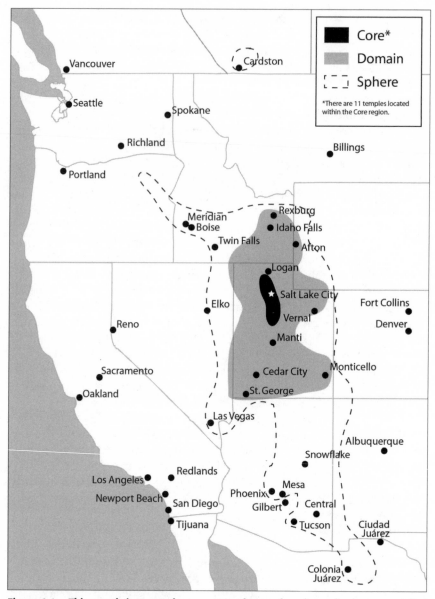

Figure 6.1. This map brings out the concepts of core, domain, and sphere as applied to a distinctive culture region. *Source:* Meinig (1964). Used with permission from Taylor and Francis.

majority of the population. This domain might also include places that are more diverse, but where the Mormon culture and religion held sway. Those places outside of this domain have a smaller Mormon proportion, much less than a majority, where the concentrations are more scattered. It is within this cultural "sphere" that Mormons maintain a less-robust presence but where they also enjoy the benefit of long-standing occupance. Outside of this overall region are places where many Mormons live, such as the major cities on the West Coast, but which lack the history to consider them part of the Mormon region.

The second issue is based on scale. There is no prescribed size for a region. It can be large or small; covering several countries, or just an urban neighborhood. This applies as well to a culture region. Vidal de la Blache pointed to smaller areas in his depictions, often encompassing a city and the countryside surrounding it. In their discussions, geographers like Meinig and Conzen have described culture regions that encompass several counties, and sometimes part of several states. These are regions that include both cities and countryside and comprise a large contiguous area. Yet urban geographers will often describe ethnic neighborhoods, which in effect are culture regions at a smaller scale. The scale often determines the nomenclature we use. When viewing national separatism or ethno-regional movements the scale is often based on more expansive territories, which themselves include several cities and the countryside. When we consider something like segregation, however, it is nearly always focused on the neighborhood scale within the city.

Scale is a dynamic attribute. The scale of regional concern can shift alongside major political changes. The construction of the Union of Soviet Socialist Republics, while following the contours of the Russian Empire, was a self-consciously multinational entity composed of separate, ethnically defined republics, plus smaller regions that were often stamped with an ethnic designator. While this model was not necessarily how power was shared in the system, this multinationalism was encouraged, and was an important feature of Soviet identity. When the Soviet Union collapsed, the official ethno-territorial divisions already in place were used as the basis for newly independent states. But each of these new states in turn contained a number of ethnic minorities. In an ironic twist, very often these new minorities were the same Russian people who had dominated the entire Soviet Union. The situation in Ukraine has recently made the news, as Russia successfully annexed a part of the territory (Crimea) and sent forces in to preserve the political autonomy of the easternmost parts of the Ukraine (Trenin 2016). This division was in some ways foretold, as the newly minted Ukrainian state contained large proportions of Russian-speaking ethnic Russians and Russian-speaking ethnic Ukrainians.

ETHNIC PLACEMAKING

At its foundation, place is simply a mark on the map that can be identified by location and boundaries. Sometimes places are synonymous
with a function. Retail malls and shopping centers, auto strips and
downtowns, are places after all. Or, places can represent the geographical manifestation of a community. We may speak about the wealthy
part of town, but mean the neighborhoods where rich people live. Some
places are quite clear and are demarcated by political boundaries, or
streets, or natural features such as rivers. There is nothing more discrete
than an island. But there are many instances where places are geographically ambiguous; their boundaries may be defined many different
ways. Unless the zoning is quite rigid, "downtowns" are rarely marked
off. Rather there are gradations, from the core blocks constituting all
the features of a downtown, to outer blocks where downtown functions
bleed into industrial or residential places.

A city is made up of many little things that frame its identity. Kevin
Lynch in 1960 and Grady Clay in 1980 identified lots of elements that
could be used to organize the city. Lynch identified landmarks, but also
corridors, edges, nodes, and districts. Clay included iconic districts, urban
fronts, sinks where all the undesirable items are dumped, commercial
strips, and turf in his basket of urban elements. To both authors, these
elements were more than functional; they had personality. Places are not
just the elements within them, but also develop recognized identities. The
type of meaning ascribed to a place depends on who is doing the perceiv-
ing. Mental maps drawn by individuals can fill up numerous details of
familiar places: places where people live, work, shop, or just happen to
spend a lot of time (Curtis 2016). The place significance here is far more
complex and even conflicted, because it includes so many impressions.
But as one reaches less and less familiarity, place meaning is simplified,
perhaps stereotyped. All the details and nuance that populate the imagi-
naries of people who live in a community give way to broader impressions. For outsiders, their views of places are patched together from these
rough strokes making up their own mental landscape (Buttimer 1980). A
neighborhood will be mentally classified as "poor" or "crime-ridden,"
when the reality is far more complex.

The intensity of ties between our subjective impressions and a place has
been well described by Tuan (1974) in his book *Topophilia*, literally "love
of place." Tuan shows how places instill particular emotion in contexts
ranging from types of natural environments to urban places. Our modern
cities inspire a response on the basis of imposing landmarks. Large religious edifices like cathedrals are an important part of a city's identity, as
are massive government buildings and skyscraping office towers. Around

the world, cities sport a distinctive skyline that defines them. Many cities will also create their own structures, which then become a huge part of that urban identity. The Eiffel Tower is a late nineteenth-century iron edifice which still defines Paris. Dubai, an emerging urban center, boasts the Burj Al Arab, described on its own web page as "more than just a stunning hotel, it is a symbol of modern Dubai" (http://www.jumeirah.com/en/hotels-resorts/dubai/burj-al-arab/).

Ethnic groups have considerable opportunity to construct their own places, although they may not have as much control over the meaning. As new groups move into an area, the area undergoes a transformation. But the changes are usually the accumulation of many small changes in elements of the neighborhood. Key landmarks shift with the construction or repurposing of new landmarks. In Chicago, Islamic mosques and Hindu temples create a new religious landscape (Numrich 1997; Tillman and Emmett 1999). In that same city, African Americans converted many storefronts to churches, creating new spaces for worship. Toronto's metropolitan area contains about 100 mosques and 70 Buddhist temples (Qadeer 2016).

These new structures—associated with a particular ethnicity—change the texture of neighborhood life, and have sparked protests. Among newer religious institutions, mosques have been singled out. Among the best-known examples in the United States was the proposed development in 2010 of an Islamic Center and a mosque near the site of the World Trade Center terrorist attack. Yet this was also accompanied by protests against mosques near less hallowed ground in other U.S. cities. Objectors have claimed that mosques will inculcate terrorists, be used to store ammunition, and spread Sharia law (Goodstein 2010). Another source of consternation has come from the building of extremely large houses by Chinese immigrants in Vancouver. The objections have less to do with the ethnicity of the new neighbors, and more to do with the feeling that the mansions will destroy the character of the neighborhood (Qadeer 2016).

While Japan is a homogeneous population, ethnic placemaking also can be found there, coming for the most part from its significant Korean population. In Osaka, Koreans are concentrated in one of the central wards of Ashihama (Hester 2002). Ashihama was once a Japanese village on a floodplain. With Osaka's expansion and the subsequent in-migration by Koreans, actively recruited by Osaka's rubber factories, the district became the heart of Osaka's stigmatized Korean community. The development of a Korean shopping street from the 1930s on also inscribed a strong Korean presence in this particular neighborhood. As the neighborhood came to be conflated with Korean identity, the very name "Ashihama" conjured its Korean residents. For outsiders, it also evoked dirtiness and overcrowding.

If given the opportunity, ethnic groups inscribe a particular space with a characteristic style. There are certain architectural tropes associated with various parts of the world, from the half-timbered houses and extended roofs associated with Bavaria, to the interior courtyards and wind towers of the traditional Arabian house. Transplanting such designs—or at least elements of such designs—to a neighborhood conveys as clearly as anything the presence of a particular group. Sometimes this is expressed in a small way, such as with the use of the national colors. But sometimes an ethnic group goes for much more. The Little Saigon neighborhood of Westminster, California, has adopted many architectural styles that come from Vietnam including covered colonnades, tower gates, archways, green tiles, and stylized dragon heads (Mazumdar et al. 2000). This is consonant with what other ethnic groups attempt to do. But beyond this, Vietnamese American residents have been successful in establishing a design standards manual that codifies that this Little Saigon village "use architectural elements similar to those found on buildings constructed in Vietnam in the early 1900s in the French colonial tradition" (Mazumdar et al. 2000, 323).

The transformation of corridors or strips coincides with the establishment of new ethnic shopping districts. New immigrant-owned businesses altered the cultural complexion of a single street in Nashville, from Anglo to Hispanic (Chaney 2010). A corridor in St. Paul, Minnesota, sprouted new Vietnamese shops and services in old warehouse spaces (Kaplan 1997) just as Vietnamese immigrants in a Washington, DC, suburb create places to shop and worship while also marking the landscape with their own identity (Wood 1997). Edges are developed, too, as the boundaries of ethnically defined spaces harden. These lines may occur because of tensions between groups, because members of a group choose to cluster in particular streets, or as part of a strategy by the majority population to isolate a minority neighborhood.

Many edges are drawn based on the desire of neighborhood residents to define and develop their turf. A study of the white ethnic neighborhood of Fairmount in Philadelphia showed there was a great deal of internal cohesion among the primarily white ethnic population—but much of this was bolstered by huge mistrust aimed at the neighboring African American population (Cybriwsky 1978). This social exclusion was manifested by graffiti, physical threats, and discrimination. Such consistency forged an edge that was sharp enough so that most black neighbors shied away from crossing it, or would only enter Fairmount to make the point that they had a right to this space as well.

The assemblage of items found within a place is often much greater than the sum of its parts, and we may find that these places do develop potent meanings. Over time, neighborhoods that have been imbued with a variety of these ethnicity-inflected landmarks, corridors, and edges emerge as districts of their own, and become significant parts of the city. Some ethnic places are quite well known, found in some of the largest cities, and even become tourist attractions in their own right or perhaps districts of ill-repute to be avoided. Other ethnically constructed places are mainly known locally. Within the ethnic community, though, the development of a place binds a community together and forges a sense of identity otherwise unavailable. And of course, in a negative sense, the conflation of a people with a place can also be used to stigmatize.

Ethnic places—whether landmarks, strips, or districts—can be permanent or transient, clearly visible to all or mostly just visible to insiders. Landscapes can be altered in a matter of hours, and so ethnic groups can mark a place with a festival or a parade that can transform an otherwise ordinary space into something imbued with particular meaning. Likewise, ethnic places do not need to be external and visible to everyone. Some of the most important ethnic spaces may be found in nondescript buildings or in homes that passersby would not even know existed. Yet for the people who are a part of this group, these places can be vital for cultural affirmation and interaction. It also bears mentioning that the meaning of place will vary considerably, depending on specific individuals (Massey 1991).

In considering all the main factors together, Hardwick (2010) discusses why certain ethnic groups are able to make a strong cultural impression. One key factor is the overall number of ethnics and their proportion of the population. The "Great Migration" of African Americans from the rural South transformed many northern cities in a relatively short period of time. Restrictions on where the new migrants could live ensured that certain sections of these cities would contain extraordinarily high proportions of blacks and cast a powerful imprint. The attainment of majority status in particular neighborhoods and even entire cities furnishes the demographic wherewithal to affix a cultural, political, and economic stamp. Another important factor is that of economic success, since certain populations can make an impact well beyond their numbers, based largely on their economic power and wealth. This is found among South Asian enclaves in major east African cities like Nairobi, Dar es Salaam, and Kampala (Kristiansen and Ryen 2002). Chinese populations in Southeast Asia have also created a strong presence despite fairly small numbers. These groups established businesses and were able to develop neighborhoods to their liking (which, unfortunately, also caught the ire of resentful local populations). Finally, the ability of a group to maintain internal cohesion—based on common values and an awareness of its own distinctiveness—allows the group to develop institutions that can strongly impact a place. While vastly outnumbered in the Prairie Provinces, French Canadian settlers were able to establish important beachheads in places like St. Boniface, Winnipeg, Manitoba. Their devotion to Catholicism and other aspects that encourage identity maintenance, such as their own educational system and French language associations, helped their cause considerably. Residential segregation also played a role, both as an outcome of strong ethnic boundaries and also as a factor preserving these boundaries (Driedger 1979).

CONSTRUCTING AND CONSUMING ETHNIC SPACES

Ethnic spaces come about in a variety of ways. Such spaces often come about organically. To be sure, economic, political, and social forces create conditions favorable to ethnic clustering, but the creation of an ethnic neighborhood occurs in an unselfconscious manner as the consequence of many individual decisions. This is different from those cases of ethnic neighborhoods created by design. For instance, many historical ghettos were established quite deliberately by municipal authorities as a way to isolate a group. But ethnic neighborhoods can be intentionally developed for positive reasons as well. Such neighborhoods are constructed, branded, and broadcast in and beyond the city. If the branding is particularly successful, it may become a reason for people to visit the city in the first place. To be clear, it is rare to see an ethnic space developed out of whole cloth; more likely, it is fashioned from a nucleus of ethnic concentration.

Planning becomes a large part of trying to develop just the right mix of places and to ensure that the community contains at least some semblance of authenticity. Development of ethnically branded neighborhoods derives from the same impulse that has created ethnically branded rural towns (Hoelscher and Ostergren 1993). Some examples are New Glarus, Wisconsin, which promotes a Swiss identity, and Cambridge, Minnesota, with a Swedish cast. German heritage tourism is promoted in the Texas hill country (Adams 2006). The United States is not alone in such promotions. In fact, the Chinese government steers people to Yunnan Province to engage in ethnic tourism. Yet the Han majority controls much of this tourist activity (Yang and Wall 2008). In Xishuangbanna, the Golden Peacock Tour Company—a company run by Han interests—has become the most successful tour company. Han dominate most of the businesses, while telling the minority Bai culture how to maximize their tourist potential (Yang and Wall 2008).

Ethnic Tourism

So why deliberately develop an ethnic neighborhood? One reason is that ethnicity has become a component of tourism and, since tourism is primarily invested in the selling of places, ethnicity is seen as a way to create more places that will attract outside consumption and revenue. Additional value is created from packaging the various components of a place into a single identifiable neighborhood. A well-packaged ethnic neighborhood benefits the local entrepreneurs, other ethnics who are looking for specific goods and services, city residents in search of something exotic, and visitors who may decide that the best place to get Greek food would likely be in, say, "Greektown." We see this in ethnic neighborhoods in Toronto, developed at the behest of local actors to create Little Italys, Indiatowns, and Greektowns (Hackworth and Rekers 2005). Other places, such as Little Tokyo in Los Angeles, serve much the same function and have been developed largely with the input of the Japanese American community (Smith 2006).

It is useful to know the variety of ways in which ethnic businesses, especially as part of an ethnic economy, are able to make places. This can be considered in light of their importance to both insiders and outsiders. From the insider perspective, ethnic establishments provide goods from home, people who understand the language, and an opportunity to socialize. In her study of the Ethiopian community of Washington, DC, Chacko (2003) describes these as sociocommerscapes. The idea is that these ethnic landscapes include ethnic commerce, but ethnic commerce also doubles as meeting place. The obvious sorts of businesses that provide this service are restaurants and cafés. Depending on the openness of the establishment, these may attract not just members of the community, but also culinary tourists. But among the Ethiopian community in Washington, as with ethnic communities everywhere, much of the social activity occurs outside of these more obvious sites. Grocery stores specializing in native foods are places where people often can get together and where the signage is in Ethiopia's primary language, Amharic. Establishments selling various sundries and bric-a-brac are also places where commerce is combined with social interaction. These establishments promote their Ethiopian identity through the use of the language, but also use of flags, posters, and other ways that advertise Ethiopian identity.

Toronto is a city that has a higher proportion of immigrants than almost any other city in the world. When combined with second- and third-generation ethnics, this creates a true ethnic mélange, with many different groups engaging in activities. The Portuguese community in Toronto is spatially quite concentrated, anchored by Dundas Street, with institutional completeness and a fairly self-contained ethnic economy (Teixeira 2006). The Portuguese are able to marshal tremendous resources in retaining their customer base, finding co-ethnic employees, and creating a true central place among Toronto's many neighborhoods. To be sure, many Portuguese live outside this neighborhood, but it continues to serve as a focus. Toronto's large Chinese community, on the other hand, exhibits

Figure 6.2. The Pacific Mall is a large, Chinese-themed mall in Markham, Ontario containing about 450 stores and services. *Source:* **Lucia Lo.**

a pattern of "concentrations within dispersion" (Lo 2006, 93). There exist Chinese districts that are more likely to serve Chinese customers, many of whom are more inclined to patronize grocery stores where they can find the foodstuffs they require for day-to-day cooking (Lo 2009). In recent years, massive Chinese shopping malls have emerged in the suburbs, offering a complete shopping experience for all of Toronto's considerable Chinese population (see figure 6.2). Most people who shop at these malls travel there by car and live in a number of different places, but the very fact of establishing an ethnic mall is significant testimony to the power and promise of concentration.

From the outsider perspective, some of these identifiers are obvious, whereas others go completely unnoticed. Many ethnic spaces are intentionally built to promote tourism and the consumption of ethnic products. Many of these communities create places intended only for insiders, but have also been successful in developing areas well known to outsiders. The immigration of South Asians to Great Britain has created numerous spaces—many of which are private—but others highlight the greatest gift of these immigrants to England: Indian curry. Manchester's "Curry Mile" is a well-known strip of restaurants that attracts large numbers of non-Asians (Barrett and McEvoy 2006). Interestingly, Curry Mile did not develop in an existing ethnic enclave, nor is it owned by Indians. Most proprietors are Pakistani. But Curry Mile is marketed as a tourist experience to business travelers and leisure travelers alike. The placemaking here points to the fact that ethnic communities create their own spaces, and that one of the most powerful ways to do this is through the development of commerce. Ethnic entrepreneurs are businessmen and -women to be sure, but many also see the value of ethnicizing their places as a means to promote new shopping and dining experiences to members of the general population. After all, if people can be enticed to go to an ethnic district, they are likely to buy a meal, perhaps shop for a few knickknacks, and maybe even pick up some groceries.

The end result of all this is an attempt to draw more people into neighborhoods in order to consume products, and becoming a part of what Marilyn Halter (2007) calls "shopping for identity." Businesses realize that ethnic marketing can be a winner. Members of an ethnic group themselves appreciate the familiarity and the nostalgia—especially those ethnics who have long left the enclave. Those people outside the group desire something out of the ordinary. Ethnic-themed places can provide this. Singapore has made a concerted effort to create so-called historic conservation districts, which are intended to be places that will attract tourism. Along with designation as a historic district comes a variety of regulations that are supposed to contribute to the ethnic meaning of the neighborhood. For example, Singapore's Little India has been developed at the insistence of insiders who see an India theme center attracting both business and pleasure tourists, as well as becoming a focal site for a variety of retail outlets, restaurants, and services (Chang 2000).

Ethnic Festivals

Ethnic festivals are similar to contrived ethnic neighborhoods in promoting ethnic identity. And these neighborhoods provide excellent backdrops to the staging of festivals, heightening the ethnic sentiment that exists there already. An example would be the Tet festival held once a year in Little Saigon, Westminster, California (Mazumdar et al. 2000). Within a vibrant ethnic space, this festival helps to connect past to present and to provide people with an additional opportunity to appreciate their heritage. However, many ethnic festivals also occur in a non-ethnic space and render it into an ethnic place for that moment. Festivals are different from ethnic neighborhoods because, while branded ethnic neighborhoods display everyday aspects of cultural identity, ethnic festivals bring in dramatic expressions: showing off music, dress, dance, athleticism, art, theater, and, almost always, food. These festivals are also more readily controlled than ethnic neighborhoods. Festivals allow ethnic communities to decide which aspects of their culture they wish to promote, and to leave aside those they wish to exclude (Bramadat 2001). Like ethnic neighborhoods, ethnic festivals must reconcile many different goals (Dawson 1991). Do they attempt to provide a more nostalgic, traditional view of the ethnic culture, or present the manner in which these groups adapt to modern society? The idealized culture of the past—with all of the deprivation and persecution magically wiped away—is exhibited, whereas the lived culture of the present is ignored. Often this revival is used more to sell the culture to tourists and, as such, becomes a commodity just like the branded ethnic neighborhood.

Many ethnic festivals are oriented toward the outside population, but they can become an important part of maintaining ethnic identity among a diffuse population. In the United States, Tamil culture is reified in a series of festivals, many of which take place indoors (Devadoss 2014). These festivals are organized by the local Tamil Sangam, which charges a membership fee and is open primarily, but not exclusively, to Tamil ethnics. The events often take place in distinctly non-Tamil venues—city halls, schools, auditoriums—but here they recreate the landscapes and soundscapes of home (Devadoss 2014).

Ethnic Theming

The efforts of insiders to develop their own ethnic places are often amplified by the work of cities in theming these places. There is an economic incentive, since it promotes tourism and retains some of the local money inside the community. There is also a strong cultural component. Ethnic neighborhoods create a vibrant city, which goes hand-in-hand with greater cultural diversity. Chicago, for example, has made it a priority to bolster the various ethnic neighborhoods that exist in that city (Johansson and Cornebise 2010). Urban diversity is part and parcel of what it means to be a global city, and cultural neighborhoods provide the "umph" that helps the city land conventions, major sporting events, and a more upscale workforce.

Sometimes the theming is conducted with very little help from the insider community. Brisbane, Australia's Chinatown, was inaugurated in 1987 in an inner-city location, yet a Chinatown had never existed at this place (Ip 2005). Most Chinese ethnics lived elsewhere in the metropolitan area; in fact, most had left the inner city years before. Yet the symbolism demanded an inner-city neighborhood with the requisite icons of Chinese culture, all packaged up into a place commodity.

Certainly, ethnic neighborhoods vary considerably in perceived and actual levels of authenticity. In regard to ethnic communities within the United States, Zelinsky (1990) has stated that ethnic neighborhoods really do not exist in any form that would be considered authentic. Instead, he says that they are kept up mainly as a means of promoting consumption or as a type of ethnic museum. In Zelinsky's colorful turns of phrase, "they are specimens of a larger tribe of roadside attractions that include synthetic Wild West frontier towns and those garish Indian villages to be found in western North Carolina's Cherokee country and elsewhere" (1990, 34). I would not go nearly this far. While many ethnic spaces indeed do fit under the category of "roadside attraction," others continue to have a great deal of purpose and meaning. To be sure, the intentional planning of ethnic spaces chips away at their authenticity because the meaning is imposed from the outside, rather than emerging from inside the community itself.

Historical occupation is sometimes sufficient to drape the legacy of an ethnicity on an entire neighborhood. This is not the case for Brisbane's Chinatown and a few other places, where the designated ethnic commercial district in no way coincides with any kind of presence. More common, however, are cases in which ethnic neighborhoods develop from some historical root, yet the ethnic population has dwindled, with many living in other locales or even outside the city. The neighborhood composition does not correspond with its own designation. We see this in Toronto, where the four ethnic neighborhoods studied by Hackworth and Rekers (2005) have few ethnic inhabitants. Only 15 percent of the residents who live within Greektown are actually of Greek ethnic origin. In fact, many of these neighborhoods are quite attractive to immigrants, but immigrants of the "wrong" ethnicity. This is also true of the "Swedish" Andersonville neighborhood of Chicago, where Johansson and Cornebise (2010) found that fewer than 5 percent of the locals trace their ancestry to Sweden.

While light on residents, such neighborhoods may make a concerted effort to develop as ethnic business areas. Ethnic enterprises provide the necessary signatures to label the neighborhood and help ethnically oriented businesses to prosper. The Toronto neighborhoods studied by Hackworth and Rekers (2005) have a higher percentage of ethnic businesses than ethnic residents; the most dramatic difference would be the Gerrard India Bazaar. Here less than 6 percent of the residents identify as Indian, and yet 72 percent of all businesses are South Asian, which includes Pakistani and Bangladeshi enterprises. For Chicago's Andersonville, the Swedish identity relies heavily on just a sprinkling of Swedish businesses. These sorts of businesses may have located there precisely because the location was themed.

CONTESTING PLACEMAKING

Neighborhoods are subject to differing interpretations. There may be contrasting views regarding what the place should be, with local authorities thinking that it should be one thing but residents feeling that it really should be something else. Arguments occur over exactly what basket of attributes can be bundled into a particular designation. As one group stakes out its part of the urban landscape, other groups will challenge that very space. A landscape signature also carries different sets of meanings, depending on who is doing the signifying. This creates competition for the actual space inhabited by members of a group or of several groups.

This competition occurs when an ethnic group considers a space its own based on demographic dominance or economic power. If left unchallenged, the territory begins to acquire these ethnic characteristics. But it often happens that other groups are also interested in claiming this particular space. An example from Seattle shows what happens when different populations compete over a Chinatown (Hou and Tanner 2002). In this case, there exists a great deal of spatial politics within an area that once incorporated Japanese and Chinese residents, but became more Chinese after the Japanese left during and after World War II. Since then, immigration brought more Vietnamese and, as their numbers grew, the newer residents felt that they had a right to much of the space as well. Sometimes this contestation erupts over simple things. For instance, the Vietnamese and Chinese disputed the colors of columns that were painted on the freeway. Rather than just the red for the Chinese, the Vietnamese also wanted yellow to represent their presence. There are also challenges over stores and other introduced items. The Chinese organizations in Seattle protested the introduction of a large Japanese supermarket, claiming that this would hinder emergency vehicles. The concerns over the free flow of traffic may have also contained worries that the big Japanese supermarket could encroach on existing Chinese identities (Hou and Tanner 2002). In the Little India near Los Angeles described in chapter 4, the concern was that the name of the neighborhood—taken at the behest of some Indian entrepreneurs—was misleading and exclusionary, considering that the vast majority of people in the area were not themselves Indian (Sheth 2010).

Neighborhood change certainly adds to the complexity of neighborhood identities. Neighborhoods rarely remain stable, so the signifier of a neighborhood persists even as it bears very little resemblance to what transpires in real terms. Urban areas are festooned with such designators, suggesting a period of time that has long since passed. In Cleveland, Ohio, a place like Slavic Village still retains a few Polish and Ukrainian businesses, but has increasingly become African American and Hispanic. Little Italy in New York contains many of its iconic restaurants with their red-and-white tablecloths, but this neighborhood is gradually being pushed out by an expansion of Chinatown, which itself has become more pan-ethnic Asian or East Asian in character.

At times, ethnic businesses may be seen as unwanted intrusions, and the resentment toward ethnic-owned businesses can flare up in a number of different contexts. Ethnic-owned businesses are convenient targets because they contribute to the ethnic economy and are generally quite visible. During the 1998 riots in Jakarta, Indonesia, it was Chinese-owned establishments that were burned to the ground. As discussed in chapter 3, the Chinese were often hated members of the middleman minority set up by the Dutch earlier in the colonial period. Tensions between Arabs and Jews over Middle East policy also flared up in the summer of 2014. French demonstrations against Israel bombing in Gaza led some demonstrators to attack Jewish-owned businesses in the Parisian suburb of Sarcelles.

An additional aspect of contestation involves the interpretation of particular ethnic places. There is a lot of romanticism about ethnicity, and promoters enhance aspects thought more attractive to tourists. An area in the central city of Albuquerque, New Mexico, considered to be part of the Hispanic homeland, has also been effectively co-opted as a center for idealizing the Wild West (Dürr 2003). While the Hispanic district has a strong historical basis, it has been dressed up to serve its tourism purposes. Observers are invited to see real Indians practicing their native crafts. Hispanics are also characterized in a very nostalgic way. The commodification of this place, which many Anglo shop owners see as a true cultural, economic asset, rankles many Hispanics, who see this as a significant homeland, and Indians, who feel that they are prostituting their identity in order to sell culture and place.

The example of San Antonio is instructive as an example of how different meanings have been projected on particular "ethnic" landscapes (Arreola 1995). In this case, Anglo investors determined what the "Spanish" neighborhood should consist of, and this had very little to do with the wishes of the existing Mexican population. These differing projections resulted in two distinct places. One is a Euro-Texican place created primarily by Anglos in the first half of the twentieth century as a way to idealize the Spanish background of this neighborhood. This district is popular among tourists who want to walk along the San Antonio River and shop in this romantic landscape, which includes all kinds of Spanish colonial revival architecture. Yet, most Mexicans consider this place a fake; the actual Mexican district is found several blocks to the west. The latter commercial landscape, operated chiefly by ethnic Mexicans for the benefit of co-ethnics, varies greatly from the commercialized quarter that has been created primarily for visitors.

PLACEMAKING UNDER THE RADAR

We are accustomed to thinking about ethnic landscapes as something clear and visible—readily apparent to even the most undiscerning eye, and sometimes with signposts! Perhaps the most blatant example is the gated entrance, the "chinoiserie" that provides the architecture of a stereotypical Chinatown (Lai 1990). Other ethnic communities have their "tropes" that emphasize what they are and what they are doing.

However, there are elements of ethnic placemaking that are not easily visible to outsiders, and in fact may not be externally visible at all. In many respects, this is due to the fact that many ethnic groups are not concentrated. Especially in an age of heterolocalism, in which ethnics may live in a dispersed setting and use their cars to travel to gathering places, the sort of tight concentration that gives rise to distinct ethnic markers may give way to more nuanced elements (Zelinsky and Lee 1998). This can occur in several ways. Rather than having the ethnic landscape be outside, many landscape elements move to the inside, into interior spaces like a church or a meetinghouse. Another way is to display landscape elements outside, but so subtly that it is impossible for all but the insider to understand the significance. Finally, specific ethnic landscapes could be developed on a periodic basis. What exists is there for only a few days or weeks, and then it vanishes.

Many ethnic groups exemplify this more muted placemaking. Indian ethnic groups in the United States—in contrast to those in the United Kingdom—tend to live in dispersed areas. Because the average socioeconomic status of these populations is quite high, there is a tendency to inhabit suburban residences. Unlike the communities of well-off Chinese, there is less of a tendency among Indians to establish anything resembling the suburban Chinatowns we see in the United States and Canada. Skop's (2012) examination of Indian residential and commercial patterns in the Phoenix metropolitan area demonstrates the impacts of this dispersal. To be sure, an automobile-dependent city like Phoenix will be far more dispersed in general. Without the few old-fashioned or new urbanist–designed pedestrian-oriented neighborhoods, most Phoenix neighborhoods sprawl in such a way as to discourage real ethnic identity. This, paired with the tendency of Indian Americans not to cluster, results in a landscape of suburban dispersal. There is no "Indiatown" or really any form of what we might consider an ethnic landscape. Instead, this defines ethnic community without propinquity.

Just because the Indian landscape in Phoenix flies under the radar, invisible to the outsider eye, does not mean that it does not exist. Defining such a dispersed, low-key landscape depends on noting its various elements. This partly has to do with the more scattered religious institutions. Many Indians are Hindu, and their temples can be found in dispersed locations. Such temples, when constructed grandly as many of them are, make a strong cultural impact. However, other temples have been repurposed from other uses and may not be as readily apparent as temples. This is true of the Phoenix temple found in a building formerly occupied by the Church of God (Skop 2012). Moreover, an ethnic imprint may be only found inside, particularly when it is part of a faith not normally associated with that group. Christian churches minister to many South Asians, as well as provide fellowship, but may not be readily apparent to outsiders.

Ethnic groups also establish cultural centers that are meant to provide meeting places large and small. These meetings combine with religious functions, and they almost always have space available for festivals. But among a dispersed population, these places may be found in nondescript neighborhoods, away from where most participants live. The Indo-American Cultural and Religious Center, a huge warehouse-like building north of Phoenix, exemplifies this trend (Skop 2012). Space is available for all types of functions, including a big yearly festival. Interestingly, this center welcomes all Indian groups and faiths—despite significant differences in ethnicity, language, and religion. In Northeast Ohio, a region with a fairly large proportion of South Asians, there are centers similar to this, the India Community Center in Cleveland Heights being a good example.

For smaller communities, such as the Tamil population, the assembly of a diffuse population for a festival is an important marker of identity and a way to bolster community. But these communities cannot justify a stand-alone center. So festivals are held in university or civic auditoriums where, for the day at least, the space is transformed (Devadoss 2014). Something similar happens in Phoenix, where a local second-run movie theater is co-opted on Saturday mornings to show films from different regions in India (Skop 2012).

Finally, an ethnic landscape may be invisible because so much of it is found behind closed doors. Just as civic centers or movie theaters may be transformed for the day, ethnics create interior landscapes that highlight their identity. Interior public spaces are modified to represent the ethnicity through wall hangings, furniture, paintings, sculptures, and other items. The bland building façade opens into an interior bursting with ethnic vibrancy. Here may recur pictures of the homeland, or actual symbols that represent the particular ethnicity. For example, the Latvian population in North America employs the *saule* or sun symbol, and this is found in such items as stained-glass window hangings, wrought-iron decorations, pottery, wooden door carvings, and prints, as shown in figure 6.3 (Woodhouse 2005). The same display of significant motifs can be found in private interior spaces, which provide the most intimate means by which an ethnic group can broadcast its identity. The U.S. Tamil community is not numerous or visible enough to display a robust external ethnic stamp, but it is successful in replicating many important aspects of Tamil culture in members' homes. Residents reaffirm their Tamil-ness from the Indian spice used for cooking, to the Tamil script that appears on items, to the final coup de grace—the prayer room—which highlights all the deities and is meant to replicate that region in India (Devadoss 2014). Other ethnic groups, such as the Portuguese within Toronto, work to transform the interior of their homes by building basements and wine cellars and using these as places to entertain (Teixeira 2007).

Figure 6.3. This print, found in Chicago's Lutheran Church, shows Mother Latvia caught between two images of the sun. Incorporations of Mother Latvia serve as a constant reminder of the motherland. *Source:* Kathleen Woodhouse.

MAKING ETHNIC PLACES

The capacity of ethnic groups to construct their own spaces and to truly make places is conditioned by the size and dominance of the group, its own internal cohesiveness, and its relations with other groups. One key aspect relates to the process by which the ethnic neighborhood comes about. Many neighborhoods emerge based on structural and economic forces, combined with all of the individual choices discussed in chapter 4. We might consider these ethnic neighborhoods to arise organically inasmuch as they develop bit by bit, with population clustering and the establishment of businesses and institutions. Other ethnic neighborhoods are developed more intentionally, or an existing ethnic neighborhood may be spruced up and branded to appeal more broadly. These efforts can come from inside the ethnic community or from outside actors.

The intent of placemaking determines the look and feel of the community. Placemaking of all sorts serves a variety of objectives, and these can be perceived based on how the communities themselves are developed. Are ethnic places more internally oriented, or do they seek to appeal to a wider crowd? Are ethnic places created as byproducts of some other activity, such as ethnic commerce, or is the very act of place creation the primary intent? How much do ethnic places broadcast tensions and divisions between groups, or are the boundaries that separate ethnic neighborhoods fairly permeable? The answers to these questions provide a great deal of insight on how the ethnic community functions, how it serves the members of the ethnic groups, and how it is situated within the broader urban environment.

7

꒜

Ethnic Spaces Created from Exploitation and Conflict

The last chapter examined the role of ethnic placemaking and described it as a process that marks space occupied and characterized by an ethnic group. While sometimes contested and other times imposed, we often view such activities in a positive light, leading to the sort of "good segregation" described by Peach (1996). But other ethnic spaces are developed in quite different ways, with adverse results. This is especially true where the ethnic clustering results more from constraints than from choice; where discrimination leads to confined spaces with their attendant economic, social, and political marginalization. At times, a certain degree of economic interdependence brings ethnic communities together, but one community is clearly ostracized once their work has been completed. At other times, the community is stripped of resources altogether, and given little opportunity to partake in mainstream society. Divisions such as this occur at all spatial scales—from large regions within a metropolitan area to the kind of microsegregation experienced in all different contexts. Constraints can be more political in nature, having to do with the defensive needs of the ethnic group to secure some territory and to be physically separated from members of a rival group. Here, we can speak of spaces that result from political divisions that cut across cities just as they divide countries. Sometimes the division is quite extreme, in cases where groups are actively at war. Other times, the division is softer, as groups seek succor and support in their own spaces.

ECONOMIC INTERDEPENDENCE AND ETHNIC SPACES

The combination of ethnicity and the labor market render many different types of ethnic spaces. Immigration is the principal manner by which new ethnic groups enter into a society, as most people go to other countries in order to find a better life. Once they arrive, many immigrants find that the society they entered is not nearly as welcoming as they would have hoped. They encounter hostile people who resent the intrusion, but immigrants remain because they are able to find some sort of work and because remaining within the society, even on the fringes, is preferable to returning home. The economic interdependence between the immigrant population and the native population has a number of important attributes. On one hand, most newcomers arrive very poor, and many have very little in the way of documentation. Yet they are attractive to employers because they cost so little and are often willing to do jobs that the native labor force shuns.

This sort of dynamic has occurred for a long time. European Jews originated from many different countries, and became a common presence in medieval trading cities. Early on, they were identified as traders and artisans. The passing of such skills from one generation to the next was partially responsible, but also at work was the fact that Jews, even more so than other foreigners, were prohibited from owning land and from pursuing other means of livelihood. This placed them in an economic niche that at once provided them with a place in the overall medieval economy, while also stigmatizing them as they were compelled to follow vocations—such as moneylending—off-limits to Christians, thus exposing Jews to opprobrium. Despite occasional monetary successes, the Jewish presence was always probationary, and Jews would often be forced to flee a place on very short notice (Nirenberg 1996).

In an echo of medieval European controls on its Jewish population, post-colonial governments throughout Southeast Asia established a number of indigenization laws that gave preference to the native population and often restricted the occupations open to their Chinese minorities. In Indonesia, the Chinese population had also entered society to perform particular tasks, but these economic roles in turn placed them at odds with the majority of Javanese society. As a result, "no country harbouring a Chinese minority possesses a blacker record of persecution and racial violence than Indonesia" (Pan 1994, 214). Indonesian frustration, often abetted by the government or the army, boiled over into several pogroms in the 1960s. These violent episodes may have calmed for a while, but were again rekindled in 1998 (Panggabean and Smith, 2011).

Modern immigration in Europe continues this state of affairs. As several countries grew wealthy following World War II, they also found themselves in need of labor. Populations that were not growing as rapidly as before, combined with a labor force that was unwilling to perform certain types of jobs, meant that opportunities existed for new workers. In many cases, the initial idea was to capture the benefits of labor without making a long-term commitment. Germany's "guest worker" program that was popular in the late 1960s and early 1970s was a case in point, as it seemed to provide a solution to the labor shortage by offering immigrants one- to three-year stints in Germany (Martin 2002). Original labor recruitment was intended for the agricultural sector, but as Germany became more industrially powerful, it found that a large number of workers were needed for some of the less desirable factory jobs. At the end of the contract, the foreign labor was expected to go home. Most of them did, but many remained and had families of their own. The Turkish migration, along with the later migration of other groups, effectively made West Germany and then the whole of united Germany a country of immigration— a situation finally admitted to by mainstream political parties (Castles 2006). And while Turks were never more than a third of the total number of foreigners, in many ways they became the face of foreigners who did not integrate as readily into German society (Martin 2002).

The geographical result of this migration is witnessed in a series of increasingly Turkish spaces sprinkled across German cities. The Turkish presence has functioned apart, sidelined in many respects, and lacking access to the fruits of the broader Germany economy. Continued language barriers and education in lower-level schools limit opportunities and keep unemployment high. Turks in Germany continue to live in a parallel society in which they engage with little interaction beyond their own community (Mueller 2006). This has positive benefits to be sure, including strong connections to their faith, strengthening local attachments as well as engagement with communities in Turkey (Ehrkamp 2005). More and more, Turks can claim some pieces of space as their own. But the marginalization of the Turkish society relative to German society continues.

The immigration flows within European countries expanded considerably in the 1990s and 2000s based on two major factors. The first was the liberation of the so-called Eastern bloc countries in 1989, followed by political transformations in the Balkans and the breakup of the Soviet Union itself. Residents of these Eastern European countries were now free to leave, and many took advantage of this. The second factor has been the further development and expansion of the European Union (EU), which began in the 1950s as the European Common Market and has since expanded to become a political-economic union of 28 countries (though this will fall to 27 pending the expected exit of the United Kingdom in 2019). Many Eastern European countries joined the European Union in the first decade of the twenty-first century. Following the Maastricht Treaty of 1993, all peoples within the European Union are granted access to employment across the continent, which enabled unfettered migration.

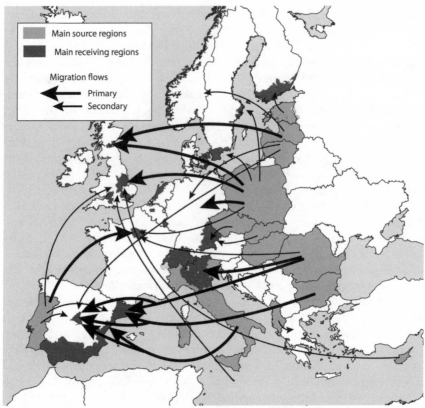

Figure 7.1.   Some of the main migration flows from source to destination regions within the last several years. *Source:* Map produced by Jennifer Mapes, partially based on data from Bell et al. (2010) and other migration sources.

These two changes have sparked increases in immigration from both within and without Europe. Figure 7.1 displays some of the dominant flows within Europe itself.

The case of Greece during the 1990s and into the 2000s illustrates this new immigration. While Greece is considered one of the least prosperous parts of the European Union, during the 1990s it became a beacon of hope for many immigrants arriving from nearby countries. Initially, much of the immigration came from Asia Minor, where there was a significant population of ethnic Greeks. In the 1990s, Albanians—newly freed from the oppressive Stalinist regime of Enver Hoxha—decided their prospects would be a lot better in neighboring Greece. A poor people, made poorer by a corrupt government and some very shady economic dealings, Albanians did not have the wherewithal to simply enter Greece through the front door. Instead, many of them came over the mountains and arrived initially without any authorization. The rural population of Albanians found work in Greece's extensive but small-scale agricultural sector (Papadopoulos 2012). They were often attractive to farmers who were looking to pay laborers less than half of what they would have to pay native-born Greeks. At the same time, most Greeks did not accept the Albanians (Lawrence 2007), considering them dirty, untrustworthy, and simply not as frugal or hardworking as the Greeks felt themselves to be. The mixing of Albanian and Greek groups has led to increasing levels of racism, where the Albanian population is considered to even have different physical and moral differences than the Greek population (Lawrence 2010). And because Albanians constitute such a large proportion of immigrants, particularly in the rural parts of Greece, nearly all immigrants are labeled as Albanians (Lawrence 2007).

The spatial evidence of the Albanian population varies. In the larger valley villages Albanians keep to themselves, inhabiting decrepit housing abandoned by the Greek population. They stay away from public spaces to avoid the scorn of the native-born (Lawrence 2007). In the hills, where the Greek population is more accepting and where the immigrants often work individually for specific farmers, many Albanian families live right next to the farmers themselves, sometimes in outbuildings and sometimes in the basement (Papadopoulos 2012). The segregation is piecemeal, depending on the level of economic interaction.

BELEAGUERED SPACES

When members of a group occupy a heavily segregated space, this often resembles a ghetto, as discussed in chapter 3. These beleaguered spaces take many forms, but the upshot is that they are based on constraints placed on the inhabitants. In the past, such spaces were mandated by law or customs so extreme as to be inviolable. Today, we are more likely to discuss ghetto formation where a group is isolated in a neighborhood or block of neighborhoods. This is based not on law but on a series of acts, behaviors, and attitudes that cause members of a group to be confined to a particular neighborhood and where the vast majority of people living in these neighborhoods belong to this group. These could be considered de facto ghettos. Such a condition denotes extreme segregation, as evidenced by high scores of unevenness and isolation. And such a situation does not occur by chance.

The experience of ghetto living varies a great deal. While the form and extreme segregation may be the same, there can be major differences in the level of economic interdependence and vitality. Marcuse (1997) makes a distinction between the *classic ghetto* and the *outcast ghetto*. History is replete with examples of classic ghettos, where segregation is involuntary and residents are exploited. These ghettos have even been walled at times. The classic ghetto quarantines an entire population physically, but normally allows the members of the population to participate in some way in the economy of the society as a whole. But Marcuse argues that the outcast ghetto, which shunts residents into the margins of urban life, is something "new and unique" because residents of these spaces are divorced from the rest of society. The separation is both vertical, as a form of racial separation, and also horizontal, since it is only the lowest class who inhabits this ghetto; those more fortunate have escaped it long ago. Wilson (1987) has described this formation most evocatively in tracing the exodus of working- and middle-class blacks out of these ghettos and into more prosperous neighborhoods.

While some like Anas (2006) take a broader definition of ghetto to encompass all manner of ethnic segregation, the nature of ghettos is such that it seems like something imposed on a group rather than a voluntary choice. Wacquant (2011, 6) likely states it best when he describes a ghetto as an "instrument of closure and control." Even when no laws are involved—and they can still be involved indirectly—individuals living in ghettos are placed in these neighborhoods because of the majority desire to have as little as possible to do with them. But it goes further than this, because ghettos entail a stigmatization of the subjected population along with their spatial confinement (Wacquant 2011). This desire is backed up by a series of restrictions, discriminatory actions, and even threats of violence that make ghetto residence inevitable. Those living in ghettos are cut off from opportunity within the mainstream, and the neighborhoods in which they reside are often stigmatized. The development of public housing projects in the United States, and many social housing projects in European cities and suburbs—often occupied by specific ethnic groups—have deepened the ghetto experience. Ghettos were deliberately created in the United States and, even if not deliberate, housing projects in many cities came to be identified with particular groups, leading to de facto ghettoization. The development of social housing on the outskirts of Paris has long been tied to immigrants from North Africa and their children (Robine 2011).

Vancouver's establishment of a Chinatown in the late nineteenth century provides a characteristic example of how ghetto residence has been inflicted on a minority population (Anderson 1987). In this situation, Chinese immigrants found themselves occupying a very few blocks, enforced indirectly through an 1893 bylaw prohibiting the establishment of a washhouse or laundry outside prescribed limits. The neighborhood itself was characterized as a "Chinatown" due to the concentration of Chinese immigrants, and it was viewed through the racist prism that prevailed at the time. This resulted in quite unflattering stereotypes that effectively conflated the impoverished conditions of a place with the people who lived

Figure 7.2. Stereotypes of Chinatown by cartoonist N. H. Hawkins, from the British Columbia *Saturday Sunset*, August 10, 1907, page 1: "A typical home of Vancouver white workingman"; "A warren on Carrall Street."

within, as shown in figure 7.2. So Vancouver's Chinatown represented a ghetto not only by virtue of its concentration of Chinese residents—who were essentially prohibited from living elsewhere—but by the manner in which the neighborhood was invested with all manner of deviant stereotypes, from opium addiction to criminality to general dirtiness. Such

Chinatowns were also grimly regarded in the United States, and were further scapegoated because of the high proportion of men compared to women. In a cruel instance of blaming the victim, these communities were prohibited by law from admitting Chinese women, but the bachelor society that resulted was then given as one additional example of Chinese deviance (Lin 1998).

MICROSEGREGATION IN ACTIVITY SPACES

The marginalization experienced by members of an ethnic or racial group is not always geographically fixed. Indeed, segregation can follow people as they move about their daily lives. Oppressed people have long been excluded from various places as an indicator of their status. When the Nazis took over a city, one of their first actions was to exclude Jews from a variety of places, forcing them outside the mainstream. This type of segregation can be self-imposed as well. Boal (1969) discussed it in terms of *activity segregation*, in which individuals move about constrained by their ethnicity. In Boal's example of Belfast, Northern Ireland, Catholics and Protestants would use separate bus stops, walk along different streets, and essentially move in divergent circuits—occupying distinct parcels of the same city.

The African American population long suffered from restrictive policies, and these increased in force during the late nineteenth and early twentieth centuries. In fact, Jim Crow laws, named after a nineteenth-century pejorative term for blacks, were instituted in all the former Confederate states (and in other states to a smaller degree) and some were passed as late as the 1950s. Jim Crow laws severely curtailed access to public facilities: schools, courts, transit, hospitals, restrooms, parks, and drinking fountains. This was followed by the exclusion of blacks from all manner of private facilities, including restaurants and hotels. The effects of these policies limited the freedom of movement among African Americans in a most pernicious way. Their intent was to minimize contact between whites and blacks, making it difficult for blacks to feel themselves anything other than a stigmatized minority.

After black Americans moved in large numbers to northern cities, occupying new spaces and enjoying new opportunities, they escaped some of the worst aspects of Jim Crow. While discriminatory, the fine-grained segregation imposed in the South was not as virulent in these parts or, at least, the terrain was known. Moreover, many blacks began to buy automobiles and to enjoy some of the freedoms that went along with this new mobility. However, this mobility was still greatly constrained. African Americans traveling through unfamiliar territory were subject to an aura of uncertainty, as black travelers never really knew what they would go up against (Seiler 2006). When African Americans decided to go back to their childhood homes in order to visit family members, they were confronted by a landscape of restrictions. Simply stopping for a meal was not possible, since many restaurants were closed to black customers. Most hotels also excluded blacks. Preparation was vital—and a big part of that preparation was a directory of places open to black travelers. Two guides were published during the mid-twentieth century: the *Travelguide* and the *Negro Motorist Green Book* (see figure 7.3). These captured

Figure 7.3. One issue of the *Green Book* that African American motorists used to find establishments that would serve them before discrimination was prohibited.

both the newfound freedom of the black middle class, and the continued oppression that all blacks experienced wherever they went (Seiler 2006). The *Negro Motorist Green Book* introduced its listings by stating:

> For some travelers, however, the facilities of many of these places are not available, even though they may have the price, and any traveler to whom they are not available is thereby faced with many and sometimes difficult problems. The Negro traveler's inconveniences are many and they are increasing because today so many more are traveling, individually and in groups. (1949, 2)

This was followed by numerous listings of hotels, tourist homes, restaurants, barber shops, beauty parlors, garages, nightclubs, drugstores, taverns, liquor stores, and anything else that was available. The guide included all the then 48 states and Washington, DC, as well as Canada, Mexico, and Bermuda. These entries showcased an archipelago of safe houses that African Americans still had to traverse in their journeys. The *Travelguide*'s covers always showed prosperous and sporty looking women, with the motto: "Vacation & Recreation without Humiliation" (Seiler 2006).

POLITICALLY DIVIDED SPACES

Ethnic divisions within the city are always more than just what happens in the city itself. This is especially true when ethnic divisions correspond to divisions between rival national groups or represent the actors in a sensitive geopolitical situation. There have always been divided cities, but such cities usually were subjected to political regimes that did not suffer rival nationalities. These groups were forced into quarantined spaces, or forced to assimilate, or driven out altogether. Today there are a number of cities where the divisions correspond to boundaries between distinct nationalities, but where these divisions have been recognized and accommodated to some degree with varying levels of dissatisfaction. The number of such cities is legion: Jerusalem, Belfast, Montreal, Beirut, Brussels, Nicosia, and Sarajevo. These and other examples reflect strong political tensions in urban space. Here the segregation patterns are not simply local, but reverberate internationally as well.

The development of such politically divided cities differs markedly from cities occupied by immigrant or other ethnic groups. Whereas urban form in most ethnically plural cities results from land value considerations, planning policy as desired by the state, and the nature of ethnic relations, the morphology of politically divided cities is dictated primarily by geopolitical considerations. In particularly tense cases like Jerusalem, geopolitics is preeminent, as it concerns the divisions between the Palestinian Arabs, the Israeli Jews, and the entire international focus on these relations. In more relaxed cases such as that of Brussels, these divisions often result from ethnic or linguistic policies that determine where people live and how they create their space. In any of these cases, however, placemaking becomes quite charged and urgent, since it may determine the relative safety of those residents who live within an ethnic place. The boundaries between such ethnic places—rather than blurred and porous—are more likely to be fixed and hard, with any breaches portending potential trouble.

These ethno-political ruptures are bound up with scale and the tendency for situations in politically divided cities to jump scales. Ethnic location involves more than neighborhoods. Rather, it involves nations who are often in competition for power, which takes place at a much larger scale. Take the case of Montreal, which is among the more relaxed side of the spectrum of politically divided cities. The French-speaking and English-speaking populations have never really gone to war against each other, at least since the early nineteenth century, and despite a few terrorist incidents in the 1960s, violence rarely occurs between the two groups. However, the configuration of neighborhoods in the city and its suburbs signal much larger issues occurring country-wide. Montreal is the principal city in French-speaking Quebec, and those English speakers who live there are considered by many Francophones to be relics of an era when Anglophones dominated the majority French. The jockeying between Anglophones and Francophones on the island mirrors the larger contest between Quebec with its majority French speakers, and the rest of Canada with its majority English-speaking population. The Quebec government has initiated measures to make Quebec and Montreal more French and to compel many of the English-speaking population to educate their children in French, to use only French language signs, and generally to reduce the power of this minority group. English speakers have responded by hunkering down in a few of the Anglophone west-side neighborhoods and nearby suburbs. Many have also made the decision to just move out of the city altogether. Yet those who remain will assert their sense of place, sometimes even if it means flouting the imposed law. Some of these maneuvers have been found in similar cities, such as Brussels, where the French population is encircled by a ring of Flemish-speaking villages.

While battles between competing linguistic-national groups can get heated and uncomfortable, those cities divided by religion suffer the most venomous conflicts. Jerusalem—an actual city that includes Israeli Jews, Palestinian Arabs, and a few Christians—is also the focal point for the three religious traditions of Islam, Christianity, and Judaism. It symbolizes the conflict between Israel and her Arab neighbors, and most notably the Palestinian Arabs who occupy many of the same lands. Jerusalem has been divided for most of the twentieth century. During the Ottoman Empire, each religious group secured its own neighborhoods. Under British control, a boundary line—a green line—was established to separate the Jews from the Arabs in Jerusalem. Each community on either side of the line provided its own services, and there was virtually no interaction between them. The situation continued with the development of the state of Israel, but as Israel gained control of the whole of Jerusalem after the 1967 war, it incorporated more of the previously Arab lands to the east. In this respect, the boundary that separated the Jews from the Arabs shifted to accommodate these new facts on the ground (Shlay and Rosen 2010). Ethnic placemaking in the context of Jerusalem is politically supercharged. The development of Jewish spaces in former Arab territory is perceived either as a just consolidation by the Jewish majority, or as a horrible affront by the Palestinian population. These so-called ethnic spaces have emerged as the key flashpoints in the conflict between Palestinians and Israel.

Just north of Jerusalem, Beirut has also experienced similar conflicts. In a politically sensitive situation, the demarcations between ethnic neighborhoods do not allow for easy transgression. Beirut, once considered the Paris of the Middle East largely because of its cosmopolitan character, turned into a site of internecine war between its Muslim and Maronite Christian populations during the 1980s. These groups had always occupied separate neighborhoods, but with the coming of conflict, neighborhoods became even more segregated and fortified (Genberg 2002). Public space was one of the casualties of this conflict. A fortified barrier was placed along the boundary between the Christian and Muslim sectors, and the three gate crossings were effectively closed to all but international diplomats and militants (Calame and Charlesworth 2009). Some areas were taken over by one population as part of their neighborhood, but much public space was in fact simply left deserted. The city government has made efforts to develop more of these spaces where interaction between different groups can take place (Genberg 2002), but it is a long process.

It is interesting to note how groups in politically divided cities are often empowered to develop parallel institutions. We can see this in a place like Bolzano in the South Tyrol section of northern Italy. Bolzano is also a creature of geopolitical shifts, specifically Italy's acquisition of the South Tyrol from Austria after World War I. Mussolini decided it was his duty to alter the ethno-linguistic makeup of this Germanophone city. He Italianized what was then Bozen by developing industry and encouraging masses of southern Italians to move up north to work in these new factories. German speakers were passed over for employment and housing. So Bozen/Bolzano went from being·nearly exclusively German to having a majority Italian population, which it does to this day, smack in the middle of a German-speaking countryside. While a minority within the city itself, German-speaking Sud Tiroleans maintain distinct neighborhoods, most notably in Bolzano's historical city center. Conflicts between these groups—which at one time grew quite heated—have simmered down. But resentments persist, and neighborhoods are sharply drawn. Moreover, completely parallel institutions have developed. Ethnic Germans and Italians are educated in different school systems, they frequent different shops, they listen to different news, and they support different political parties. All of this further encourages their separation. There are of course public spaces—as the level of violence that one finds in some politically divided cities is not found here—but at the same time, these spaces do not seem to be built as much for interaction as for tourism, and members of the different groups pretty much keep to themselves. It is a situation that Carlá (2007) has termed "living apart in the same room," and it renders Bolzano into a strangely divided sort of place.

The division of a city becomes more evident when a city is divided by a quasi-political boundary. To some extent, this applies to Sarajevo, where the inter-entity boundary line between the Serbian and Bosnia/Herzegovinian halves of the country slices just to the southeast of the city, cutting off the increasingly Muslim main city from the suburbs where many of the Serbian residents reside (Bollens 2002). The divisions in Nicosia are starker. Once the unified capital of Cyprus, the city has mirrored since the Turkish invasion of 1974 the division of the entire island, with a line separating the northern, Turkish Nicosia (now capital of the Turkish Republic of Cyprus) and the southern, Greek Nicosia, the capital of Greek Cyprus. While tensions between the groups in Nicosia are less recent and raw—compared to Bosnia, the conflict resulted in few casualties and atrocities—the city is divided by a wall, and moving between neighborhoods entails a thousand miles of airplane travel. Parallel city administrations and services are on each side. But an encouraging sign is that the mayors of the two Nicosias have exhibited a fair degree of cooperation, and urban planning has proceeded with the idea that the city may be unified once again (Bollens 2012).

EMBATTLED ETHNICITY

While all people belong to a culture, individuals do not feel fully the extent of their own difference until they find themselves confronted by hostility. Throughout history, most newcomers have not been welcomed, but instead pilloried, persecuted, and pushed away. Societies have promoted divisions between mainstream, dominant groups and those groups left behind. Space has not been used kindly, but instead has furthered minority marginalization. Minorities can be kept away by driving them into a ghetto, keeping them on the outskirts of the city, forcing them to use separate facilities, and building symbolic or physical walls. Segregation can be promulgated at both large and small scales.

Unlike the placemaking described in chapter 6, this sort of geographical marginalization is rarely due to choice or, if it is, it is a false choice based on fear. Initially at least, ethnics find themselves without many options and must make the most of their limited choices. Circumstances may change over the course of time, and what had been a space of exclusion and confinement becomes a space of enablement. Once a group obtains some resources, marginalized spaces can be transformed into valued ethnic places. If left alone, businesses and institutions can ameliorate some of the harshest conditions. How many neighborhoods that were once beleaguered are now regarded with a kind of nostalgia? Of course, the availability of resources to some ethnics might also lead to further decline as more successful ethnics seek a way out, leaving their more disadvantaged brethren behind.

Once ethnic spaces are established, they play a fundamental role in shaping the life chances for those who inhabit them. These consequences arise from how spaces were created in the first place. Whether ethnics cluster as a result of societal constraints—including ghettoization, discrimination, or some other factor that forces members of the group to live in particular places—or whether they stay together in order to achieve some benefit, will determine the level of control these groups have over the consequences.

8

⨪

Positive Consequences of Concentration

We have all heard the real estate mantra: "location, location, location." Indeed, how well an individual does within a society depends to a great extent on where she lives, a fact borne out in study after study. This is most certainly true in the case of ethnic or racial concentration. Even clustering at a relatively small scale affects how different ethnic populations make their way in society at large: their ability to promote their own culture, to advance their economic interests, and to project their political voice within the larger society. Clustering can confer tremendous positive advantages on members of a group. It can also have consequences that are quite negative, based on the segregation itself and its interaction with other social ills. Sometimes, positive and negative elements might occur in the same place, at the same time.

While it is impossible to be exhaustive, we can try to make sense of these outcomes by considering them in a couple of different lights. First, outcomes are not neutral, but are mostly tilted toward the negative or positive side of the ledger. Outcomes range from bad to good; from the hopeless to the hopeful. On the negative side, space operates as a constraint, preventing members of particular groups from exercising their fullest potential. The concentration can become a tool of oppression and persecution in its own right. On the positive side, the clustering of ethnic members operates as a kind of resource, helping the ethnic group promote its own interests. Second, the types of outcomes, both positive and negative, can be usefully categorized into several related themes, each carrying a particular kind of effect. What is more, a group may suffer from a specific negative consequence while still employing space as a means to further its goals in a positive way. In all these cases, space is more than simply a container within which the activities of individuals occur. Instead, space allows actors to utilize it for particular ends. Concentration carries profound consequences for identity formation. It divides some identities, while bringing others together. It impacts the relationship between groups within society, even as the distance and lack of interaction can breed stereotypes and mistrust. The nature of the impacts depends on the groups involved, the societal context, the state apparatus, the nature of the majority group, and the presence of other minority groups.

CONSIDERING THE CONSEQUENCES

The clustering of culturally similar people can bestow several benefits. There is the benefit of enhanced social capital: people feel they can trust one another, even if they do not personally know each other very well. There is the benefit of familiarity: one's own language, foods, and just a general way of doing things can be obtained in an environment that is otherwise quite alien. There is the benefit of knowledge: as insider information is provided to people about opportunities, dangers, and other aspects of life. Finally, there is the benefit of transmission: immigrants want to pass along the culture of their native lands without worrying that their children will lose this heritage.

Each benefit requires both a certain degree of proximity and a minimum population size. Consider the desire to transmit culture to children. This could be done informally—within or between families—but is more effective within some sort of school or camp. So let's say there is a desire to open a Sunday school where children are taught in their parents' native language. Such a school would be virtually impossible without a certain number of people who are willing to help run the school and without a certain number of children who would be interested in attending. The desire to provide people with familiar foods requires a grocery store, which needs a number of customers who are willing to shop there.

Most of the benefits of ethnic clustering demand a certain threshold population. As we begin to scale up potential ethnic institutions—welfare societies, legal assistance, and banks—each requires a larger population than the one before. In years past, before widespread mobility, the maintenance of these institutions required members to be within walking distance. For groups whose religious observations prevent members from driving on the Sabbath, this is still a consideration. However, many groups in the modern era are able to maintain thresholds over wider geographic areas. Yet their institutions still need to be accessible.

Within the same city, the ability of an ethnic population to utilize its own spatial concentration depends very much on its location vis-à-vis other actors within the society. The same goes for the degree to which any type of segregation can exert a negative impact on its own, independent of other factors. Such variations will be even more pronounced between countries. We cannot even begin to consider how concentration operates unless we consider the particular context and the scale within which it occurs. Focusing the scale from a large overview down to a finer scale of resolution may reveal other types of consequences that come into play (Lacoste 2006).

Positive consequences may be considered thematically. The first outcome might be the *cultural/symbolic ramifications* of ethnic concentration. As we saw in chapter 6, ethnic placemaking reinforces ethnic identity in a profound way. Clustered groups are more capable of maintaining institutions and commercial activities that cater to residents and provide a much firmer footing in society. This may even extend to religious practices, especially those making use of territory. The *emotional aspects* of ethnic clustering connect to this, and have to do with the ways residents may find living within a neighborhood of co-ethnics more comfortable and less threatening. Group sentiment can effectively encapsulate the residents from too much outside influence (Robinson 1984). Ethnic clustering brings with it *economic rewards*. Space, along with available ethnic resources, can provide ethnic entrepreneurs with the grounding they need to develop a successful business. Ethnic solidarity ensures a loyal labor force and faithful customers. Finally, spatial concentration often bolsters a group's *political profile*, and provides a sense of *physical security*. Concentrated ethnic settlements form the territorial basis for ethnic interest-group voting. Especially in an electoral system that promotes district-based voting, ethnic groups may use their local majorities to elect one of their own to municipal councils, regional legislations, and country-wide parliaments. In less peaceful situations, ethnic neighborhoods may even provide a clear-cut way for members to defend themselves.

CULTURAL AND SYMBOLIC RAMIFICATIONS

Most of the positive consequences stem from the aspect of choice, as discussed in chapter 4, but not all the time. In some cases, it is whether a group can extract some good from a bad situation, if members can promote their own agency within an otherwise oppressive structure. This can be observed in efforts to turn stigmatized neighborhoods into points of pride. One famous instance comes from the branding of Harlem in

New York City. Harlem was created because of the deepening segregation foisted on the black population coming north. This was an area that had first been colonized by affluent whites looking to obtain more breathing room uptown, but between 1900 and 1920 became a center for black settlement (Osofsky 1971). By the 1920s, Harlem came to represent the premier African American neighborhood in New York City, and this symbolic attachment deepened with the emergence of establishments like the Cotton Club, the Apollo Theater, and others that manifested the urban black experience (McGruder 2015). Such neighborhood symbols are historically useful as well because they reinforce past events and sentiments. This increases their influence on present-day ethnic attachments.

Ethnic communities have long been marked by the religious institutions within them. Any overview of an urban landscape could easily encompass a variety of different institutions—whether they be Serbian Orthodox churches, Jewish synagogues, or Polish Catholic parishes. These tend to reflect, if not the present status of that neighborhood, at least how the neighborhood was shaped in the past. In fact, the development of different ethnic neighborhoods in a place like Chicago was accompanied by the distribution of a variety of different parish churches, which represented the Italian/Irish/Polish/other ethnicity of the congregants, as seen in figure 8.1 (Kantowicz 1995). Compared to Protestant churches, Catholic churches were often quite place-based—congregants would attend their neighborhood church. But ethnically mixed neighborhood parishes were unrealistic in a city awash in numerous newcomers. Each nationality requested separate parishes, with priests who could speak to them. As a result, multiple parish churches might be established in the same district.

In Dar es Salaam, Tanzania, the South Asian population is found in the Asian-dominated downtown and the neighborhood just to the west. These neighborhoods help to anchor the communal gathering sites of different South Asian groups. There are many such venues, but among the more meaningful are the major Hindu temples, Catholic churches, and Shiite mosques. These establishments bring together ethnics from different classes and castes, and provide cultural education and social life (Nagar 1997). The gathering areas, made possible by the concentration of South Asian groups in Tanzania's principal city, help to shape and maintain the individual ethnic identities.

Some religions continue to require proximity to a religious institution and may require the establishment of particular spaces. The Jewish creation of *eruvim* districts exemplifies this. An *eruv* is a circumscribed territory marked off by invisible perimeters that are rooted in actual features of the landscape (Vincent and Warf 2002). It is also land that is symbolically leased from local authorities. During the Sabbath, eruvim allow observant Jews to carry outside the home those things they would normally only be able to carry inside (Rapoport 2011). The eruv thus creates an imaginary

CHURCHES

A - All Saints
B - St. Bridget
C - St. David
D - Nativity of Our Lord
E - St. John Nepomucene
F - St. Anthony of Padua
G - Immaculate Conception
H - St. George
I - St. Barbara
J - St. Mary of Perpetual
    Help

Bridgeport, circa 1910.

Figure 8.1. Roman Catholic immigrants to Chicago found comfort within their own churches, as evidenced by this map of the Bridgeport neighborhood in 1910. *Source:* Kantowicz (1995). Used with permission from Eerdmans Publishing.

enclosure of private space, but people must live within these confines in order to take advantage of its benefits. Eruvim can be big or small, and do not have to be composed exclusively of Orthodox Jews. In fact, some are as large as a city (Vincent and Warf 2002). But eruvim establishment, and the fact that Orthodox Jews are required to walk to the synagogue on the Sabbath, certainly promotes clustering. It is their symbolic dimension—which enhances the solidarity and community of those Orthodox Jews living within them—that provides for an ethno-spiritual home.

EMOTIONAL VALUE OF CONCENTRATION

While often members of a group are forced to live in more segregated spaces, and perhaps denied access to other areas, they may develop some positive emotional reasons for living in a concentrated space. An ethnically defined neighborhood comforts its residents and helps create a barrier against outsiders. It allows ethnics a way of maximizing their contact with friendly faces and avoiding contact with hostile ones. It promotes familiarity and keeps anxiety and uncertainty at bay.

This is especially true for many maligned groups who may find that segregation, while foisted on them by antagonistic outsiders, has its share of compensations. The residences of Japanese burakumin mark their identity. The burakumin develop a distinct community, bound to each other by emotional and psychological ties. While these neighborhoods are stigmatized, they also enable their residents to avoid contact with other Japanese. Burakumin are less likely to experience feelings of rejection as long as they remain within the community (De Vos and Wagatsuma 2006).

Wealthy communities may realize the emotional benefits of concentration as well. The Chinese in Southeast Asia have succeeded in business and become quite prosperous (Wang 1991). They must also confront a great deal of intolerance in many societies in which they have settled (Pan 1994). The Chinese are viewed as exploiting the native peoples. They are seen as blocking the development of native enterprise. When there is economic trouble in these societies, the Chinese feel the wrath of the discontented. They are also seen as potentially disloyal, even blamed for actions undertaken by China. The ethnic Chinese have been kept at arm's length by native attitudes, and have kept themselves at arm's length as a result of their own sense of distinctiveness. This distinctiveness is manifest in segregated communities. The Chinatowns that have emerged across Southeast Asia are clear targets during conflict, but they are also places where the Chinese can turn for emotional support. These communities shelter their residents from social and political hostility. It is not the resentful faces of the indigenous that they need to see on their strolls about town, but the faces of their compatriots. In fact, Chinese spaces in Jakarta are articulated even further: some

Figure 8.2.   Chinese walled neighborhoods in Jakarta, Indonesia. *Source:* Harald Leisch.

are traditional, some are new, some are from different origins, and some have different levels of prosperity (Leisch 2002a). The example in figure 8.2 demonstrates that outside hostility and the desire to separate have led some wealthier Chinese who request the "best possible security" (Leisch 2002b, 349) to embrace gated community life.

Segregated neighborhoods may appear as a positive refuge for some groups, but at a certain point they may become an unwanted crutch. The legacy of segregation lives within people's minds and creates a sense of comfort. For example, Muslim Asians who live in some northern English towns often feel out of place when traversing urban spaces dominated by whites. Both men and women are wary of their reception. Muslim women in particular may feel that the outward expression of their faith—their dress in particular—opens them up to negative interactions; as one stated, "it's all the publicity that Islam has had 'cause they don't know you as a person, they just know that you're a Muslim" (quoted in Phillips 2008, 186). This makes it psychologically easier to remain in a friendlier neighborhood. Yet many ethnics evince a strong desire to live as equals among other groups, in a more heterogeneous community. They yearn to break free of their ethnically isolated quarters and live in more diverse circumstances, provided these are accompanied by tolerance (Phillips 2008). The process of integrating places must occur across several steps, as pioneers move into an uncomfortable situation and create more opportunities for others. In these English towns, it has been middle-class white areas with younger populations that have held the most promise as places where Muslims and other ethnic/religious minorities may venture.

ECONOMIC VALUE OF CONCENTRATION

One of the defining features of any ethnic neighborhood is its mixture of ethnic businesses. Business establishments allow some members of the ethnic group to make a living, while providing other members access to goods and services that may be otherwise hard to come by. Ethnic businesses confer social advantages and help maintain ethnic identification. Grocery stores—to take one common business—provide more than specialized ethnic foods; they also facilitate social connections and become significant elements in the ethnic landscape (Oberle 2006; Odoom 2012). At higher levels of ethnic economic development, banks have emerged to facilitate the flow of credit to ethnic members for their own personal needs and for the establishment of ethnic businesses (Li et al. 2006). Beyond this, ethnic businesses provide a focal point for the ethnic community, and serve as the entryway into the ethnic community itself.

In considering ethnic economic activity, the scale varies from a few isolated businesses to a series of stores, services, banks, and firms that accommodate the goods and service needs of their community and connect with one another, allowing economic transactions to multiply. A handful of isolated businesses may carry a great deal of meaning for the community, but hardly constitute an economy on its own. But a greater density and diversity of businesses does begin to resemble an ethnic economy.

How does concentration figure into this? Spatial clustering allows certain ethnic groups to take advantage of both ethnic and spatial resources. Most immigrants have very little money, few of the necessary skills, and a weak grasp of the native language (Light and Karageorgis 1994). Ethnic resources provide an additional set of resources that can be tapped. Ethnic resources may include a level of trust that facilitates the acquisition of investment capital from other co-ethnics (Portes and Zhou 1992). The community can provide easier access to co-ethnic employees who may be willing to work for lower wages and are more trustworthy (Bailey and Waldinger 1991). They may also provide a protected customer base, which is loyal to the establishment even if it does not provide the absolute lowest prices (Aldrich et al. 1985).

Spatial resources stem from clustering, facilitating ethnic economic ties and fostering an ethnic customer base (Kaplan 1998). Spatial proximity is especially valuable in those communities where customers may need to walk to the stores they patronize. The same holds for co-ethnic employees, who live close to the businesses (Zhou [1992] 2010). Proximity may also spur more linkages between businesses. In turn, these businesses interact with each other by buying and selling each other's goods and services. In addition, concentrated business activity allows the overall market to increase (Aldrich et al. 1985). This increase in market and business combines to create an ethnic "central place"—a focal point recognized by members of the community, both ethnic and non-ethnic. The social and cultural ties of an ethnic population are buttressed by economic relations (Min 1993).

One of the best-developed ethnic economies is found among the Cuban population of Miami. Cubans used their economic success to create an alternative to incorporation in mainstream Anglo society. Miami long had a special connection to Cuba, being the southernmost U.S. city near the Caribbean islands. However, when the island was taken over by Cuba's Communist Party, a mass exodus of middle- and upper-class Cubans came straight to Florida, aided and abetted by U.S. policy. This was a group with a great deal of human capital resources and financial resources as well (Abrahamson 2005). Many Cubans were well trained, well educated, and several had business experience. Favorable U.S. policy that often provided Cuban refugees with financial support, along with the then underdeveloped nature of the Miami economy, allowed Cubans to occupy sections of the city—especially the quarter that came to be known as Little Havana—and begin developing their own businesses (Boswell and Curtis 1984). Additional refugees who arrived in 1980 and the substantial resettlement of Cubans from other parts of the United States to southeast Florida hastened this well-developed ethnic economy.

Miami became an ideal example of a concentrated ethnic economy because, first, there was a clustering of Cubans in Miami and large numbers of Cuban-owned businesses. Second, the businesses employed other Cubans. Many of the new workers had very little experience with American culture, knew little English, and were thankful for the opportunity to work for another Cuban; the job might even become something of an apprenticeship that would allow them to someday operate their own business (Abrahamson 2005). Third, the new stores catered primarily to a Cuban clientele. Refugees who came into Miami were looking for a comfortable place to shop—hearkening to the emotional benefits of concentration—and they also needed particular goods that only Cuban-owned stores could provide (Portes and Stepick 1993). Fourth, the Cuban American economy has developed to the point that Cuban firms do business with other Cuban firms, resulting in several linkages (Wilson and Martin 1982). As a consequence, this particular ethnic economy allowed Cuban American to live and work entirely within the community, to a level where many observers argue that it has provided an alternative to the mainstream Anglo economy. Many Cubans decided to effectively create a parallel society that would allow individuals to live within Miami without very much exposure to Anglo culture, even a society that may provide higher wages to some workers. An influx of additional immigrants from Central and South America have only added to the Latin character of this city and provide an additional labor force. The Cuban influence on the landscape and the ability for the Cubans to "make" this place has been enormous.

Spatial resources can also apply to the clustering of ethnic businesses without a lot of residential settlement. This can occur as ethnic businesses grow to rely on customers outside the neighborhood, or the business district becomes so active that most participants prefer to live elsewhere. Los Angeles includes two solid examples where ethnics make a place from businesses in areas where the majority of their populations do not reside. The enclave of Koreatown stretches about one mile along Wilshire Boulevard, and is festooned with a huge array of Korean establishments. Yet the vast majority of Koreans in the Los Angeles area do not live here. Instead, Koreatown is used primarily to house visitors and furnish a sort of display area for the city's Korean American community. Just a couple of miles east lies Little Tokyo, and this is even further removed from where most Japanese Americans live. Little Tokyo is quite neatly bounded, with its edge bordering Los Angeles's skid row. And while most Japanese do not live here—with the exception of the few apartments and some hotel space—many of them choose to regularly make the trip in order to procure different goods, but also as a way to participate in some of the festivals and other ethnic-themed activities in this quite distinct neighborhood (Smith 2006). A trip to Little Tokyo may also be accompanied by a trip to a peaceful garden styled next to a Buddhist temple, as shown in figure 8.3.

Figure 8.3.   This garden is found at the Nishi Hongwanji Buddhist Temple, on the corner of Third Street and San Pedro in Little Tokyo, Los Angeles. *Source:* James M. Smith.

POLITICAL EMPOWERMENT

One area where ethnic concentration can be a clear advantage lies in the political arena. To gain this advantage requires the realization of citizenship—which can be a major hurdle in many countries—and on being fully enfranchised. Efforts to prevent certain groups from voting, as was done in the American South against its black residents, could effectively shut down the political rights of a population. But once those rights are attained, many groups have pressed for political power. Actual elections are one approach, but this is also accompanied by the development of political institutions.

Demography leads to political power, in many contexts; the question is how well this power can be deployed. The situation in greater Moncton, New Brunswick, is instructive in this regard. While Canada itself is officially bilingual, most provinces are effectively monolingual in English or French. New Brunswick is the one province with a fairly even split, and within this, the Greater Moncton area has a substantial Francophone minority. These minorities deploy a number of territorial strategies, depending on whether they are a minority in one city (Moncton) or a majority in the adjoining city of Dieppe. In what Bourgeois and Bourgeois (2005) describe as administrative nationalism, French-speaking minorities seek control over various institutions—particularly school boards and health boards—by utilizing territorial strategies.

Immigrant populations coming into the United States followed a path of gaining some political power first, before they were able to achieve anything close to economic equality. The Irish immigrants wore a path in this regard (Marston 1988). Their loyalty to each other—based on ethnicity rather than class—and their settlement in spatially distinct neighborhoods were key to their political success. Prior to gaining political power, the Irish developed cultural institutions that helped to stage events like parades and molded a positive image of the Irish. These associations unified and mobilized the Irish population, and created ethnic political solidarity. Residential clustering facilitated this mobilization and would later serve as a springboard to electoral success. The emergence of ethnic political "machines" from the late nineteenth century into the mid-twentieth century testified to the power of strong ethnic ties based on distinct neighborhoods (Cochran 1995).

Most minority groups rarely have the numbers to challenge majority candidates at larger spatial scales like states, provinces, or countries, at least not initially. Political empowerment often comes at smaller spatial scales, such as within a municipality. In this instance, residential segregation can emerge as a political resource. If voters elect someone primarily on the basis of ethnicity—and this type of voting is common throughout the world—then the ability to concentrate that vote can allow that ethnic candidate to prevail. When African Americans left the rural South, where they had been denied political rights, to venture into the urban North, they were shunted into segregated spaces and discriminated against economically. But they were able to use their spatial concentration and ethnic solidarity to accrue political power. The black ghetto became the base of black power, and shattered the political barriers of municipal power (Browning, Marshall, and Tabb 1984; 1990). Several African American politicians gained a voice through this process, and later many took over as mayors of some major cities—just as earlier ethnic politicians had done years before—though in many cases, continued success required electoral coalitions with other ethnic groups (Douzet 2009).

Ethnic political concentration can be a double-edged sword. Segregation certainly fosters electoral opportunities, leading to greater minority political engagement. In fact, under the Voting Rights Act of 1965 and especially as amended in 1982, electoral districts were supposed to be configured to provide representation to all groups. But this was taken to mean that districts should maximize the concentration of particular groups—primarily African Americans—in a number of oddly shaped legislative districts. This form of gerrymandering, in which districts concentrated minority populations, left surrounding districts with very few minorities. So the underrepresentation of minority interests was "remedied" by providing for a handful of officeholders, but this concentration of minority voters into singular districts meant that minority concerns were completely absent outside the districts. This decreased support for minority-sponsored legislation, and could reduce the incentive for voter turnout (Cameron, Eppstein, and O'Halloran 1996; Weber 2000).

In Europe, the types of immigrants, the stage of the migratory process, the electoral systems, and the political cultures vary from one country to another. One key difference comes from how countries open or restrict citizenship and the voting franchise for both immigrants and their children (Martiniello 2009). Some European countries allow non-citizens to vote, at least in part. Others are generous in giving expatriates a say in the process. Some countries employ a list system, where much of the voting is at large, whereas others are more district based. In Britain, a country that employs district-based voting and also has a relatively generous immigration policy, religious minorities vote in higher numbers where they are most concentrated (Fieldhouse and Cutts 2008). This aligns with the idea that ethnic concentration favors mobilization (Schlichting, Tuckel, and Maisel 1998; Hero and Tolbert 2007). By contrast, populations in segregated neighborhoods in France tend to have lower rates of citizenship, voter registration, and electoral participation. During the 2010 French regional elections, the participation rate in highly segregated suburbs was much lower, and those same suburbs experienced a great deal of unrest. This drop in participation signaled disillusionment and alienation from voters.

ACCENTUATING THE POSITIVE

The desire of people to live among their own drives much concentration. To some, this can be a reaction against outside hostility. To others, it can provide a means of preserving community. If members of an ethnic group make this choice voluntarily, there is a good chance that the concentration will confer positive benefits and allow the group to reap more ethnic resources. It also means that the group is able to realize greater levels of bonding social capital, and thus strengthen group ties.

One question is whether this sort of concentration is something that drives greater levels of intolerance between members of the ethnic community and everyone else. Much of the distaste for segregation comes from the notion that it is an unhealthy state of affairs that harms the overall society, even if it provides some short-term benefits to members of the society. Some of this is shaded by a society's views on incorporation, and whether assimilation is perceived as the ultimate goal. In cases where this is not as important, the spatial sorting of different groups can allow these groups to function as somewhat autonomous societies and economies, while leveraging their geographical concentration to have a greater political impact. The discussion of multiculturalism in chapter 10 addresses this issue more fully.

In all discussions of consequences, we need to be careful not to overstate the homogeneity within the ethnic group itself. While ethnics enjoy a great deal of commonality, based on their cultural similarities, they are also individuals with distinct life circumstances. Some members of a particular group are going to enjoy outcomes quite different from that of other members. To take one example, while many ethnic businesspeople can enjoy the protected customer base, co-ethnic labor, and other ethnic resources of their community, a truly successful ethnic entrepreneur will soon transcend the limits of his community and provide goods for the broader society. This will no longer be an "ethnic" business, but a mainstream business that happens to be run by an ethnic person.

9

ॐ

Negative Consequences of Concentration

While concentration certainly carries with it positive benefits, there is also a much darker side. Oftentimes people live apart because they are not allowed to access certain neighborhoods. Most societies have a history of enforcing this kind of segregation, in which a dominant group spatially marginalizes a certain minority population and excludes them from a number of different spaces. The spatial marginalization reaches extremes in the most repressive and racist regimes, but is present even within some of the most benign societies. Where this occurs, the overall consequences of concentration tend toward the negative for those groups affected. This is partially because spatially marginalized groups are usually discriminated against in many other ways—socially, economically, and educationally—and this makes it difficult for them to obtain their share of resources. These handicaps are based on income, education, and other individual attributes that shape their standard of living, and so people who are compelled to live in segregated neighborhoods are among the poorest members of society.

But segregation also operates as an additional layer of deprivation, intensifying poverty and other social ills by reducing access to those types of people and places that could improve a person's life. The type of consequence is determined by how concentration came about, which in part is determined by the nature of the group itself, the context within which it operates, and the scale being examined.

CONSIDER THE CONSEQUENCES

Research continues to show that segregation carries material consequences. Just as the residential choices of some groups are constrained through formal discrimination, economic disadvantage, or the pressures and preferences of other groups, segregation also multiplies the negative material aspects of poverty (see Massey and Fischer 2000). Segregated populations tend to be less well off anyway, and the process of segregating a group testifies to that group's undesirability within a particular social context. But the question remains whether the consequences of such potent segregation are compositional or contextual. A *compositional* effect occurs when a neighborhood with a high percentage of a given group may demonstrate deprivation because members of the group are individually deprived. If a large proportion of a neighborhood's population has incomes that place them under the poverty line, then the neighborhood itself will appear as a high-poverty neighborhood. Segregation concentrates people who are already deprived, and so that sums up to overall neighborhood deprivation. A *contextual* effect is something else altogether. In this case, the concentration itself may add an additional layer of deprivation. Individuals who live within a segregated neighborhood experience their own individual-level poverty, but they also experience impoverishment by virtue of their location. It is a classic case of the sum being greater than the parts.

The first effect could be considered along the lines of a resident's *physical well-being*. This includes much poorer health outcomes due to structural problems—like lead paint or higher levels of pollution—or simply lack of access to health care. It might also be manifested in lack of access to decent foods, as poor, segregated neighborhoods are often bereft of decent choices. Segregation has also been associated with outbursts of violence, or at least the heightened level of attention given to violent acts that occur across a segregated urban landscape. The recent example of a black man shot in segregated Ferguson, Missouri, or older examples such as the Los Angeles riots of 1992 or the *crise des banlieues* in Paris in 2005, has brought into sharp relief the racialized landscapes of metropolitan areas in the United States and France.

The second effect has to do with the lack of *economic well-being* among residents, many of which result from neighborhood circumstances themselves. Poor segregated neighborhoods suffer a huge lack of employment opportunities, which may persist even if the overall economy is relatively healthy. Low property values compound these financial disadvantages, leading to blighted housing. The discriminatory impacts of predatory lending—focused like a laser on the most vulnerable neighborhoods—leads to foreclosures. Some of this reflects the operations of the urban land market, and the reluctance of many merchants to open businesses in disadvantaged and often segregated quarters; some of this evinces the truly malicious operations of people who seek to swindle susceptible people.

The third effect relates to the diminished opportunities found within many of these neighborhoods, and the lower levels of *human capital*. One clear way in which this is evidenced is through the inferior quality of schools and the lower level of educational opportunities in general. But it may also be seen in lower levels of human welfare, which makes it more difficult for individuals to overcome their poor circumstances. In such neighborhoods, the lack of opportunities can breed a variety of social pathologies—drug abuse, teen pregnancy, and crime—that spur even more negative outcomes.

Finally, the neighborhood has the capacity to do real *psychological harm* to its residents. Part of this is internal, as the threat of persecution and violence makes people uncomfortable and too fearful to get out and about. Even the police may be seen more as agents of oppression than of security. Part of this is the way in which residing in a neighborhood itself can serve to marginalize residents from the wider society, or even define them in unflattering ways.

CONCENTRATION, PHYSICAL DEPRIVATION, AND VIOLENCE

Segregation itself has been shown to lead to much poorer material outcomes among members of the segregated group. Segregation within Accra, Ghana, exists to some extent between tribal groups (Agyei-Mensah and Owusu, 2010). This is particularly pronounced between the less well-off Ga group and the more privileged Akon group. Segregation exacerbates pressures on housing and on scarce municipal resources, as the more deprived members of the Ga group live within specific Accra neighborhoods that are marked by blighted housing, few services, and poor sanitation. These neighborhoods are clearly unhealthy, according to Weeks and colleagues (2006). In their study, the percentage of Ga within a neighborhood was an independent predictor of higher levels of child mortality.

Similarly, there seems to be a strong association between residential segregation in Nairobi, Kenya, and several measures of human welfare. In a study by K'Akumu and Olima (2007), the focus is on the "racial" segregation established between the African, European, and Asian populations. This has promoted a system of "systematic and uneven spatial distribution of public services" (94–95) that includes education, transportation, sanitation, and health. These early colonialist divisions set in motion the entire trajectory of Nairobi's socioeconomic development.

Squatter settlements laced through and around Nairobi sprang from colonial-era segregation. Similar patterns are found among many other growing third-world cities. For example, nearly 50 years after independence, an examination of the divisions within Dar es Salaam, Tanzania, shows the legacy and continued persistence of colonial-era segregation (Smiley 2009; 2010). The Germans and then the British enacted the types of building ordinances that effectively segregated the population, even without the type of explicit racial zoning implemented in South Africa. The city continues to be divided today. For modern-day expatriate Europeans, life is lived within the upscale Msasani Peninsula and, to a much lesser extent, the downtown.

The question is, are there any additional factors related to the segregated context of that group? Teasing this out requires a sophisticated analysis. Multivariate regression demonstrates how residential *isolation* is related to the prevalence of intravenous drug use among African Americans, while residential *concentration* is not related to this form of drug abuse (Cooper et al. 2008). An even more elaborate analysis is provided in Grady's (2006) examination of racial disparities in low birthweight. She uses multilevel modeling to assess the role of context, and found that residential segregation exerts an independent effect beyond what is accounted for by individual factors.

One topic receiving a great deal of attention has been the relationship between certain neighborhoods and the availability of healthy foods. So-called food deserts are defined as areas where people suffer economic and physical barriers to procuring healthy food (Shaw 2006). The food deserts are correlated with the socioeconomic and racial segregation within a city. Lack of affordability is one thing, and this can reflect a neighborhood's lack of means. Residents simply may not have enough assets to afford healthy food that is otherwise available nearby (Shaw 2006). But many neighborhoods also lack the physical proximity to healthy food markets at any price. Gordon et al. (2011) sought to measure food deserts in New York City and found that neighborhoods with few supermarkets and many fast-food eateries also corresponded to areas with the highest proportion of black residents and the lowest median income. A study of Toledo, Ohio (Eckert and Shetty 2011) did not identify a systematic relationship, perhaps owing to the more heterogeneous nature of many of the city's neighborhoods, but the authors were able to identify "areas of concern." Kwate (2008) also showed how racial segregation—via pathways of population concentration, an anemic retail environment, and neighborhood characteristics and stigmatization—increases the predominance of fast-food establishments in black neighborhoods.

Sampson (2012) argues that *collective efficacy* is an important factor related to levels of violence. Collective efficacy refers to residents' belief in their ability to shape the destiny of their community by controlling what goes on there. It would be difficult to disregard pernicious effects of violence in detracting from the physical well-being of neighborhood residents. Study after study has shown that violence is much more prevalent in poor than in wealthy neighborhoods. The stresses of poverty, the breakdown of the social order, the high level of illegal economic activity, and the absence of constructive police engagement are all factors within these communities. This association applies especially within segregated minority neighborhoods. As a result, crime and violence tend to come to the fore and create conditions leading to much lower levels of well-being and a diminished sense of collective efficacy among the residents. Moreover, people with means will move to safer neighborhoods, therefore reinforcing segregation. Those without the opportunity to move may just decide to stay home, participating less in the community. As people spend less time with neighbors, they trust their neighbors less, miss opportunities to build social ties, and participate less in civic life (Ellen and Turner 1997).

In truly desperate cases, collective action can work in ways counter to the maintenance of order, and there have been notable examples of segregation driving collective ethnic violence (Jones-Correa 2009). Segregated and deprived neighborhoods may erupt in frustration and protest as competition for space and community resources trigger racial unrest (Abu-Lughod 2007). European cities, with fewer and smaller segregated neighborhoods, have experienced less of this sort of mass violence. Yet the spatial concentration of poor, immigrant populations increases competition for resources between groups. These tensions are exacerbated among segregated youth, and can result in gang violence (Sauvadet 2004). In 2005, a British official warned that riots in Bradford, Oldham, and Burnley were the result of severe segregation and that Britain was sleepwalking into American-style ghettoization (Peach 2007). One study in Sweden demonstrated a clear connection between the number of car burnings—considered a proxy for delinquency or violence—and the degree of minority isolation (Malmberg, Andersson, and Östh 2013). The authors found that it was not immigration per se that was significant in determining the level of car burnings; rather, it had more to do with the segregation of these immigrants.

It would be remiss not to mention how minority individuals are so often the target of collective violence directed against them. I have already discussed the plight of Chinese in Indonesia. The South Asian population in East Africa suffered similar episodes. The indigenous populations here felt that they were being bypassed, and directed much of their frustration at those they saw as interlopers. This frustration was more muted while the countries were still under colonial control, but flared into something much bigger after independence. The most ex-

Figure 9.1. Concentration and relative wealth made Asian East Africans a suspect population from the start. When Idi Amin rose to power in Uganda, he kicked all South Asians out of the country, including many who had lived there for generations. This photo shows Ugandan Asians on a train to Mombasa, Kenya, after being expelled in 1972. *Source:* ZUMA Press, Inc./Alamy Stock Photo.

treme situation occurred in Uganda, where President Idi Amin blamed the South Asian population for unfair trading and in 1972 kicked nearly all of them out of the country, including many who had lived there for generations (see figure 9.1). In addition, all the property held among these peoples was confiscated and redistributed to Ugandan natives (Van Hear 1998). In the early and mid-twentieth century United States, much of the violence was aimed at blacks moving into cities. This in-migration set off a string of violent reactions among the majority white population. This caused riots in 1917 in East St. Louis, 1919 in Chicago, and 1921 in Tulsa (Lieberson 1980; Massey and Denton 1993). Riots and personal harassment continued well into the 1960s.

SEGREGATION AND ECONOMIC DISADVANTAGE

Ethnic communities that are segregated under duress are far more likely to be impoverished as well. This has to do with the compositional effects, of course, since so many of the residents are poor and otherwise disadvantaged. But the contextual effects of segregation also create a negative feedback in which segregation exacerbates poverty, and segregated, high-poverty neighborhoods discourage any incoming economic activity. Poverty begets poverty, and all is situated within highly segregated circumstances.

Among contemporary scholars, two sociologists, Douglas Massey and William Julius Wilson, have done the most to systematically articulate why ghettoized neighborhoods incur contextual deprivation. For Massey, the empirical evidence demonstrates that concentration amplifies the degree to which an individual experiences poverty by increasing the spatial isolation of the poor. As he says, while all racial and ethnic groups have experienced harmful effects owing to structural changes in the economy—a shift from manufacturing to services—because of high levels of segregation, "the consequences were uniquely deleterious for blacks in American cities" (Massey and Fischer 2000, 688). In their 1993 book, *American Apartheid*, Massey and Nancy Denton provide some additional detail as to why such spatial isolation can be so damaging. The impacts of the neighborhood environment include the evaporation of legitimate retail and banking services, often replaced by price-gouging convenience stores (preventing residents from stretching out the little money they have), check-cashing outlets with outrageous interest rates, and the scourge of predatory home lenders. All of these factors make life in a segregated ghetto more expensive and less rewarding than it has to be.

For William Julius Wilson, segregation becomes especially pernicious when combined with poverty. In his foundational books, *The Truly Disadvantaged* (1987) and *When Work Disappears* (1997), Wilson argues that many inner-city neighborhoods were once transformed by white flight, but that the main problem facing them today is black flight—the outmigration of the middle and working class into more congenial suburbs. This leaves behind a socially truncated population without a middle class, or even much of a working class. The interaction of poverty and race leads to extensive social instability, a lack of marriageable men, and a set of behaviors that contrast drastically with those of mainstream society. The job deficit within these neighborhoods, often a result of the segregation and the skittishness of potential store owners, pushes unemployment rates into the stratosphere and compels residents to find other ways to make a living.

In the American context, at least one of the factors blamed for the lack of employment opportunities within many of these neighborhoods has been described as a *spatial mismatch* (Kasarda 1989; 1990). The aftermath of World War II led to the suburbanization of many factories, retail outlets, and other businesses. This corresponded with the influx of many African Americans from the rural South into inner-city neighborhoods in the urban North (Kain 1968). We also could see the in-migration of certain Latino populations into the same inner-city neighborhoods, particularly Puerto Ricans within the Northeast cities (Glazer and Moynihan 1963). Unfortunately for many of these residents, they arrived too late to take advantage of job opportunities which were rapidly disappearing into the suburbs. So there was a spatial mismatch between available jobs and people who might be able to fill these jobs. Many of the jobs that did appear in the downtowns, places which were accessible to some of these inner-city residents, were corporate command-and-control jobs, marketing jobs, and legal positions that were simply off-limits to those without much education.

A study (Kaplan 2001) looking at the situation in Cleveland in 1990 showed that, while there was no significant difference in job opportunities between poor and better-off neighborhoods, the racial composition of these neighborhoods was a key factor. Many African American neighborhoods, and especially highly segregated African American neighborhoods, had fewer jobs available. The average low-income black neighborhood had about half as many job opportunities as the average low-income white neighborhood. Similar results were shown by Howell-Moroney (2005), who untangled the effects of growing up in a segregated neighborhood with lack of access to job opportunities. Both effects were consistent and statistically strong. These effects are less apparent, though still present for blacks, Latinos, and native peoples, in some Canadian cities (Walks and Bourne 2006). And they were found also to block the occupational mobility of Chinese women living in Chinese residential enclaves in the San Francisco metropolitan area (Wang 2009). These women ended up with niche jobs that offered much lower wages.

Beyond the difficulties that many residents within segregated inner-city neighborhoods experience in finding gainful employment and a reasonable income, there are also difficulties associated with accumulating wealth. For most Americans, wealth creation comes from home ownership—generally achieved through acquiring a mortgage. As described in chapter 4, minority groups, specifically African Americans, were prevented from acquiring reasonable mortgages even as the rest of the country took advantage of home finance throughout much of the twentieth century. The beginning of the modern mortgage instrument, backed by quasi-federal agencies like Fannie Mae, was exclusionary. Certain neighborhoods were "redlined"—considered too risky and excluded from all investment—and so residents within these neighborhoods were normally precluded from buying their own home. Even after fair housing protections were installed in the 1970s, poorer black neighborhoods still had limited access to mortgages of any kind. Banks were not physically present, loan volume was small, and denial rates were high.

In the 1990s, a new and invidious form of mortgage financing came about. So-called predatory lenders peddled mortgages that were over-priced and loaded with a number of economic time bombs, such as extremely high interest rates or rates that automatically reset, extra fees added to the cost of the loan, penalties placed on households that de-cided to secure a better loan, and/or loans that exceeded the value of the property. These often led individuals to default on their mortgage, forc-ing houses into foreclosure. Many of these predatory loans were targeted at those segregated neighborhoods that had hitherto been avoided by conventional mortgage providers. The results of these predatory lending practices—as accounted for by numerous research studies—were that beginning in the late 1990s and early 2000s, a large number of homes in inner-city neighborhoods went into foreclosure. The people who had bought their homes were no longer able to retain any of the assets that they had assiduously built up. These individual tragedies accumulated into a larger tragedy for the neighborhoods involved, as wealth was stripped away from what had been poor communities on the mend. Research indicated that African American and Latino communities were inordinately affected by foreclosure, even holding other neighborhood attributes constant (Kaplan and Sommers 2009). This was true through-out the country, but began in many industrial cities in the Northeast and Midwest, such as in Akron, Ohio (figure 9.2).

CONCENTRATION AND EDUCATION

People in segregated neighborhoods rarely enjoy the same level of train-ing, education, and positive role models present in more advantaged neighborhoods. Schools are a vital part of how people realize opportu-nity, and people who can afford it actively seek superior school districts (Owens 2016). The importance of schools in matters of segregation is clear from two monumental U.S. Supreme Court decisions on schools that bounded the era of de jure segregation and enforced racial disadvan-tage. *Plessy v. Ferguson*, written 120 years ago, declared that schools could be racially segregated, and legally confirmed a dual system for blacks and whites. This was then overturned in 1954 by the landmark *Brown v. Board of Education* decision, which argued that segregation in education was inherently unequal, and mandated that schools be integrated. The actual implementation of this decision took a long time to put into prac-tice, and the outright banning of black students from white schools and colleges continued apace into the 1960s. Afterward, there was still some progress—school segregation levels declined for a time—but have since shot back up. Within larger metropolitan areas today, black and Latino

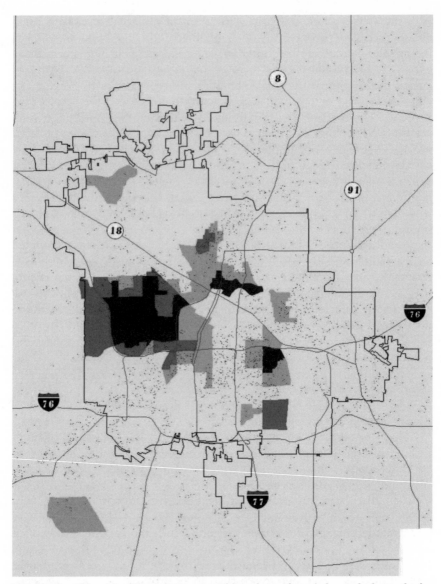

Figure 9.2. This map of Summit County, Ohio, where Akron is located, shows the location of foreclosures between 2001 and 2003 overlaid on the percentage of minority residents by neighborhood. Even when holding other factors constant, race proves to be a powerful indicator of where foreclosures occur. The dots represent foreclosures; the darker areas indicate a higher proportion of African American and Latino residents. *Source:* David H. Kaplan.

students are found in schools that are at least 70 percent non-white, and over 90 percent non-white in the urban cores (Orfield and Frankenberg 2014). It is not just race at play here; intensely segregated schools suffer also from a high poverty rate, bringing together race and class (Orfield and Frankenberg 2014).

Nearly three decades ago, the journalist Jonathan Kozol wrote about the inequality in schools within U.S. metropolitan areas. His book, *Savage Inequalities* ([1991] 2012), exposed massive disparities between high-performing schools in prosperous white communities counter-poised with broken, underperforming schools found in disadvantaged minority areas. The physical quality of such neighborhood schools was terribly unsanitary, with leaking pipes and peeling paint. Worse was the pressure put on teachers and staff who were overwhelmed by the over-crowding, lack of preparedness, and need. Many of the teachers were not prepared for these challenges.

The results of these differences in school quality are not hard to see. Dropouts in the United States are concentrated within segregated high-poverty schools. Schools with a majority minority population often graduate less than half of their class, whereas predominantly white schools with high dropout rates are exceptionally rare (Orfield and Lee 2005). Schools located in segregated areas show performance indicators markedly inferior to schools outside such districts (Mickelson 2001; Borman et al. 2004). Gaps between blacks and whites are much more pronounced in high-minority schools, and these gaps tend to get wider over time (Lleras 2008).

One factor in why segregation is detrimental to learning results is dif-ferences in funding levels. At least in the United States, many communi-ties are funded through property taxes assessed at the municipal level. Wealthy communities end up with more property tax money to spend on schools compared to poor communities. The richer communities can provide lots of extra benefits and a fair degree of classroom enhancement. Poor communities often end up with a higher tax rate, but on a smaller tax base—related to the depressed property values discussed before—result-ing in less money. What is more, these poor communities must pay for a big basket of problems, from enhanced security to students who have little knowledge of English.

Another factor is that minority schools have an exceptionally hard time retaining good teachers; the better, more experienced teachers find their way into school districts where they get paid more, deal with fewer prob-lems, and can teach high-achievement courses. Poor segregated schools do not have the middle-class parents who are less likely to be intimidated by the educational system, more likely to press for additional opportuni-ties, and hold schools accountable to their demands.

It is important to note that other countries also experience school disparities, even if they do not utilize the same school funding formulas. This is particularly apparent as immigrant populations rise, causing an increase in visible minorities and in ethnic segregation. In Sweden, for example, the share of foreign born residents has increased to nearly 14 percent, many of whom come from non-European countries. This has found its way into the school system. The highest levels of low socioeconomic status and ethnic segregation are found in regions with a high share of visible minorities. And within these regions, there are significant disparities in student performance, with high-minority schools doing worse than low-minority schools. These types of disparities may be getting worse as Sweden experiences a larger influx of the visible minority population, lowering the support for schools in these districts (Andersson, Östh, and Malmberg 2010).

THE PSYCHOLOGICAL PERILS OF SEGREGATION

Segregation also affects residents emotionally. As discussed in chapter 4, segregation is normally a product of social distance—meaning that a group is considered unworthy of associating with members of the mainstream society. Higher levels of segregation correspond with greater social exclusion, and a ghetto is a place where these elements are at their most intense. As Castañeda (2012) puts it, ghettos are demarcated by an external boundary placed around the individuals who live within them, and they are described by the stigma attached to all ghetto residents. For those who live outside this bounded space, the territory often becomes conflated with the individuals who live within it.

At times, the neighborhood is the key method of identification. The Japanese burakumin are nearly impossible to single out from other Japanese based on physical features, names, or even many cultural characteristics. As an outcaste group, burakumin have long been confined to specific neighborhoods, and these have emerged as places of stigma. The very word comes from *buraku*—the Japanese word for hamlet—that were slums on the outskirts of town to which the outcaste population was confined (Neary 2009). This residence became such an important marker that those who wished to "pass" and deny their burakumin identity were required to move twice. The first move would be to some place outside of what were euphemistically termed "special villages." However, since the Japanese registry also records the previous residence, and the registry is often a requirement of applying for a job, a successful passer would need to move again to erase any trace of burakumin residence (De Vos and Wagatsuma 2006). It is interesting to what extent the knowledge of burakumin in general is so much related to their geography, and how quickly geography becomes an indicator of stigma. According to Fielding (2004, 82), "knowledge of the buraku districts forms part of the fiercely secret mental maps of every long-term Kyoto resident, reproduced and re-enacted generation after generation." Tracing someone to a buraku district becomes proof of his or her identity. Geography itself becomes an agent of deprecation.

Other groups are not necessarily defined by the places they live, but their neighborhoods come to acquire a great measure of their own identity. This has been the case in many communities where ethnic groups are concentrated. Chapter 7 described Vancouver's Chinatown around the turn of the twentieth century, where the neighborhood inhabited by immigrant Chinese residents was disparaged, and the residents were demeaned as a result of living in these places. Today we see a similar phenomenon in Paris, where the immigrant poor are normally found outside the city, in the suburbs or *banlieue*. While the levels of concentration found here are far lower than what prevails in black or even Latino inner-city neighborhoods in the United States, the popular imagination—aided by the press—often conceives of these immigrant areas as ghettos, evoking American-style concentration, lack of choice, and poverty (Douzet and Robine 2015).

Does this outward impression of people living within concentrated, impoverished, and disparaged neighborhoods have an impact on residents' own perceptions? Louis Wirth (1927, 71) said it best when he argued: "The ghetto, be it Chinese, Sicilian, or Jewish, can be completely understood only if it is viewed as a socio-psychological, as well as an ecological, phenomenon; for it is not merely a physical fact, but also a state of mind." In Wirth's day, individuals were clearly marked by their location, outside and in. As to how this applies to modern-day ghetto residents, studies have shown that these do indeed exert a negative effect on an individual's psychology. In Paris, immigrant youth living in the suburbs feel trapped and marginalized, and also believe the neighborhoods they inhabit serve to demean them in concrete ways (Douzet and Robine 2015). The police appear far more hostile, the schools are not as good, and they feel as if their own identity as French people is compromised because of where they live.

Many accounts of segregated and economically deprived spaces point to a set of social pathologies that are evident and measurable. Such neighborhoods do indeed suffer from numerous social ills, including high rates of teenage pregnancy and single motherhood, massive unemployment, and a high prevalence of drug use. These maladies can affect most clearly the folks involved, but they also cast a shadow on the neighborhood itself and particularly on the psychology of people who are growing up within the neighborhood. Many of the behaviors associated with poor minority residents of ghettoized spaces are linked to the interaction of poverty and high levels of segregation (Massey, Gross, and Eggers 1991). This ends up aggravating negative social outcomes—specifically teenage childbearing and single motherhood. One example of this disturbing trend is that intravenous drug use among African Americans in isolated black census tracts has been far higher than for those in less isolated tracts (Cooper et al. 2008). This could be a result of greater availability, the psychological harm of witnessing neighborhood violence, and the generalized effects of poverty.

BLURRING THE LINES

While it might seem that there is a clear line between the positive and negative impacts of clustering, often the lines are blurred. A minority group's apparent choice toward clustering could result from a majority group's aversion to living with members of that minority. We see this clearly in the case of "tipping," discussed in chapter 4, in which whites move out of a neighborhood in response to the in-movement of African Americans. It is also important to keep in mind that segregation and its outcomes are part of a dynamic process and a recursive process. It is dynamic, because these consequences depend on today's circumstances and on what the group perceives for the future. People who see a situation with little hope for improvement look at things completely differently than those who see hope on the horizon. It is recursive, because the various outcomes of segregation will shape future segregation. People who perceive clustering as a benefit are simply going to make different spatial choices than people who perceive it as a trap.

Then there are those cases where different groups are able to deploy spatial concentration so as to enhance various aspects of their experience. Perhaps concentration helps generate a better economic outcome, or it improves the political prospects of residents and their ability to look after their community, or it enables group members to better preserve their identity as a group. While these can be presented as binaries, any given group may experience multiple outcomes that put them at different levels of advantage or disadvantage vis-à-vis their spatial location. So, for example, an economically deprived group may find that its spatial concentration enables it to exercise greater political power than would otherwise be the case. This is true of many African Americans who live in inner-city neighborhoods that have a whole host of other problems, many of them related to excessive segregation, but that do allow for election of representatives who can then promote their interests at a higher level.

10

ɔ͡

Multiculturalism and the Spatial Configuration of Ethnic Groups in the City

When different cultural groups coexist in some fashion, we have a situation of multiculturalism. Multiculturalism refers to a philosophical position, cultural diversity as found on the ground, and to a set of government policies used to promote certain ideals. Multiculturalism also works to produce beneficial outcomes for certain ethnic groups, as well as some outcomes that can be quite harmful to other groups or to the polity as a whole. To some extent societies choose how they handle such differences, and these choices will change with the times. What may have been one set of conditions in the past can evolve into something else. Groups that were perceived as unmixable or part of a separate caste may at last find their way into the national fold. Others remain outside, either by choice or perhaps because they have no other option.

Most states and nations in the world today must contend with multiculturalism. As the map in figure 10.1 shows, countries include diverse populations contained within their boundaries. For example, China's government recognizes 55 official ethnicities in addition to the dominant Han ethnicity that comprises some 90 percent of the population—and numerous regional distinctions exist even within the Han group (Walcott forthcoming). India includes some 50 separate languages and major fissures among its Hindu, Muslim, and Sikh citizens (Jenkins 2008). And as we have seen, several societies also create their own distinct groups—often outcaste groups—which then add to the overall difference. In addition to this intrinsic diversity, rare is the country that does not grapple with the cultural effects of immigration, as people move by choice or by force. Immigration has long been a defining feature in settler societies like

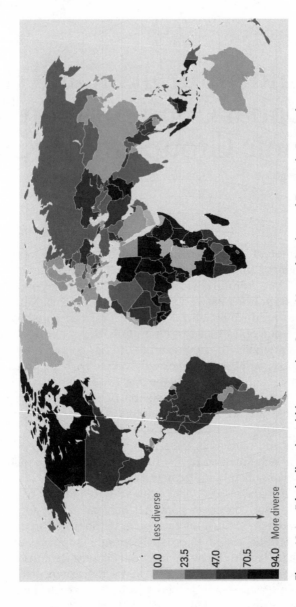

Figure 10.1. Ethnic diversity within countries. *Source:* Harvard Institute of Economic Research.

the United States, Canada, New Zealand, Australia, and Argentina. Yet countries not often thought of as immigrant destinations experience this as well. Immigrants are a fixture everywhere, from places that are well off to places that are destitute. They arrive for all kinds of reasons, and must be incorporated in some manner.

In this chapter, I seek to furnish a better understanding of what multiculturalism means and how it operates in everyday life. We are also speaking of cultural categories that may shift, and are never completely fixed. The history of ethnic and national identity shows that such constructs change and their boundaries can move. Government policy codifies certain practices, and these practices end up reifying specific categories or even creating new ones. The history of race in the United States is an example of how such categories have been created. The contemporary story of Muslims in Europe demonstrates anew the extreme power of categorization—what some have termed "othering" or Orientalism (Said 1978). While the initial categorization may not necessarily reflect what is on the ground, the new categories take on a life of their own and become factors that must be considered.

WHAT MULTICULTURALISM MEANS

So, what does multiculturalism really mean? It is important to emphasize that what is termed multiethnicity, multinationalism, or multiracialism does not by itself directly lead to "multiculturalism" as it is commonly understood (Qadeer 2014). But the demographic facts of diversity—the existence of different cultural groups—compel the acceptance or rejection of multiculturalism at some level. Multiculturalism is a term or an ideal that has spawned philosophical reflection, been enshrined in policy, and been grounded in empirical reality (Kallen 1982). At a fairly shallow level, it acknowledges the existence of other cultures, and some demonstration of their particular cultural traits. Celebrations of ethnicity, as discussed in chapter 6, belong to this genre. Kymlicka (2012) argues that many depictions of multiculturalism involve a focus on specific cultural traits—an attempt to create a colorful tapestry of customs, clothing, and cuisine. This marketing vision of multiculturalism misleadingly makes it all seem so uncomplicated, when true multiculturalism can be quite complex.

An authentic multiculturalism involves a series of societal and political choices that go beyond lip service to "diversity." These involve providing each cultural group with 1) legitimacy, 2) sufficient resources, and 3) a basket of "rights" determined in some manner. Legitimacy entails recognition by national, regional, and local governments of the existence and salience of groups beyond the dominant group, and bestowing these groups with a certain standing. Members of a group have a right to retain their cultural distinctiveness as part of their overall human rights. Beyond this, each group should be treated fairly because for so much of history, cultural differences have been used to stigmatize, to marginalize, and to oppress.

Resources provide the means and opportunities for each group to develop institutions for its maintenance. Religious institutions are generally a key aspect for most cultural groups. Some groups are empowered to provide schooling to their members. Welfare institutions can help co-ethnics in times of need, and present a much softer face to immigrants who need help in a strange new society. The establishment of organs of communication—such as a newspaper or a television channel—allows a group to communicate with its members. In truth, most immigrant groups do this formally or informally, but in some cases the government may assist with outreach or funding.

The basket of rights involves the legal ability for members of a cultural minority to exercise group rights or to be legally perceived as a protected class. For immigrants or even children of immigrants, this may involve the right to dual citizenship, the right to separate laws, or the right to opt out of certain requirements. In the United States, the Supreme Court exempted the Amish from mandatory education requirements at the high school level (McConnell and Hurst 2006). In cases where multiculturalism is mapped onto specific regions in a country, these rights may transfer to the government of the region itself. For example, Italy recognizes five "special" regions based on their cultural distinctiveness (figure 10.2).

Societies vary in how they deal with these needs. Societies that are firmly assimilationist in their outlook establish that cultural differences should be sublimated to the larger society. Such societies can focus on the rights of the individual, as opposed to the rights of the group. They may also make it clear that citizens must pledge allegiance to their country, but affiliation with some intermediary group is frowned upon. Any demonstration of cultural distinctiveness, such as headscarves, is only allowed privately. A pure homogenizing regimen would soften and eventually eliminate all such symbolic or personal cultural distinctiveness.

Other societies allow for "diversity," maybe even celebrate it, but do not promote meaningful group establishment with resources and rights. Or they can establish institutional shells with scant effective power. The former Soviet Union promulgated a whole series of nationality and multicultural rights in its constitution, even created separate geographical spaces such as republics and oblasts, but these were mostly false fronts (King 1998) until the dissolving of the state made them effective. China also recognizes many official minority groups, but provides each with little true autonomy or cultural rights (Walcott forthcoming).

Figure 10.2. Italy's five special regions.

Societies that are truly multicultural in their orientation take a different approach. In these countries, groups have certain rights and privileges that redound to the group itself. Canada is often held up as an exemplar of this type, with French and English charter groups, greater institutional support for ethnic groups, and solicitousness toward the native Canadians or "First Nations" (Kymlicka 2012). Post-apartheid South Africa has also sought to call itself a multicultural, multiracial society, though whether it has succeeded is an open question inasmuch as it has failed to incorporate the South African "underclass" (Bekker and Leildé 2003). Many cultures have always existed in Spain—especially the Catalans, Basques, and Galicians—but these were only able to exercise their rights after the dictator Francisco Franco left the scene (Richards 1996). Ideally, each group in a multicultural society is able to maintain its own culture while coexisting peacefully and harmoniously with other groups and with the state as a whole.

Multiculturalism at the state level may or may not apply to the level of cities. If a country carves out different territories for its culture groups, then the cities within these territories may be fairly uniform. A country like Belgium, with its two language regions and the Francophone capital of Brussels, is much like that. There is no more diversity within Belgian cities than would be found if the entire country itself was monocultural. It is just that some cities are French and some cities are Flemish. Multiculturalism at the urban level involves a mixture of groups, and these can be reflected in any number of ways, as discussed in chapter 3. A city may seem diverse, but each group may be sorted into its own neighborhoods with less opportunity for cross-group interaction. Multiculturalism at the neighborhood scale, where different groups live together and interact on a daily basis, is more likely to foster a true diversity and familiarity with other cultures.

MULTICULTURAL STRATEGIES

Various models of multiculturalism determine how group rights fit within the national polity, and this in turn concerns the role of the individual citizen (Eade and Ruspini 2014). The ideal of *liberal multiculturalism* begins with the recognition of diversity, and provides many group rights. Each group may be provided with state assistance to promote cultural institutions, allowed to control its own education, and furnished opportunities for dual citizenship. In cases where there are recognized inequities, some redistribution of resources may also be practiced. The value for society can be great tolerance. This perhaps comes closest to Kymlicka's (2012) ideal, and is partly the manner by which a country like Canada has pursued a multiculturalist path.

This form of multiculturalism, however, may come at a cost. Greater group divisions can undercut the opportunities for people across groups to work together or socialize. Individuals keep to their own group and may not engage in the larger community. Putnam (2007) warns that too much diversity could create a situation in which individuals do not communicate across groups. In fact, even the bonds within groups may be weakened. In considering this type of multiculturalism, there is also a problem of how specific groups are constructed. Since ethnic boundaries are fairly fluid, it is a challenge to find a true voice that represents all prospective members. There may be many voices claiming to speak for a group, or the organization that prevails may not really do all members justice (Malik 2015). Sometimes the authorities make the decision as to who will represent the group—privileging one organization over other contenders as the group representative (Vertovec 1996). This choosing of representatives is almost guaranteed to marginalize particular viewpoints and maintain the status quo. And whether or not there is agreement on the composition of the groups, the end result of strong group solidarity is the prospect of what Sen (2006) describes as "plural monoculturalism" with cultural groups "co-existing side by side, without the twain meeting" (4). Another worry is that multiculturalist policies weaken the larger national community. The fissiparous tendencies of separate group identities can prove too strong to counter those forces bringing members of the nation together. Etzioni (2011) argues that this sort of "radical multiculturalism" unleashes major practical problems, causes political backlash and, ironically, results in a loss of community.

Some argue that these worries are overblown. Multiculturalism enables people to live in dignity, acknowledge their roots, and provide cultural community. It also guards against a mindless nationalism, instead recasting national identity in a more positive light—moving it away from ethnic to more civic conceptions (Uberoi 2008). It bestows pride to all members of the society. Kymlicka (2012) maintains that multiculturalism has itself become a source of Canadian identity. Yet this Canadian multiculturalism is something of a double-edged sword. After all, it is more a creation of English Canada—and while it was French Canadian prime minister Pierre Trudeau who was its strongest proponent, English Canada's embrace of its many ethnic groups and celebration of group identity are viewed as ways to counter the French Canadian claim to their own nationalism distinct from that of their English-speaking compatriots (Mann 2012). So, in a sense, the Canadian multiculturalism as practiced masks a greater division within the Canadian polity as a whole. It has been argued that multiculturalism does little to strengthen the sense of an overall, shared Canadian identity.

It is in response to this latter objection that another model of multiculturalism comes about, one that involves the inculcation of universal moral values shared by the entire polity. In this model, described as *communitarianism*, plural differences are acknowledged and even championed, but there is a higher purpose to which all groups subscribe (Eade and Ruspini 2014). Cross-cutting allegiances that bridge the entire society counter excessive group differences. This might be described as "diversity within unity that allows each group to maintain its culture as long as it does not conflict with a shared ethos" (Etzioni 2011). The British have promoted this communitarian philosophy, which allows people ample opportunity to practice their faith and to adhere to many aspects of cultural norms. However, when cultural norms collide with the larger values of British society—for instance in their differential treatment of women—then these norms are considered unacceptable. Of course, the issue then becomes: whose norms must be paramount under this system? Continued challenges to this idea have been the experience in most multicultural societies.

Societies that subscribe to a multiculturalist ethos must legitimize the expression of group cultures, while acknowledging that the groups themselves are not fixed, that they are not the be all and end all of participation, and that these should be subordinated to an overarching national unity. Not an easy task. Controlled multiculturalism balances the needs of the group with the needs of the broader society. And the overall political system is responsible for providing the necessary resources and controlling the pace of integration. While groups are allowed a set of institutions within which they can maintain their identity, they are clearly expected to familiarize themselves with the mores of mainstream society. They cannot simply practice their culture without acknowledging this authority.

The Netherlands has been held up as an example of this trend. The country provided a set of parallel institutions, including schools (Doomernik 2003). However, the Dutch began to alter their support for multiculturalism in the 2000s, and insisted on some measure of integration (Fincher et al. 2014). The Dutch have been more eager than most other countries, for instance, to even out ethnic groups within housing estates. For instance, any separation by Surinamese or West Indians is moderated by policies that allocate housing on the basis of need and so attempt to undercut segregative tendencies (Musterd and Smakman 2000). Dutch policy now supplements any support for cultural institutions with a series of integration steps, including stiffer language and cultural exams that make sure all ethnic groups acculturate (Fincher et al. 2014). Therefore the so-called Dutch model, based more on controlling than embracing multiculturalism, now has been adopted by several other European countries (Lesińska 2014).

In considering how best to approach multiculturalism, it helps to consider exactly which facets of multiculturalism are emphasized. Measures of multiculturalism (Kymlicka 2012; Koopmans 2013) seek a more structured understanding of multicultural societies, and a way to rate them. The multicultural policy index, championed by Banting and Kymlicka (2006), looks at policies, resources, and also affirmations of multiculturalism found within each state. The indicators of citizenship rights for immigrants, developed by Koopmans (2013), is similar but focuses more on religious rights, which tend to be more salient in many multicultural contexts.

In part this explains why multiculturalism has been so hotly debated in European countries. Here the overall immigrant percentages are a bit smaller than in the classic settler societies, but the percentage of Muslims is higher and, according to Koopmans (2013), Muslims make more claims for religious rights. This involves accommodating Muslim religious practices outside of the mosque, building more Muslim cemeteries, and allowing for rituals, religious schools, clothing choices like headscarves, and many other items. Ironically, this is where the key tensions have arisen. Countries like France, which have little tolerance for religious displays, fall short on this religious dimension. Germany and the Scandinavian countries have allowed some concessions, but balk at the obvious religious displays and do not accord Islam the same prestige as Christianity and Judaism (Meer et al. 2015, Heckmann 2003). It is in this instance that the Netherlands, which has changed much of its rhetoric to be more integrationist, is far friendlier to Islamic religious assertions, providing full recognition, resources, and relatively few boundaries to Islamic expression (Koopmans 2013). Beyond these forms of accommodation, it is necessary to add that multiculturalism has also sparked a backlash in many democracies, as populist movements demonize immigrants and other minorities as avatars of economic misery and "globalism" (Vieten and Poynting 2016).

ASPECTS OF MULTICULTURALISM

There are five aspects to consider in looking at multiculturalism. The first aspect entails where the multiculturalism is coming from. This book considers ethnicities based on national groups brought into a singular state framework, indigenous populations steamrolled by the settlement expansion of the majority, importation of forced labor groups, and immigrants who have entered into a new society. These different types of groups arguably have different claims to receiving cultural protection. In Spain, one might consider a Catalan—a member of an historical nation on the Iberian Peninsula—differently from a Peruvian immigrant. However, in Peru, the washing of a colonial Spanish culture over indigenous Indian tribes opens a cultural distinction unlike that of the later immigration of Japanese to the country (Takenaka 1999).

The second aspect concerns the scope of potential forms of multiculturalism. What, and how extensive, are the opportunities for the different groups involved in a multicultural community? Is multiculturalism practiced in the political realm via political parties, consociational governance, and the like? Is multiculturalism practiced in the economic sphere with the development of distinct ethnic economies, differentiated places for consumption like ethnic shopping malls, and even a dual or triple labor market? Social relations must also be considered, inasmuch as different groups occupy separate social networks and maintain their respective institutions. And finally, the religious sphere can lead to extremely controversial decisions. The influx of Muslim immigrants into predominantly Westernized, somewhat secular societies has led to much hand-wringing regarding just how many aspects of the Islamic religious expression can be retained and still maintain compatibility with majority society. All these spheres may be developed under conditions ranging from relative equality to severe structural constraint as access to coveted political, economic, and social goods is denied members of some cultural groups. This is also multiculturalism—just not the same as proponents like to consider it.

The third aspect concerns scale, and this is vitally important in considering how multiculturalism operates in every society. To say a society is diverse really tells us very little without knowing how this diversity is practiced and at what scale it is manifested. At a large scale, there may be distinct groups occupying separate territories within a country. If large enough, these groups have the ability to maintain themselves as holistic cultural communities and provide a powerful counterbalance to the central state. In some states, these groups and their territories gain tremendous autonomy: Quebec, Catalonia, Scotland, and Okinawa are examples of this scale of multiculturalism. Here groups define themselves as subnational and culturally distinct. Under the right conditions, they may press for autonomy or even independence. Or there may be groups that feel that their rights are being violated, and may seek secession or attachment to another polity. The Russian-speaking Crimean Peninsula resistance to further Ukrainian control and its (re)attachment to the Russian Federation in 2014 is a recent example of this.

Below this level of regional multiculturalism, a middle scale might exist where groups occupy clearly defined spaces in the city or countryside. This does not necessarily have to be based on proximity—as we saw in our discussion of heterolocalism in chapter 4—but it always has a geographical basis, either through the carving out of distinct spaces or the deliberate nature of flows from one place to the next. The diffusion and regional formations of Amish populations demonstrate this development at a rural level. The carving out of Latino spaces in Los Angeles County illustrates how this might operate at an urban scale. These configurations can create culturally defined worlds within worlds, and allow a resident to live most her life without encountering people from the outside.

At a still smaller scale is the sort of multiculturalism found within places, as groups maintain some distinctiveness in a venue of high proximity and tremendous contact with members of other groups. Some of these spaces are fairly monocultural—occupied by one particular group. More often they are made up of several groups that come together and share a space. At this smallest neighborhood scale, intercultural contact is a common aspect of everyday life. But this does not necessarily impede the opportunity to forge separate spheres, or in many ways to create separate lives. It is just that these will often look and feel different than when multiculturalism is present at a coarser grain.

The fourth aspect concerns the purpose of multiculturalism. Arguably, most ethnic diversity throughout history has been accompanied by extreme discrimination. The presence of separate groups in a society establishes a pecking order. Most societies layered ethnicity onto class, while other societies adamantly affirmed the inherent inequality of their residents—using this to justify abject poverty, limited rights, and even bondage. The newer advocates for multiculturalism argue that diversity does not have to be unequal. In fact, they speculate that allowing individuals to attach themselves to an intermediary group between the family and the nation is a form of cultural liberation. It provides for more expression, easier communication, and stronger bonding. A truly equitable multicultural society has been fairly rare historically and is still uncommon, though not beyond possibility.

Finally, official proclamations of multiculturalism need to be distinguished from the actual characteristics. The type of society that is championed from on high can diverge greatly from the reality on the ground. It is important and helpful to analyze government documents and the statements of politicians in order to examine an official policy. Much of Banting and Kymlicka's (2006) checklist takes these policies into consideration. It is also possible to note formal access to political rights, notably citizenship, which varies tremendously by country (Zapata-Barrero and Gropas 2012). Until recently, Germany did not even have a multicultural policy, but over the years has come to grips with the increased pluralism that exists there (Schönwälder 2010). France has long held a strong ideology of assimilation that attempts to sublimate ethnic differences. Yet, it is also one of the most multicultural countries. Outside of the traditional settler societies and Europe, East Asian countries like South Korea—long used to considering itself an ethnically pure society—have acknowledged and even embraced officially the growing fact of greater cultural diversity (Kim 2015). Hong Kong is an example of a change in official policy as political circumstances altered (Law and Lee 2012). Always predominantly Chinese, with a 5 percent mixed minority population, Chinese control in 1997 occasioned some basic changes, including a strong emphasis on operating in Chinese (which tended to hurt many ethnic groups who were more comfortable in English) and non-recognition of these minority groups as Chinese nationals.

The policies of multiculturalism promulgated at the state level are operationalized at the local level (Fincher et al. 2014). Local plans in turn play a large role in shaping how diversity is in fact experienced. Other societies have long attempted to control their multiculturalism—and the loudest voices often belong to those who want to vanquish it altogether. But multiculturalism persists and grows, and as it does, it continues to be a messy affair, with various governmental strategies leading to uncertain outcomes.

MULTICULTURAL INCORPORATION

Official approval and facilitation does not always translate into truly multicultural cities, but it does help the process considerably. Multiculturalism can be promoted in many different ways. A very positive take on this is provided by Qadeer (2014, 122), who discusses the development of ethnic enclaves that are the products of "market choices and revealed preferences where ethnic institutions and businesses create a wholesome community life." Such multiculturalism involves the establishment of centers of worship, linguistic concessions, ethnic music and the arts, and a multicultural curriculum in the schools. Sometimes ethnic members really want to remain close by family and co-ethnic neighbors.

It is unlikely that this form of multicultural incorporation is found in its most pure form, but several excellent examples exist that help provide a sense of how these may work out spatially. Wei Li (1998) and Min Zhou ([1992] 2010) describe situations where voluntary ethnic enclaves are established and, most importantly, tend to persist across generations. Both authors describe the development of Chinese enclaves within the United States. Zhou's example of Chinatown in lower Manhattan showed increasing numbers of Chinese, coming largely from Mainland China, Hong Kong, and Taiwan. This neighborhood expanded and deepened, and has also defied the logic of assimilation as "both the population and the physical boundaries of Chinatown are growing at accelerated speed" (Zhou [1992] 2010, 187). The enclave continues to flourish some 25 years later. Li's (1998) well-known example of ethnoburb (see also Fong 1994) allows us to see how enclaves can be established outside of the inner city, where these traditionally grow. The San Gabriel Valley in the Los Angeles metropolitan region has provided a rich set of destinations for Chinese who prefer single-family houses and a more suburban style of living. It has created both a "mosaic of residential areas" and "a complex of business districts" (Li 1998, 497). This creates the conditions under which people remain.

The issue of scale comes up repeatedly. The classic stereotype of distinct enclaves spanning several blocks (or in Li's example, whole towns) shows activity at a larger scale. The groups form part of an overall multiethnic tapestry, but at a fairly coarse weave. There have been examples of this enclavization among Chinese groups in North America, Bangladeshis in London, Arabs within Israel (Falah 1996), and Cubans within Miami (Alberts 2006). Such neighborhoods may be somewhat multiethnic—at least among immigrants—but are influenced by the activities of a particular group. The opportunities for true multiethnic interaction are more limited.

Multiculturalism at finer scales involves ever greater opportunities for interaction and a very different feel. More commonly witnessed, both historically and among many ethnic populations in diverse cities, is a fair degree of mixing at the neighborhood level. This mixing may be among two or more ethnic groups sharing the same space, and it may include members of the majority group as well. The mixing at this geographical scale may or may not be reflected in shared social and economic activities. However, to maintain aspects of cultural distinctiveness, there is a point in which each group goes about many of its own activities. The neighborhood of Belleville, in Paris, provides one of the best examples of this tendency, as it includes residents who are Tunisian in origin (both Muslims and Jews), Chinese, and a few West Africans—all mixed within a block. Despite the fraught nature of interfaith relations in France as a whole, Muslims and Jews get along quite well and even participate in many shared social and economic activities. Yet they retain their distinctiveness through different modes of worship. The connections between the Chinese and the other groups in the neighborhood are fairly limited. Though they share the space, they do not share other aspects of life. This pattern of separate lives within a shared space is a feature in many cities, and can also be found among ethnics who conduct social and economic activities over much more dispersed spaces.

MULTICULTURALISM AND ETHNIC IMPRINTS

The majority of ethnic groups throughout the world are not strictly segregated. Instead, most groups at various scales of resolution find themselves intermingled with either the dominant population or with other groups. Johnston, Poulsen, and Forrest's (2009) schema, described in chapter 5, reflects this state of affairs more quantitatively.

While there is a robust academic discussion of exactly what multiculturalism means and how it can be implemented socially and politically, there is less attention paid to exactly how this applies to the types of ethnic settlements and the nature of ethnic imprints. Multiculturalism as practiced at a large scale would involve separating groups into distinct territories. Folks have their own spaces and, often, their own governments. This is better described as plural monoculturalism, in which interaction only takes place at a high level, and almost never during everyday life. Multiculturalism as practiced at a small scale is something entirely different. This involves people sharing neighborhoods, streets, businesses, and perhaps even joining together in community organizations.

So how do groups continue to maintain their ethnicity under such conditions? In studying multiculturalism, Patrick Simon (2010) described how ethnics can live together but also live apart. They work and shop in a shared neighborhood. They interact on a daily basis. Under cordial conditions, there is ample opportunity to bridge many of the divisions and create a more harmonious habitus. At the same time, each ethnic group maintains a private culture—activities and associations that can only help bolster its identity. They can utilize the ethnic and spatial resources that come from ethnic concentration, while avoiding the mistrust and isolation that comes from segregation. Cohabitation within a neighborhood does not lead to integration, but promotes a true diversity.

Of course, this represents an ideal case—particularly the extent to which the outcome is harmonious. Other examples may not be so ideal. Multicultural or multiethnic neighborhoods may simply be neighborhoods in transition, moving from dominance by one group to dominance by another. Such neighborhoods may also be way stations on the road to assimilation, as each group blends into the mainstream society and forfeits its distinctiveness. Or such neighborhoods can be sites of contention, where groups jockey for resources and where they limit contact with one another, as much as is possible. Any effort toward a positive solution to a multicultural population needs to grapple with how multiculturalism actually plays out on the ground.

11

✌

Distances and Diasporas

Movement, and the distance that requires such movement, have been the key factors in creating ethnicity. This is something that has been true historically and is true today. Moving over long distances created many ethnic groups in the first place, as peoples from other lands and cultures migrated and mixed (in a variety of ways) with existing populations. Ethnicity is a marker of difference between members of one group and the members of other groups within a society, especially including the majority or dominant group. And the migration across distance was the main way in which such differences were revealed. The individual acts of immigration created new cultural groups that adapted to the dominant society in some manner. In other cases, the immigrants were the dominant ones, either colonizing lands occupied by indigenous societies or setting up a few individuals as a dominant ethno-class, entrusted with administering the new colony and keeping the natives in line. The colonizers could also solicit members of other groups, through force or enticement, to settle in a new territory and fill a niche. All of these interactions created ethnic differentiation. But they also created something more. This was particularly true of members of a group that never quite settled in the new land, preferring by whatever means possible to continue ties to the old homeland, perhaps with the idea that they would somehow return.

A group with continued ties to an historical homeland—no matter the current reality of that homeland—has become known as a *diaspora*. This category once referred principally to the Jewish diaspora, which involves the widespread dispersal of the Jewish population far from its homeland and with only tenuous connections to the countries in which it has settled. The idea of the diaspora was then transferred over to any number of different populations that had dispersed from some or another homeland and settled, perhaps uneasily, within other societies. Thus, the term describes far-flung communities that are anchored to a particular state, but also populations that are fairly decentralized, with few ties to the state and stronger ties with each other. In contrast to an ethnic group situated within a particular society, diasporas connote a global community (Dufoix 2008).

This chapter explores how these different forms operate out in the world, how they influence the nature of ethnicity, and the ways that ethnics establish themselves on the landscape. So much of what we think of as being new is, in fact, an extension of what has always taken place. Groups have always traveled long distances; they have long maintained ties with their homelands. The modern difference entails the advantages of new transportation and communication technologies. This allows people to travel more easily, but most importantly, allows people to communicate in real time across those great distances that once presented such a barrier.

DEFINING DIASPORA

The term "diaspora" comes from the Greek, and refers to the scattering of seeds. This metaphor became a powerful way of referring to the experience of a particular group that was dispersed outside of its homeland and into a wider world. For most of its terminological history, "Diaspora" was capitalized and reflected only the Jewish experience of exile and dispersal. In recent years, the term has gained great popularity in describing the experience of many groups. In fact, the number of such groups has been growing with increased labor migration. In an introduction to a volume on diasporas, Sheffer (1986) defines a diaspora as a group that leaves its homeland either voluntarily or through forced expulsion, becomes a minority population in another country controlled by others, preserves a strong identification as a distinct ethnicity, and continues to maintain transnational contacts. The homeland is vital, even though relations between the diaspora and the homeland are sometimes uncertain and the homeland itself is artificially constructed (Sheffer 1986; Connor 1986). Cohen (1997) adds that, in the diaspora, many communities share a strong political commitment to their homeland and a desire to return.

Diasporas constitute a type of ethnic group. Members of a diasporic community are distinct from members of the dominant society in the country which they currently reside. This is a result of the boundaries that they place around each other and, commonly, the boundary placed around them by the other members of society (Royce 1982). At the same time, it is a common mistake to conflate a diasporic population with an ethnic group. All members of an ethnicity are not truly diasporas. For instance, Italian Americans who may share some elements of ethnic distinctiveness do not constitute a diaspora. Yet there is sufficient fluidity to make the term applicable to a wide range of cases. In truth, it is often applied to groups that are hardly diasporic at all (Tölölyan 1991).

Safran (1991) and Cohen (1997) have come up with some key ways in which members of a diaspora are distinct. They begin with the idea that diasporic populations have a homeland from which they are dispersed. This homeland does not have to be sovereign or autonomous, but it must exist in the community's imagination. The dispersal also rules out distinct populations, such as the burakumin, who have been created within a particular place. Groups that have been forcibly dispersed within an existing country, such as many of the American Indian tribes, could conceivably qualify.

The second key notion is that diasporic populations still exist uneasily within the lands to which they migrate. As a group, members of a diaspora are immigrants. They enter a society and build homes there. But they part ways with other immigrants in a key regard: they either do not desire to incorporate within the receiving society, or they may not be allowed to do so. Conceptually, this rules out groups that assimilate after the first generation. Assimilation is an uneven process. Segmented assimilation, for example, would indicate that groups may incorporate in some manner, but perhaps not in a way that allows them to enter fully into mainstream society. This would likely rule out groups such as the many Spanish, Portuguese, and Italians who have entered countries like the United Kingdom and may maintain some ethnic traditions, but are still comfortable within their new society. The various waves of settlers who have entered into a country such as Argentina would also not easily fit under this criterion.

The third criterion, and arguably the most significant, refers to the idea that diasporic populations are always interested in returning home. The notion that their host country will never be more than a place to sojourn—to stay for a limited time, even if this transcends generations—is something that keeps that group distinct. It also suggests a variety of powerful transnational linkages between communities in the various host lands and those in the home country, and can include an intense desire to be involved in the affairs of the home country or even to attempt to manipulate the way in which governments in both home and host countries deal with one another. There is often a backdrop notion that once the home country is "free," the diaspora will return. The Cuban American population is especially instructive, since this group has long maintained a strong belief in eventually returning to Cuba once it is no longer communist. This criterion also rules out historically marginalized groups such as African Americans, whose descendants came to this country from various regions of Africa in shackles but, with the exception of a paltry "back to Africa" movement that was riddled by scams, have shown little desire to return to this continent except as tourists, essayists, and as a form of pilgrimage (Campbell 2006).

One variant of this third criterion concerns groups for which the homeland ties are sublimated to ties that exist across the diaspora itself. In other words, their affiliation is less to the people living in some territorial homeland and more to the other members of the dispersed diasporic population. The connections here span all of the distinct communities scattered among far-flung locales, united by a singular identity but comprising individuals living in many nations. The best example of this would be the Chinese diaspora in Southeast and South Asia, discussed below.

These three criteria show how diaspora communities can be described as *transnational*, in connecting several countries. Many diasporas are also extremely national, in that their identity is bound up with the homeland to which they share a cultural and political loyalty (Esman 2009). These external loyalties can create tensions both within the diaspora community and between members of the diaspora and the country they inhabit (Tölölyan 1996). For example, the long-standing Armenian diaspora has been transformed from a diaspora of exile, whereby various institutions spring up among Armenian settlements situated among a panoply of countries, to a diasporic transnationalism, spurred by the emergence of the Republic of Armenia (Tölölyan 2000). This has been especially clear in foreign policy initiatives, in which the Armenian diaspora seeks to influence the foreign policy of its various host countries, but also affects the policies of the newly independent Armenian homeland (Baser and Swain 2009).

So-called divided loyalties become a key issue for individuals within the host country, who see the diaspora as a threat. Such communities may be less likely to pledge allegiance to their host society, but instead focus their attention on building up their individual enclaves. In these cases, we can see diasporas as potentially challenging the nation-state in fundamental ways (Cohen 1997). It is for this reason that some of the more notable diasporas—the Jews, the Japanese, and the Chinese—are often looked on with suspicion as a possible "fifth column" that may be employed to undermine the national polity (Burton et al. 2002).

Definitions composed of criteria are useful, but potentially misleading. As with most things involving human activities, the diasporic elements are not binary, but are better seen as arranged on a continuum. Some groups make it their expressed purpose to return to a homeland once given the chance. Other groups are not so eager, but still maintain meaningful ties with their home countries. Over time, the attitudes of a group shift as some become more assimilationist over generations while others become less so. Also, of course, while an identity is a powerful thing—framing ethnicity and particularly diasporic ethnicity—it includes many different attitudes.

Today, diaspora communities can still refresh and sometimes even generate a sense of nationhood. According to Eriksen (1993), the sense of Mauritian nationhood is strongest in the European diaspora; the experience of being outside the country helps to minimize the ethnic cleavages that divide Mauritians at home. The nationalism of Nevisians is "deterritorialized" in that diaspora (Olwig 1993), where the contacts between Nevisians outside the island are more important than any national project within the island.

THE JEWISH EXPERIENCE

The diasporic definition referred first to the Jews who, from the fourth century BCE, were more likely to be found outside the Holy Land than inside, and were often forced to live among more hostile peoples (Kalra, Kaur, and Hutnyk 2005). The Jewish diaspora had both an incredibly powerful connection to its homeland in the lands around Jerusalem, but also had little control over that space (Safran 2005). Their experience in the many countries where Jews settled ranged from grudging acceptance to horrific persecution. And unfortunately for these clusters of diasporic Jews, popular and official opinion could change in an instant, depending on who was in power, natural calamities for which a scapegoat was needed, or the recrudescence of political or religious passions.

The key feature of the Jewish diaspora was exile. The decision to live outside of the Holy Land was not a voluntary one, but the product of persecution and expulsion. The connection with this homeland created a powerful imagery of a specific landscape of longing, one to which each Jew would vow to return. For the present, most Jews had to endure a life of impermanence, often suffering from legal restrictions that prevented the ownership of land—always a good determinant of creating a presence in a country. The more benign reaction among members of societies that "hosted" Jews was essentially marginalization. The Jewish response was a form of placemaking, if this was at all possible. In chapter 3, I discussed the creation of the Jewish ghetto, first in Venice and then in other medieval European towns. The experience of the Jewish diaspora, while often oppressed, did allow for the development of cultural institutions and the preservation of religion in many societies. Under more forgiving regimes, major Jewish communities appeared in cities like Krakow, Poland, which hosted an enormous range of Jewish institutions and a Jewish population of nearly 60,000, about 25 percent of the city before the Nazi invasion (Kugelmass and Orla-Bukowska 1998). The Russian Jewish Pale was an area in western Russia (formerly a part of Poland/Lithuania) where Jews were compelled to live (Rowland 1986). Within this Pale, about half of the Jews inhabited larger cities, reflecting a tendency of Jews throughout the diaspora to disproportionately reside in cities. Yet the Pale also included many small Jewish settlements, of the sort memorialized by Anatevka in *Fiddler on the Roof.* Unfortunately, the concentration of Jews within the Pale allowed for periodic pogroms incited by the government, in which Jewish houses, businesses, synagogues, and the Jews themselves were targeted for destruction.

The Jewish experience differed greatly depending on the context. Such is the case of Jews who arrived in the southwestern coast of India, in what is now the modern state of Kerala. Why Jews came to the Malabar coast in the first place is not clearly established, but they likely came when the local prince invited merchants to settle there, helping to enhance the economy of the region. The new settlers found a tolerant society, so many stayed and established their own society. Katz (2000) maintains that the Jews were able to adequately acculturate to the various societies they landed in, but that they never assimilated, preferring to maintain their own identity. There was relative harmony between the Hindu powers, and the Jewish and Christian communities established under their aegis. Landmarks of Judaism, especially synagogues, were allowed to flourish in the region (figure 11.1).

Persecution is part of the legacy of the Jewish community and a reason for its persistence. It was difficult to blend into societies where one was always considered an outsider. To be sure, the assimilative tendency among Jews in certain communities was strong. The case of German and French Jews before the Nazi rise to power betrayed the hunger of many to participate fully within mainstream society. The steady emancipation of the Jews was a goal fed by many thinkers and politicians, who thought this the best way to render Jews "more useful and happy" (Goldfarb 2009). Within the United States, among the most tolerant of those societies, many Jews maintained separate communities within major cities. The development of Jewish newspapers like the Yiddish language *Forward* exemplified this trend, as did the clustering of both businesses and residences in many large cities. The need to remain close to the synagogue and the maintenance of religious restrictions, as discussed in chapter 8, also contributed to separate communities. At the same time, assimilation—at least partial assimilation—could be especially powerful here as well.

One aspect of the Jewish diaspora that defined it politically was in the development of a Zionist ideology (Conforti 2010). For centuries, Jews had vowed to return to the homeland. Zionism, first voiced by Theodore

Figure 11.1. An interior photograph of the Cochin Synagogue, decorated for Simchat Torah. *Source:* Ellen Goldberg.

Herzl, a Hungarian Jew, advocated for the return of all Jews to Palestine and the creation of a Jewish homeland there. While Herzl was not the first person to advocate for a Jewish homeland, he rendered this into a more explicitly nationalistic framework. The increased anti-Semitism of the early twentieth century, culminating in the Holocaust, provided even greater urgency to these ideals, and helped lead to the development of the Jewish state of Israel. With a politically independent homeland, members of the Jewish diaspora could now fulfill their wishes. It also changed the nature of the diaspora itself. While there were still a number of countries, most notably the Soviet Union, from which Jews could not easily emigrate, many Jewish citizens could and did move to Israel. For the rest, "diaspora" was now a voluntary affair. It also led to many different streams of Jewish diaspora, threatening the unity of the concept. Are the fairly affluent Jewish populations in the West the same as Jews under the Soviet and now Russian authority? These variations create greater complexity—even what is described as a diaspora within a diaspora (Gitelman 1998).

THE CHINESE DIASPORA

The Chinese within Southeast Asia and along the Pacific Rim are a slightly different example of diaspora, in that the return to a homeland figures less importantly than the extensive ties across many countries. This was a diaspora borne of the poverty of their homeland—for many, Fujian province—and the operations of a colonial economy. As Southeast Asia was colonized by European powers, Chinese traders migrated to the Spanish Philippines, French Indochina, British Malaya, and the Dutch East Indies in a process that Cohen (1997, 84) calls an "auxiliary diaspora." Many who decided to leave were culturally different and socially marginalized to begin with. The decision to move was often financially positive, as many entered the host societies as middleman minorities (see chapter 3), occupying a distinct economic and social niche within the newly constructed colonial societies.

The role of these Chinese and their descendants within their new lands was one of remove. Singapore's British founder, Stamford Raffles, demarcated the town into clear quarters under the supervision of a group leader (Perry, Kong, and Yeoh 1997). The Spanish forced their Chinese population into a walled ghetto (Freedman 2000), an extreme measure that underlined the extent to which many colonial societies were systematically segregated societies and ethnic populations were separated from one another (Pan 1994). Despite their sequestration, most Chinese were more prosperous than the natives, and were roundly resented for this. They also considered their stay temporary and, at first, maintained strong ties with their home region (Cohen 1997). Yet over time, the Chinese came to comprise a substantial population in several Southeast Asian countries, especially in urban areas where they could ply their trades. Their jobs and businesses, and their position between dominant and dominated, made them prosperous, and they continue to be about twice as wealthy as the native populations (Wang 1991).

After the end of colonialism, the Chinese remained, but the attitudes of the host governments toward them varied considerably. In Thailand and pre-1975 Cambodia, they were encouraged to assimilate. In other societies, they were kept at arm's length. Both Malaysia and Indonesia allowed the Chinese population a fair degree of cultural autonomy, but also officially discriminated against them under the guise of "indigenization." Many non-Chinese Southeast Asians view the Chinese as exploiters because of their economic position and their historical role under colonial regimes. They are also viewed as potentially disloyal because of continued ties to the Chinese homeland and suspicions that the Chinese minorities in Southeast Asia are somehow subversive (McCloud 1995). The situation in the Philippines shows how changing public policies toward incorporation could have altered the choices that the Chinese population made toward assimilating (Weightman 2002). Later during Spanish rule, the Chinese in the Philippines were encouraged to intermarry, both with indigenous and European populations. The mixed Chinese and Filipino offspring were granted far more rights and privileges than full Chinese, who were persecuted. Once the United States took over the Philippine islands, these same Chinese were given many more choices in preserving their cultural identity, but both pure Chinese and their mixed descendants were constrained from assimilating into the Philippine culture.

The identity of the Southeast Asian Chinese clearly reflects the ambivalence of their contexts and of their peculiar situations. In some cases, Chinese minorities have been allowed to share in the identification of their adopted lands. But for the most part they have been kept isolated by native attitudes, and have kept themselves apart. In this case, the ties across nations define the identity. Economic networks facilitate commerce between business interests. Members of the diaspora Chinese in Southeast Asia long maintained commercial ties with each other, creating an economic network independent of the host country and of China itself (Esman 2009). With the advent of modern technologies and looser governmental controls on commerce, these linkages have intensified (Cohen 1997). Beyond the economic interests, the cross-national ties evince a sense of belonging to a singular group—the *Nanyang* (South Seas) Chinese—with a shared set of experiences.

MORE COMPLEX DIASPORAS: SOUTH ASIANS ABROAD

As the term diaspora has gained more currency, it has also come to diverge from the many elements by which a group is considered a diaspora. The Jewish diaspora consolidated aspects of a singular religion, at least, and a singular goal: the creation of a Jewish homeland. The Chinese diaspora coincided with people who shared a common ethnicity. Yet according to Werbner (2010), several diasporic groups do not fit neatly into these constraints. They are far more pluralistic in their makeup and in their ultimate objectives. Broadly construed, Werbner considers groups such as

Middle Easterners or Afro-Caribbeans as more complex diasporas in that they include several religions, ethnicities, and trajectories. At the same time, any group described as a diaspora requires some commonality. The use of the term "South Asian" as a complex diaspora can be apt, since there are at least five countries and four religions involved in the mix, along with dozens of linguistic groups. In this case, the differences are apparent, but is there any utility to assigning a common name? There seems to be. In fact, there is even an academic journal titled *South Asian Diaspora*.

Despite their differences, the South Asian diaspora has been shaped by the common experience of hailing from lands long under British domination, of being second-class citizens within their own territory, and of adapting to the British occupation—often by acquiring English and in adopting (with some variation) British educational institutions. One such common diasporic experience lies in the movement of many South Asians across the far-flung British Empire, entering as indentured servants, labor migrants, or middleman minorities during the period of British rule and then remaining into the second and third generations (Clarke and Peach 1990). In fact, while many labor migrants were given the option to return home after their contract was up, the vast majority remained, either re-upping their contracts or buying land in the new territory (Cohen 1997). This refashioned what was initially expected to be a temporary population into something more permanent. While the diversity of South Asian populations—resettling into other colonies and eventually incorporating in post-colonial societies—was quite broad, a great deal of cultural homogenization occurred as regionally distinct groups became identified under a general South Asian banner (Cohen 1997). Furthermore, aspects of caste and other social organizations sometimes diminished in the new environments, though there was also the countervailing attempt to retain these structures.

The variety of South Asian experiences is conditioned by the groups that came, where they went, their position in the new society, and their sheer numbers. Numbers matter, of course, in that large communities can maintain cultural traits and retain internal differences. The South Asian resettlement to islands like Fiji, Mauritius, and Trinidad led to substantial populations, even pluralities. The initial experience was as indentured labor, housed in mass barracks and separated from the rest of society. After these countries became independent, the ties to India were rekindled by Hindu missions from India. In these cases, though, the population was substantial enough that any diasporic consciousness would compete with a desire to set up roots in the new country of residence. Mauritian Indians were successful in gaining property after independence and in establishing a strong stake in the new country. Fijian Indians—as a substantial minority of over one-third who had been on the islands for four generations or more—were likewise eager to own land. However, this was blocked by the native Fijian population (Cohen 1997), and conflicts between these two groups have been fairly constant since independence. Many Indo-Fijians have felt a need to leave after suffering reprisals (Lal 2003).

In other contexts, such as East Africa, the overall percentages were small—perhaps 2 percent—but the impact on the economy was outsized. In these colonies, South Asians had established themselves as shopkeepers and maintained their traditions. What is more, according to Twaddle (1990), by the time British control had ended, the South Asian population was internally divided by religion, nationality, and caste and had long maintained separation. In fact, this distinctiveness from one another and from the demographically dominant African groups prevented any assimilation, and kept these communities aligned with the subcontinent (Twaddle 1990). In these instances, diasporic consciousness remained high, and was accentuated by the fact that many indigenous peoples were quite uncomfortable with the South Asian presence. The notorious expulsion of South Asians from Uganda by the Amin regime in 1972 led to a diaspora all its own. Many Ugandan Asians went to the United Kingdom or the United States, establishing new societies. Others, particularly those who had no need for employment, returned home to India (Van Hear 1998). Long after the end of Amin's reign, and with the rise of a new, business-friendly Uganda, several members of the original Asian Ugandan population were enticed to return home (Van Hear 1998).

One important aspect of a complex diaspora is that it ties together many strands of individual diasporas in the same manner that pan-ethnicities amalgamate several separate ethnicities. In the case of the South Asian diaspora, each group involved can legitimately claim a diaspora of its own: Indian, Pakistani, Nepalese, Bhutanese, Bangladeshi; Muslim, Hindu, Sikh. This is especially true when considering that these groups display considerable geopolitical differences and tensions in their homelands. The South Asian labor migration to the oil-rich Gulf States, for example, is almost completely Muslim in character compared to the Hindu or Sikh observances of other South Asian groups.

The Sikhs are another group that has stood out with its own diasporic movement. As members of a minority religion, quite distinct in culture, easily identifiable by dress, feeling persecuted by the Hindu majority, and with a clearly articulated Punjab homeland, the Sikh ethnicity is marked. Members of the Sikh community have spread mostly to North America and Britain, but with substantive populations in Southeast Asia. Sikhs in India and abroad have also called out for a measure of self-determination. Often this is something short of a fully independent Punjabi state, but certainly a change from the status quo, manifest in the desire to fashion an entity with the political privileges enjoyed by other autonomous regions (Tatla 2005). Part of the pressure to create an autonomous Sikh homeland has come about internally, but it is Sikh populations abroad that have played an important role. Groups have been established to unite all Sikhs and to lobby the governments in their host lands to apply pressure for the creation of an independent or quasi-independent Punjab (Tatla 2005).

DIGITAL DIASPORAS

As the twentieth century gave way to the twenty-first, diasporas have changed in a key way. Cheaper transportation options have made it easier for migrants to return home more frequently. Every immigrant neighborhood now includes specialized travel agencies that contract with airlines to ensure that people can keep in frequent physical contact with their homeland, even to the extent of maintaining residential ties.

However, it has been in the area of communications where the greatest changes have occurred. This began with the greater ease and cheaper costs of international phone calls (Vertovec 2004). International telephone calls used to cost a relative fortune, reserved for emergencies and quick hurried discussions. This has altered dramatically. Most phone services offer plans that feature free international calling; a family member can stay on the phone all day if she wants.

Following this was the opportunity for ethnic groups to utilize the Internet in creating online communities. The Internet offers two-way communication that is instantly updateable, providing much of the bulwark for a virtual ethnic community. This technology can be especially helpful for tiny communities that are spread around the world. For example, the population of Latvians in North American cities never exceeds more than about 7,500 (in Toronto) and 4,000 (in Chicago). Through the Internet, Latvian ethnics maintain their connections with one another (Woodhouse 2005). The scattered Nigerian population can stay in touch with each other, and create and maintain political associations and ethnic unions, even without having to live in close proximity (Abbot 2006). Asian Indian ethnics in the United States have utilized this technology handily. Many Indians reside in the suburbs, and do not maintain high degrees of visibility (Skop 2012). The Internet has allowed this population to create "bridgespaces" where they can communicate with one another and create a larger ethnic community from many isolated strands (Adams and Ghose 2003). This has the additional benefit of tying these overseas Indians back to the South Asian subcontinent. The use of digital communication does not create the sufficient conditions for a true diaspora—there must be other elements related to the desire to return, continued real ties, and even the attempt to participate in the political life of the homeland—but it does forge the necessary architecture by which these things become more possible.

In the last 10 years, the use of Skype, Facetime, and other Internet technologies have rendered another dramatic change. Not only can communication across continents be completely free of charge, but it now includes visual communication and a virtual presence. Brinkerhoff (2009) has termed this a "digital diaspora" that permits migrants to maintain virtual contact with their homeland and maintain diasporic ties in a way that would not have been possible before. This makes for a different type of diaspora because contact is continuous and permanent, with no lag time in information about what is happening in the old country. A robust use of these technologies means that immigrants never really need to leave home.

Kusek (2014) demonstrates how this works in practice among Polish migrants in London. There are websites, of course (figure 11.2), but nearly all Poles also have smartphones with up-to-the-minute communication and access to Polish television and radio. Most significantly, they use these technologies to inculcate their children in the national identity of the homeland. The result is that the Poles in London, particularly the more professional class, find themselves in a position of true transnationalism. Kusek maintains that this represents a qualitative difference between the Poles who came to London right after World War II and those who live there

Figure 11.2. This is a portal for Polish immigrants in the United Kingdom to exchange information and network with one another. The website is a virtual place where people can meet other immigrants and support each other, look for jobs, and read ads for events, services, and businesses. Many immigrants use the site to send flowers to loved ones in Poland on birthdays, name days, or Mother's Day. *Source:* Polacy.co.uk.

now. The expectation to learn English presents little problem for a new educated generation who recognize the need for English in nearly all high-level transactions. As a group, the Poles occupy British society, but keep a substantial aspect of their lives back home. As Kusek (2014, 179–80) puts it:

> In this sense, access to technology and its universalism across borders provides for continuity in their life, regardless of location. They can use the same smartphone in Warsaw and in London. They can listen to the same radio in Warsaw and in London. They can consume the same media in Warsaw and in London. They can contact their family via Facetime regardless if they are in Warsaw or in London. In that sense the Techspora is characterized not only by extremely strong connections with the homeland, but, even more so, by behaviors and identities which naturally transcend borders, and allow them to live at least portions of their lives as if they never left their homeland.

This continuous and growing adaptation of technology to serve transnational communications collapses the separation that diaspora populations would ordinarily feel. Whether it effectively cuts down on the acquisition of a new national identity remains to be seen.

DIAGNOSING DIASPORAS

As a term, "diaspora" has gained so much academic ground within the last three decades that it might have become a victim of its own success. Several journals and many, many books include diaspora in their titles. It is hard to know what the term adds that is not currently covered by "ethnicity" or, perhaps, it has emerged as a replacement for "ethnicity." However, unlike ethnicity, which is a fairly inclusive concept, diaspora has been defined more precisely with a strong set of criteria. Like the often mistermed "nation-state," a strict application would find that few alleged diasporas really fit the bill.

At the same time, its proliferation—with all groups being tagged with the diasporic label—reflects our new sophistication in understanding that identities do not simply vanish, even across generations, and that people continue to have long-standing affiliations with the places they have left behind. True diasporas describe a situation of people with literally two feet on widely separated pieces of ground: the homeland, where they continue allegiance, affiliation, and the hope of eventual return; and the host land, where they currently reside. Those "diasporas" that fall somewhat short of this ideal also include a tension between homelands and host lands. They also point to the fact that many people in the world today do not simply fit neatly into a single national identity, but instead straddle two or sometimes even more nations. This is the topic for the next chapter.

12

⚜

Transnationalism
and Hybridity

The movement across distance from one place to another, and the potential to continue that movement, can be powerful forces in unsettling newer communities. *Transnationalism* has received a great deal of attention since the early 1990s (Glick-Schiller, Basch, and Blanc-Szanton 1992). The notion that people could have connections that cross nations was not new, of course, but new technological advances, a greater sensitivity toward diversity, and the growth of nationalism itself made this perspective a part of a new analytical framework. Transnationalism entails a means of thinking about the world without relying on artificially bounded objects, notably countries, but rather considers the flows that continue to circulate between countries. It is through a transnational lens that it is possible to cut away from a world defined by fixed spaces and borders to one defined largely by flows. In this view, social, political, and economic life is oriented around networks—a way to structure the various flows between places. These flows span distance, cross national boundaries, and are also dynamic. From this change in perspective, several new insights have been developed.

Because people do not simply enter into a nation, but in fact arrive and interact with a locality, the idea of transnationalism has devolved into the notion of translocalism, which involves the idea that people move across localities and bring their experience and ties from other localities to bear on their newer localities, and vice versa. Finally, the literature of hybridity has been quite useful in noting how transnationalism and the creation of diaspora communities can lead to hybrid spaces that are betwixt two more settled spaces of home and abroad. Hybrid spaces also can beget hybrid peoples and hybrid cultures, and has become a powerful force in creating new ethnic forms and new forms of interaction.

DEFINING TRANSNATIONALISM

"Transnationalism" casts a wide net (Vertovec 1999). Diasporas certainly fit within the category, as they involve groups connected between homeland and host land. Seekers of asylum are reluctant transnationalists, desperate for safe haven after forcibly fleeing their homes. International labor migration brings people across borders in search of wages. Transnational corporations cross borders, often in search of cheaper labor, tax benefits, markets, or some other good. Transnational political networks—often in the form of nongovernmental organizations (NGOs)—reach across many societies. Even terrorists can be considered transnational because they target people and property far from the site of conflict. Transnationalism occurs over a large field or a small space, over a long period of time or in short bursts. It can involve people, but it is also applied to objects. Trade is the quintessential transnational activity.

Transnationalism is always susceptible to the frictions caused by distances. We might consider the transnationalism of the elite, the jetsetter, the "astronaut," or the cosmopolite who belongs to no nation and can seemingly live anywhere, provided it is close to modern facilities and an international airport (Ley 2010). This is the group that has historically kept its feet in various places, crossing national boundaries with ease. While the image behind this group and the world cities its members inhabit is of a sameness sanded down by the needs of global capital, Ley (2004) makes the point that they must also encounter the particularities of each community where they happen to reside. The social differences and distances from family are personally and culturally unsettling for this group, and point out that transnationalism comes with a cost. Often the cost is a rupture in family ties as elite transnationals become "prisoners of geographical distance" (Ley 2004, 162).

The cost is even more pronounced with the transnationalism of ordinary individuals, who may now live within a city but continue to have social, economic, and political relations in other communities, crossing borders in the pursuit of these relationships. While distance is certainly less pronounced than it would have been at other times—when a proto-transnationalism fueled by letters and perhaps a costly visit home was the order of the day—home is still a long way away. The transnationalism of migrants living in large foreign cities is defined by the local neighborhood, fellow nationals perhaps in other nearby cities, and then the emotionally close but geographically distant "home." The transnational conduits to such a home may lie in satellite dishes, neighborhood call centers, and travel agencies. For those with little money—the truly poor and desperate who may have fled their original homeland in search of safety—the barriers of distance are high, as are the obstacles imposed by an uncertain political situation. Would a Syrian refugee, having escaped his bombed-out city to finally gain entry into Germany, truly be able to participate in any transnational activity? Perhaps, but these activities would be limited and sporadic.

Immigration fits quite closely into the transnational spectrum since it involves the flows of peoples from one place to another. It also involves the insertion of new cultures into existing culture areas, forcing some mode of accommodation. As immigrants and emigrants move across national boundaries, they forge new networks across the different places that they touch. Immigrant activities create new interactions that result from this back-and-forth movement (Glick-Schiller, Basch, and Blanc-Szanton 1992). Transnationalism also helps to tie together those ethnics who leave the home country, either for a few weeks or several years, and those who are left behind (Levitt and Lamba-Nieves 2010).

At the same time, it is important to bear in mind that despite the high and even increasing degree of mobility across national boundaries, these flows are not unimpeded. The state continues to exert an important role (Waldinger and Fitzgerald 2004). It regulates the conditions of entry, the ease of immigration, the enforcement mechanisms, and even internal controls. The relationships between countries play a powerful role, both positive and negative, for new migrants. U.S.-Cuban relations were cast in such a way that all Cubans who managed to escape (which in fact was required due to tight Cuban control of emigration) to the United States were accorded political refugee status, and so could avoid most of the impediments faced by other entrants.

What sort of purchase is gained by "transnationalism" as a concept is open to debate since, after all, so much of what is described as trans-national is part of the historical record. The value of the concept, from people who have embraced it, lies in a few insights (see Portes 2003). Transnationalism does allow for a perspective that realizes the motility of these movements—both tangible and intangible—across networks. It also allows us to better contrast it with the more vaunted activities of governments or large international institutions. The less publicized activities of immigrant groups—welfare associations, groups that ease the transfer of people, transnational businesses, and remittances—are more grassroots activities, and an important object of study. Portes (2003) emphasizes that many immigrants, especially immigrant children, in fact do not participate in transnational networks. The old idea of symbolic ethnicity, where people feel ethnic but do not participate beyond a few minor, albeit symbolic, gestures, would be an example of this. Transnational immigrants are heavily involved in all aspects of their homeland and with other members of the immigrant archipelago. This does not mean that more assimilated ethnics are not necessarily transnational, however, since they may be among the more affluent members of the ethnic group and therefore quite involved in maintaining businesses. The social, religious, political, and economic considerations of transnational activities can be enormous.

Additionally, most host countries witness much secondary migration between local communities as immigrants work to find the best and most feasible situation for themselves and their families. *Translocalism*, or the connection between cities or other subnational localities, describes a form of transnational linkage (see Brickell and Datta 2011; Greiner and Sakdapolrak 2013; Barkan 2006 with a slightly different definition). The impetus behind translocalism is both mobility—of people and things—and fixity as it occurs within a particular place (Greiner and Sakdapolrak 2013).

NEIGHBORHOOD TRANSNATIONALISM

While the operation of transnationalism can be displayed by the demarcation of circuits on a map, pointing to the flows between places, these abstractions are made quite clear at the level of a neighborhood. Neighborhood places are made through daily activities that include shopping, praying, socializing, working, and walking. They are represented by their built environment, which comprises all the structures, stores, statues, and streets found within the neighborhood. They are also represented by a transient environment made up of street stalls, street-corner hustlers, temporary markets, or ad hoc places of worship. Permanence and transience exist side by side. New people arrive into an old landscape as the influence of the past seeps into the present. The transnationalism comes in because so much of what transpires in a neighborhood reflects the circuits of transnationalism. Massey (1991, 29) suggests that each place comprehends multiple meanings defined by different social networks, and that these identities always hearken to larger global forces "linking that place to places beyond."

The Goutte d'Or neighborhood in Paris is one example. Within this neighborhood, which has the highest proportion of immigrants within the city of Paris, three distinct communities exist: the European French, including many who have lived in the area for some time and others looking for cheaper accommodations; the Maghrebi residents, who began arriving in the late 1950s and include immigrants from North Africa and their children; and the African or Afro-Caribbean immigrants from countries like Senegal, Cameroon, Cote d'Ivoire, Malagasy Republic, and Haiti, and are relatively recent residents. Here there is an intensity of activity that marks the Goutte d'Or's position at the center of a series of transnational networks. And while many neighborhoods in many cities can be considered transnational to some extent, some neighborhoods are clearly more so than others. The level of activity within the Goutte d'Or distinguishes it from patterns in other neighborhoods in Paris, which as a whole includes all manner of transnational activities. Networks of contacts and exchanges—migrants, visitors, groceries, and telephone calls— circulate well beyond this neighborhood into the state, the region, and the world. The endpoints of all these activities are concurrently represented in every facet of life here.

The reflection of transnationalism in the Goutte d'Or is made manifest in many ways. The exercise of religion is among the most transnational of activities. There is a traditional Catholic church surrounded by a buffer of green tranquility amidst the bustle of the neighborhood. But this expression of an earlier transnationalism has been offset by the presence of Islam. Many, if not most, of the recent immigrants to Paris hail from Muslim countries and share the Islamic faith. The Islamic religion is evident in both the built environment and the transient environment of the neighborhood. There is the main mosque, the Mosquee al Fath, which has served as the most visible mosque in this neighborhood. But this mosque and an additional storefront mosque are simply not large enough to accommodate all the adherents who seek to pray in the Goutte d'Or, and the government has not provided close alternatives. Transnationalism is then reflected in the transient environment. On Fridays, blankets line one of the main streets alongside the main mosque as people pray in the street. While this expression of faith and transnationalism rankles some people, many non-Muslim residents of the neighborhood do not appear to be terribly put out by this (Barros and Marillier 2010).

The presence of Islam in the Goutte d'Or is not confined to its explicit practice. Most of the bookstores are Islamic, selling mostly Korans and other religious texts. This is in marked contrast to most other neighborhoods in Paris with their broad selection of secular bookstores, newsstands, and stationery stores. The other major feature lies in the halal butcher shops, which provide meat prepared according to Islamic dietary regulations that prohibit pork or blood products and require that the animal be slaughtered according to specific precepts. The famous French charcuterie, selling a variety of sausages made from pork, is rarely found. Bakeries, quite common throughout the neighborhood, do not serve non-halal ingredients. The significance of Islam is quite obvious in resident attire. Forms of headdress such as the hijab for women and the skullcap for men are extremely common on the streets.

The activity of shopping is another way in which transnationalism filters into the Goutte d'Or. The rue Poulet, the main shopping street, is dominated by the neighborhood's West African population. The street contains African beauty shops, African wig stores, African groceries, and African fabrics. Cheap African restaurants—some of which do not seem open to the general public—are found virtually everywhere. At this time, few West Africans own the stores in the neighborhoods, but they make up the lion's share of the customers. The operation of these stores manifests at least three transnational circuits. On one hand is the circuit of immigration—the reflection of peoples from all over the world, but primarily countries that were once part of the French colonial empire. The language of the street is mainly French, but heavily accented French, as people who arrive in Paris with their local languages use the colonial language as a bridge to communicate with others. Another circuit comes from the provision of goods imported and sold by merchants who maintain these international commercial ties. Finally, the circuit of customers is also transnational. The Goutte d'Or is a focused shopping district that provides items that simply cannot be purchased elsewhere (see figure 12.1). As a result, customers arrive from well beyond the neighborhood, the city, and even from other countries. The daily shopping is international, of course, but it is not unusual for ethnics coming from nearby European countries to make a pilgrimage to the Goutte d'Or a few times a year (Chabrol 2011).

Figure 12.1.   The Goutte d'Or neighborhood. Along the rue Poulet in Paris, an assortment of businesses cater to a largely African and Maghrebi clientele. *Source:* David H. Kaplan.

ETHNICITY AND HYBRIDITY

Related to transnationalism is *hybridity*, a term introduced into the literature by Homi Bhabha (1994). It refers to the merging of a former identity with the newer identity of the new home (Papastergiadis 2013). The concept comes from post-colonial studies that observe what happens within a colonial context when the social and cultural deck is reshuffled by the imposition of a new power, creating new manners of cultural practice. Of course, hybridity is a notion that applies to mixtures of all sorts of cultural attributes that do not give themselves up neatly to simple binaries (Yazdiha 2010).

A few examples illustrate this. There may be ideal forms of each language, but there are also blends of several tongues. Pidgins—a term used to describe these mixings—can become creoles; creoles can then become languages of their own, or alter the original language in a significant way. Just like every language spoken on earth, modern English emerged from a hybrid. Race as a category is even more problematic, as discussed in chapter 1, but we continue to use this terminology. Even assuming the value of such a designator, true racial categorization is nearly impossible. History is replete with terms such as "mulatto," "mestizo," and "mixed race" to account for hybridization. In 2000, the U.S. Census Bureau even changed its racial designators to allow people to express their racial hybridity with two or more selections. National identity—a designator far more robust than race—is still one where false dichotomies are always present. Nationalism forces a decision of belonging to a single nation and abjuring all connections with any other nation. Yet national identity is constructed from several historical trends and choices. The processes of state expansion, regional consolidation, border divisions, and our mental framing of ourselves and "others" have led to our present system of nations, but at the same time have allowed hybrid forms to appear between the cracks. The fact that the very term "nation-state" applies to so few cases testifies to this national hybridity.

In the context of ethnicity, hybridity is used to signify three important aspects, each of which has spatial significance. First is the extent to which members of a new group are sorted within a society's existing ethnic categories. Segmented assimilation describes the placing of immigrants into the existing ethnic/racial structure. Sometimes the sorting is not so clear cut, as many new groups occupy a space between established groupings. Second is the degree to which immigrant groups may change their culture as they move into a new context. Unless they keep themselves hermetically sealed off from any other cultural influences, contact will result in hybridity. Members of the group will change. For a diaspora, hybridity results from the contact of this group with the members of their adopted host land (Hutnyk 2005). In this respect, hybridity could be considered the obverse of transnationalism. Just as transnationalism denotes the extent to which groups are able to retain ties to their brethren across space, hybridity considers how a group is changed by contact with other groups, and by its placement within another context. Third is how hybridity exposes the double lives lived by members of an immigrant or any minority cultural group. To enter into a particular sociocultural context as an outsider necessitates the need to play additional roles. On one hand, there is the role that observes the culture and mores of one's ethnic group. On the other hand, there is the navigation of the culture of the dominant society. The hybridity can be complicated even further if someone represents a minority group within a larger immigrant group. As such, the roles are multiplied three ways.

As with all trendy terms, it pays to examine what value is added by "hybridity." One issue is whether the same concept could not simply be covered by the process of assimilation. After all, assimilation is the endpoint of cultural contact, as the adoption of new norms becomes complete and members of a group shed their once-distinct trappings to become, for all intents and purposes, the majority. Would hybridity then operate as a kind of way station between cultural difference and complete immersion into the dominant society? Does hybridity propose the creation of new cultural forms? Another line of questioning involves the extent to which the use of hybridity is "counterhegemonic," as many of its proponents, including Bhabha (1994), claim. Slipping between essentialist cultural categories, which is what many scholars of hybridity describe, may serve the purposes of the state and of the capitalist order (Mitchell 1997). After all, that is what we often find in regard to the creation of middleman minorities in colonial and post-colonial contexts.

HYBRIDITY WITHIN THE SOCIAL ORDER

As discussed in earlier chapters, every society contains a particular configuration of "recognized" ethnic groups, races, or nationalities—however these may be characterized. These configurations are constructed, of course, and can be quite dynamic, but they drastically impact the placement of new groups that do not fit easily into existing choices. For example, the biologically meaningless distinction of race was preceded by an equally spurious distinction based on color and the color lines employed to divide societies (Nightingale 2012). Within such a configuration, there would arrive peoples who effectively had hybridity imposed on them. They did not fit easily into the specified colors.

By the early nineteenth century, the United States had developed as a Protestant country with an African American minority, many of whom were enslaved. The American Indian populations, though present in many places, were mostly confined to the outskirts of society. Into this context came the Irish Catholic immigrant, clearly not "white" nor Christian in the way these terms had been framed (in which Christian did not include Catholic). Nor did the Irish fit within any of the other categories. Far from being accepted, the Irish were detested. From their first entry into the cities and towns of the United States, they encountered a hailstorm of invective. Efforts to retain their culture, especially their Catholic religion through churches and schools, made them even more suspect as a group and as potential saboteurs from the Pope himself, threatening to destroy the American way of life. The Know-Nothing Party, a political party quite popular in the 1850s with former President Millard Fillmore as its standard-bearer, arose to condemn these and other Catholic immigrants (Zeitz 2015). Pictures portrayed the Irish as no better than the African Americans, and sometimes even worse. In the racial politics of the day, the Irish occupied a special place—not black, but certainly not white. They were treated mercilessly in the popular press and mocked in the cartoons of the day (figure 12.2).

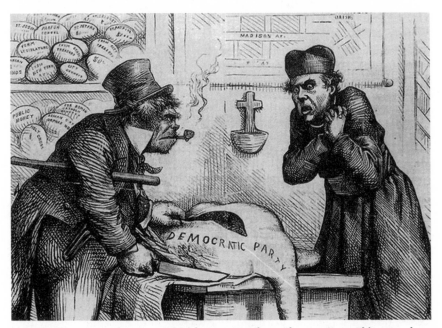

Figure 12.2. One of many anti-Irish cartoons from Thomas Nast. This one, from *Harper's Weekly*, November 17, 1871, shows an Irish man (depicted as an ape) and a Catholic priest in the process of destroying the Democratic Party.

Later immigrants, hailing from Southern and Eastern Europe, only added to the racial confusion. They arrived during a time of acute racial awareness, with diagrams displaying the different racial groups and books such as *An Essay on Inequality of the Human Races* and later *The Passing of the Great Race* popular among many of the elite. What sort of race did these people belong to? The question had all sorts of implications, particularly since true enfranchisement was accorded only to free *white* males. Those who were not Anglo-Saxon or Nordic were told they did not really fit into this category. Early twentieth-century bureaucrats, politicians, and academics agreed that they were a long way from assimilating into the "American race," differing only in whether they could eventually be assimilated (the attitude of President Teddy Roosevelt) or whether the racial difference made this impossible, as argued by the longtime director of the U.S. Census Bureau (Roediger 2005). As such, the new groups populating American cities were considered unfit for citizenship, and so were cast outside the color line. The hybrid placement of these new minorities was reflected in housing, employment (where they were expected to do particularly unpleasant jobs), and insulting epithets.

As the first generation gave way to the second, and as the virulence of anti-Catholicism and anti-Semitism diminished, these invidious categories melted away. Oddly enough, by the time that turn-of-the-century nativist Americans were railing against the Italians, Slavs, and Jews, the most despised group of the mid-nineteenth century—the Irish—had turned a corner in the popular consciousness and could now be considered "white." This was a result of many factors, most prominently the passage of many second-generation descendants of these immigrants into the professions and into middle-class respectability. The fact that the United States had defeated a nationalist vision based on making extreme racial distinctions—and what this had led to in practice—made this type of racist thinking (at least as far as Europeans were concerned) unacceptable (Brodkin 1998). And it would also be true that the absence of new immigration, brought about by the severe restrictions of 1924, hastened the assimilation of the Southern, Central, and Eastern European ethnic groups (Alba 1985).

This would end the "hybrid" character of many of these European ethnics, and this was certainly reflected in the geography of residence. With the loosening of the barriers against them, ethnic enclaves began to disappear and to become relics of what they had once been. By the 1960s and 1970s, however, new "hybrid" populations, again fitting uneasily within the black-white dichotomy, would emerge.

HYBRIDITY AND THE BLENDING OF CULTURE

Hybridity represents an encounter between a cultural group and a context. What can make this encounter somewhat tricky is that the nature, situation, and expression of the group will change as the context shifts, resulting in distinct hybrid forms. These forms are completely novel, qualitatively different from their antecedents (Dear and Burridge 2005). Examples of cultural hybrids abound. Blended languages such as "Spanglish" develop their own vocabulary and syntax and, while certainly containing recognizable strands of both English and Spanish, are in process of developing unique linguistic traits. Cuisines are in a constant state of hybridity, as aspects of two or more foodways fuse into something entirely different. So it is with the cultural characteristics of groups that emerge from the juxtaposition of two or more groups, or the placement of a particular group into an unfamiliar context. The culture of an ethnic group that persists in a new land is always going to be different from the national culture from which it originated. These alterations expose faceted features of what the groups represent, to themselves and others, and how the context constrains their expression as well.

The Japanese Brazilian or *nikkeijin* population provides a wonderful window into the separate hybridities realized by this immigrant group while demonstrating the altering contexts of both Brazil and Japan. Japanese immigrants first came over to Brazil near the beginning of the twentieth century. Japan was not yet so economically prosperous, Brazil seemed to offer the prospect of steady agricultural employment, and many Japanese were encouraged to sign labor contracts agreeing to work on one of the many coffee plantations. Unlike other labor immigration strategies, the Japanese were encouraged to come over as families, all of whom would join in the work (Yamanaka 1996). In moving, the nikkeijin migrated from the extraordinarily homogenous society of Japan to the racialized society of Brazil—the last country to formally abolish slavery. Work on the coffee plantations was tough, made tougher by oppressive plantation owners and harsh tropical conditions. Soon many of the Japanese migrants had left the plantations, some of them to rent parcels from the owners, others to form their own communities under the direction of a charismatic leader, and still others who joined in Japanese government–sponsored districts deep in the interior (Adachi 2006). Most such communities were definitively Japanese, with many in the first and even second generation staying close to their roots and sequestering themselves from the rest of Brazilian society. Even in cases where they lived near Brazilians, the Japanese chose to maintain separation (Adachi 2006). For many, their ultimate goal was to return to Japan.

With the change in fortunes following World War II, many Japanese Brazilians decided that their best path forward was to gain an education and move to Brazil's growing cities, particularly São Paulo and the smaller cities in that region (Adachi 2006). Movement into the professional ranks has created a cadre of Japanese Brazilians, often third or fourth generation, who are clearly marked as *japones* by their facial features but who have lost much of the Japanese language (Tsuda 2006). The 1.5 million Japanese in Brazil today form a clear slice of this multiracial society, but one where they are set as the outsiders, often singled out by words and the gesture of pulling up the eyes to indicate "slanted eyes." Attenuating this racialization is that most stereotypes formed by the Brazilian community, and internalized by the Japanese Brazilians themselves, are positive (Tsuda 2006). Japanese Brazilians are considered hard-working, clever, and responsible. Plus, they represent an economically successful country.

Yet the Brazilian economy still seemed to lag what might be possible within Japan itself, and beginning in 1989 many nikkeijin from Brazil were enticed to move to Japan, at least temporarily, to avail themselves of the opportunities there. The economic reason was simple: wages in Japan were many times higher than in Brazil. And Japan's closed immigration system pried open just a little bit to allow ethnic Japanese abroad entry into the country, with no restrictions on activities (Tsuda 2008). The number of Brazilian Japanese in Japan increased dramatically, despite a Japanese recession, so that it now exceeds a quarter of a million. But here too, the nikkeijin find themselves in an uncomfortably hybrid situation. Based on their physical features, they are perceived as Japanese by the Japanese, but several generations of living in Brazil have weakened their command of Japanese language and cultural mores. For many, the encounters with Japanese have been incongruous, even demeaning, as they are derided and exploited for being different than they appear. For the nikkeijin, this hybrid condition compels them to act out their Brazilian-ness in order to avoid being mistaken for a true Japanese person. This can be expressed through language (speaking Portuguese conspicuously), through dress (more flamboyant styles and colors than are standard), and even the performance of the samba (something few nikkeijin would dance in Brazil) (Tsuda 2006). Figure 12.3 shows a Japanese Brazilian store with items that appeal specifically to this clientele.

HYBRIDITY AND CODE-SWITCHING

The experience of the Japanese Brazilians illustrates how members of a single group may alter their performances depending on the context in which they find themselves. It is but one set of adaptations that must be made in the expression of group identity. Most specifically, the phenom-

Figure 12.3. **This shop, in Nagoya, Japan, is owned and operated by Japanese Brazilians for Japanese Brazilian customers. Other Japanese women would be unlikely to wear the flipflops and bikinis sold here.** *Source:* **Dorris Scott.**

enon of "code-switching" occurs whenever members of a group feel that they need to speak in one way when in one context, and another way when they find themselves within another. This may involve a shift to another dialect or another language altogether. In this instance, linguistic code-switching modulates identity depending on the circumstances. Identity switches according to the situation.

As an example of how such code-switching might work, Portes and Rumbaut (2001) conducted a massive study examining the experiences of immigrant children. These were either children who were born in the United States to immigrant parents, or who came over at a young age. From the point of view of ethnic identity, this is a critical population, because children are poised to switch identities much more readily than adults. The main proxy for this sort of switching was in the form of language retention and preference. In many cases, parents would have a limited knowledge of English, though that varied by language and by nationality. The children were nearly always fluent in English. This makes sense given their widespread exposure to the language from a very young age.

Code-switching depends on the context in which children speak. While upward of 80 percent of children preferred to speak English in general, the language at home was almost always not English. The child codeswitches between the language she uses with parents and the language she uses in the wider world. Often the child becomes a kind of linguistic emissary for the parents, when their knowledge of English is particularly poor. Interestingly, Portes and Rumbaut (2001) found that, despite a generally lower level of fluency in the foreign language, children of immigrants would often actively speak their foreign language with their friends. This could be a means of defining group boundaries, a sort of private communication, and a form of pride.

Language and identity are intermingled when ethnics speak a language that is foreign to the dominant population. (For ethnics who speak the same language, other criteria must take the place of language.) Just as the speaking of a language is flexible, depends on the situation, and changes over time, so does the identity that this language is attached to. Many children feel a sense of embarrassment about their parents, not just regarding language but also a host of other ethnic attributes including dress, social mores, expectations of children, and gender roles. They may abandon as many aspects of their identity as they can, or switch to a broader or different identity (e.g., moving from Colombian to Latino). But there may also be cases where ethnic identity is "thickened" as immigrant children define themselves by who they are not and in reaction to perceived assaults. In the wake of the anti-immigrant Proposition 187, passed in 1994, many children of immigrants felt a reactive pride and protectiveness toward their ethnicity and their language. This was particularly true of Mexican Americans, who felt targeted by the campaign.

This form of hybridity is found throughout the world, whenever an individual feels buffeted by two or more identities. Hybridity results from being the child of immigrants, and finding one's way in the journey toward eventual assimilation or the development of a different, more durable identity better suited to the context at hand. Hybridity also results from the different codes (linguistic and otherwise) used as means of establishing oneself within a group. The codes shift when the context shifts. More established immigrants, for example, may ridicule recent arrivals and the way they talk, even though they speak the same way in their home country (Bailey 2007). They may speak and act differently depending on who they are trying to please. The home domain and the public domain require different strategies and different forms of presentation. This is also true in a city like Khartoum, Sudan, with its myriad ethnic languages and a privileged position for Arabic (Mugaddam 2006), as it is in California, where dozens of languages coexist with a privileged position for English. Language may also switch as the context evolves over time. Such has been the case with language use in Montreal (Heller 1985). Once an Anglophone domain, particularly where French and English speakers interacted, the growing assertion of the French majority and the passage of French language laws changed the rules of the game. The language of choice within various spheres became much more tentative as people struggled to find the appropriate language to use. And as the dominance of English in business situations faded, it left older Anglophones more isolated, often seeking out other monolinguals. In other situations, people often used both languages, switching around to find the medium most appropriate to the situation.

ETHNICITY REGENERATED

The late Doreen Massey (1991) once concluded that one finds the "global within the local." The world can be found within a neighborhood. The ideas of transnationalism show why this is true. People do not completely move their lives from one place to another. Instead, they maintain the ties that they have from past places and times, along with new connections made in their current locale. This sort of straddling between two worlds has long been done, but the advent of faster transportation and communications makes this even more feasible. Transportation networks can be developed between countries, and as described in the previous chapter, one feature found within many ethnic neighborhoods is the travel agency set up to provide easy mobility. Communications have made even greater strides, and so the ability of people to talk inexpensively across boundaries and oceans, first with cheaper telephone calls and now with video chatting, has accelerated. The flows of information, objects, and people become an important part of the architecture of transnationalism.

In the first chapter, I discussed the notion that ethnicity is constructed. The populace is not divided by immutable ethnic categories, but rather ethnicity arises out of circumstances specific to the group and to the context, both of which can change. Ethnicity is contingent, and it is also situational. The juxtaposition of cultures and contexts brings about its own set of circumstances, one that embraces a framework of hybridity. The insertion into a particular social order, the blending of peoples, the need to change according to the situation—these all provoke hybrid attitudes and hybrid responses.

We might wonder whether transnationalism will intensify and if hybridity will become more of a common and self-conscious response. It seems that the world is becoming more complex in regard to social structures. Families now incorporate several branches and new relations borne by divorce, remarriage, and different roles for caregivers. Ethnicity has also changed a great deal. Much higher levels of intermarriage, much greater communication, accelerated mobility, and parallel worlds in cyberspace have profoundly affected ethnicity thus far. In the next and final chapter, I will discuss what I see as the future of ethnicity and of ethnic geography.

13

✧

Envisioning the Future

At the end of the 1980s, the world suddenly came apart. One by one, Eastern Europeans behind the Iron Curtain threw off their communist leaders and moved away from the Soviet orbit to join the liberal, free trade democracies of the West. In 1991, the government of the Soviet Union itself collapsed. This was more than just a series of government transitions; it represented the end of a bipolar world system oriented around the ideological conflict between communism and capitalism— a world most people had known for 45 years and had seemed poised to go on forever. France Fukuyama's (1989) article, "The End of History?" signaled an end to much of the conflict between states. Beyond what Fukuyama actually said, there was an overriding sensibility that the end of an East-West ideological battle meant that the larger fissures dividing peoples would disappear. Later books, such as Thomas Friedman's *The World Is Flat* (2005), also heralded a more open world, where differences give way to the broader forces of globalization.

In truth, the more than 25 years since the fall of the Berlin Wall has seen new forms of cleavage and conflict. Foremost among these was the presumed refracturing of the world based around culture. Samuel Huntington's (1997) *Clash of Civilizations*, Benjamin Barber's (1995) *Jihad vs. McWorld*, and other popular works heightened the resurgent role of cultural divisions in shaping the world. For someone in the 1980s to foresee that the main source of fear within Europe and North America was the growth of "radical Islam" shows how much the terms of the discussion have shifted since then.

While often couched in terms of civilizations, religions, or nationalisms, what we are seeing here is a renewed concern over cultural difference. The loci of these divisions can be world regions, but the practical impacts are found in every city. This resurgence of cultural difference has been accompanied by the rising tide of globalization, transnationalism, and communications advances that bring the world into every village and shantytown while bringing many residents of these communities into the world. This dynamism simply cannot be stopped.

FORCES DRIVING ETHNICITY TODAY

Perhaps the most impressive attribute of ethnicity is its resilience. No matter which society we are discussing, ethnic diversity persists. Existing sociocultural cleavages, conflicting national identities, immigration, the legacy of past injustices, and the continuity of current ones all make ethnicity an important and salient fixture in the world—one that shows few signs of going away anytime soon. It is a daunting task to try and summarize the forces that are impelling ethnicity in the contemporary world and may influence societies in the future, but five factors do come to mind.

The increasing range of immigration should be considered first. While the actual proportion of immigration is probably not much larger than it has been in the past, there are more immigrants today, they come from places farther away, and they affect a larger number of countries (United Nations Department of Economic and Social Affairs 2014). Economics is a primary driver of this. A globalizing economy that enables capital to travel unfettered and precipitates the movement of labor across communities and countries is a big driver of this immigration. Outsourcing of manufacturing and services moves jobs around, benefitting some communities while devastating others. The search for lower wages by corporations is matched by the search for employment by poor individuals and families who are looking for a better life.

For those settler countries in the developed world, this constitutes a continuation of long-term trends, but with a richer variety of source countries. The United States, Canada, and Australia obtained most of their free immigrants from European sources. With greater immigration from Asia, Africa, and Latin America, each country is becoming more racially diverse than was true in the past. Part of this is due to the abolition of restrictive national origin quotas, but it also comes from greater opportunities for would-be migrants around the world to try their luck in another country. Demography and aging plays a role as well, as countries in the developed world get older by the year, with some of that population supplemented by much younger immigrant streams.

For prosperous societies without a long-term history of immigration, patterns of emigration have turned to immigration. This has come as a big change, and greater ethnic diversity has required a fair degree of social adaptation. Those countries with no inclination to allow more immigrants, such as Japan and South Korea, stand increasingly alone. Immigration does not just affect rich countries, however. Many countries that are not so well off find themselves beset by people from poorer lands nearby.

While the extent of immigration is wide, the trajectories follow some logical paths. Residents of former colonies often find their way to the colonizing country. Particularly among Muslim societies, peoples from poorer countries move as labor migrants to richer countries (Fargues 2011). Political refugees also factor into this, as they seek shelter in any country that will accept them. Only a few are allowed a more permanent presence.

We have now reached a threshold where more than half of the population lives in cities. The growing urbanization of the world is a second factor altering the geography of ethnicity. In the past, many immigrants found their way into the countryside and, in the United States and Canada, they inscribed an ethnic patchwork across the prairies and plains. Immigrants who went to countries in South America, like the Japanese moving to Brazil, developed isolated, agricultural communities well away from the mainstream. This is no longer possible. Ethnic diversity is now an urban phenomenon as immigration finds its way into cities (Kaplan, Holloway, and Wheeler 2014). Even groups engaged in farming, such as the Hmong from Laos, often do this in urban or suburban settings (Kaplan 1997). New ethnic groups coming in must adapt to urban occupations and urban settlements, and steer their culture in close proximity to compatriots. While some ethnic groups can still be quite isolated in the city, such isolation must be enacted in a more intentional way, as a conscious choice of the immigrant group or of the receiving society. All else being equal, proximity increases the prospect of contact. And contact increases the prospect of adaptation, even assimilation.

Another factor of urbanization on ethnicity, especially as found within rapidly urbanizing poorer countries, is the internal migration of peoples from around the country and into the primate city. While no international borders are crossed, in many multinational societies the impact of this internal migration is effectively the same because different cultures, religions, and languages now find themselves existing side by side. The impact of immigration to Khartoum, Sudan, is instructive in that this city, like so many rapidly expanding cities, is now home to speakers of over 100 language groups, representing many different ethnicities (Mugaddam 2006).

Third, changes in the nature of transportation and communication affect ethnicity in ways large and small. While many would-be immigrants are blocked by borders or turned back from their desired destination, others can easily traverse continents and go back and forth between their home country and their new residence. For the well-off ethnic, such trips can take place on a monthly basis. And even for those without the wherewithal to travel constantly, communications advances allow them to virtually traverse these distances every day.

Ironically, though, while transportation brings the world closer together at a larger scale, at the smaller scale of the city it enables people to live farther apart from each other, stretching the geography of ethnic communities. The notion of ethnic enclaves constituting a few city blocks, where proximity was key in maintaining institutions and in enabling intra-ethnic social interaction, has moved to ethnics living in dispersed locations and driving to hubs in order to maintain community. Landscapes are still altered, but the imprints are quite different. This goes hand in hand with suburbanization, and boosts whole new forms of ethnic placement as groups begin to influence many suburban malls, shopping centers, and even edge cities. The residential ramifications may be moving toward ethnic signatures that are less obvious to outsiders, more under-the-radar, and found within interior spaces.

There have always been significant splits in the fortunes of ethnic groups. Some groups are ushered into a new society with certain advantages. The Cubans in Florida, the Chinese in Southeast Asia, and the Indians in East Africa all attest to this. Other groups straggle in at the bottom of the social hierarchy, bereft and scorned. Context, as well as the exact circumstances of the individual migration streams, can really matter here. Bhardwaj and Rao (1990) demonstrated how the Indian community in the United Kingdom, often coming with far fewer capital resources, has been largely stigmatized by the majority society, whereas Indians in the United States, who are better advantaged, have been treated fairly well and have vaulted to the top of the socioeconomic pyramid. The cultural sorting of groups comes with a heavy dose of social stratification.

In many respects, this socioeconomic bifurcation of ethnic groups—a fourth factor—will only accentuate in the coming years. There will continue to be immigrant groups with few resources arriving as unwanted guests into the society. But more and more immigrants are arriving from positions of privilege. Much of this has to do with the globalization of education and the fact that for many aspiring people in the developing world, studying in an American, Canadian, British, or French university is the best kind of education, and universities are responding to this demand. Oxford University just expanded the ultra-prestigious Rhodes Scholarships to students from the developing world. This diversity at the university level is significant in and of itself, but also propels educated immigrants into the highest levels of the professional class as many students decide they would like to stay. Of course, some countries have explicitly enticed high-skill, high-net-worth individuals by providing immigration papers in exchange for establishing companies or otherwise creating jobs (Sumption 2012). For these immigrants, the resources they can bring to the table can improve their own lives as well as the lives of many of their countrymen. Remittances prove especially transformative, and further tie localities together.

Finally, the greater income of many ethnic members allows them to fully utilize capital, human, and ethnic resources to further enhance their own sense of community. Greater levels of wealth and mobility among certain elites make possible the support of businesses, schools, welfare societies, and assorted other charities and enterprises. The money can be spent in communities at home or overseas. Latino elites in the United States, for example, help to promote ethnic human capital by fostering community development (Vallejo 2015). For wealthy Chinese in Southeast Asia, there is much the same pattern of giving to promote their community (Menkhoff 2009). As the degree of wealth being generated around the world expands, particularly for the upper echelons, some of that money will go into building ethnic-oriented institutions. Like many other aspects of privatization, this raises questions of how these various endeavors fit within the overall goals of society, as private money can be spent in any way donors see fit. This funding will alter the ways that some ethnic groups are maintained within cities, as they appeal more to co-ethnics everywhere for financial support.

THE FUTURE OF THE GEOGRAPHY OF ETHNICITY

So, after several millennia of experiencing ethnic diversity and a century of considering it formally, what does the future of ethnicity hold, and how will its geography change? We can only chart the trends that exist now; there are a variety of possible futures, and most of these will be played out in different parts of the world among separate groups. So rather than end with a recitation of all possible contingencies, let us go through some of the tensions that will be manifest at different places in time.

The fundamental tension has to do with how each society chooses to perceive the different ethnic and racial groups in its midst. All societies have a different sense of themselves, of what they mean as a nation. This broader sense informs their expectations of different groups. A broadly assimilationist society will expect each group to eventually blend in. For them, the charge that a group "refuses" to assimilate suggests that it is breaching the social compact. More explicitly multicultural societies are built to tolerate differences, up to a point. Ethiopia's constitution, for instance, allows each ethnic group within its own state certain rights, up to and including the right to secede (Turton 2006). Whether this could occur in fact is an open question since, after all, the successful secession of the one-time Ethiopian territory of Eritrea was a bloody affair. Scale matters a lot here as well. Groups with few members may be permitted wider latitude, as their isolation does not threaten the polity. More numerous groups—precisely because their removal represents an existential threat—may exercise more leverage in calling for as much autonomy as needed.

The double standards in these views are plain for all to see. Most every society sorts groups along a spectrum, from those considered "models" to those who are stigmatized for a variety of perceived sins—sins that can be based on things happening at home and abroad. Nothing shows this better than the present-day treatment of Muslims in Europe and North America. Muslims are a large group—and would certainly not be considered a singular ethnic group, as they encompass so many nationalities and languages. Yet, the discourse around a group can effectively surround them with censure. So, when a president of the United States suggested that all Muslims should be singled out as possibly complicit in terrorist activities, this demonstrates the ability to isolate, categorize, and ethnicize this diverse population. That such rhetoric is echoed by many politicians in European countries suggests the stigmatization is at a global level. Ethnonational movements, seeking to return a nation to a past that was less diverse and more monocultural, have become increasingly popular—tied into populist grievance against cosmopolitan elites. Of course, we have seen this script before, with Jews, Africans, and Chinese being targeted for perceived behavior that threatens the populace. While the current issues will change into something else in the future, it is hard to imagine a future world where such reproach does not impact groups that are perceived as different.

Just as globalization has the capacity to make far-reaching threats seem more immediate, it also allows for far more communication and contact than was ever the case. One of the arguments made for trade is that it is much harder for countries that are exchanging goods and services to go to war with each other (Hegre, Oneal, and Russett 2010). The same could be said for the type of transnational activity that brings the world into every community. Constant exposure and contact is of course not guaranteed to enhance tolerance—witness how neighbors can turn on each other when events change—but it provides the opportunity for people to get to know people as more than a stereotype.

This is not to say that the future will be a model of harmony and well wishes throughout. Yet if we take a longer view and compare the status of ethnic relations one hundred years ago with the situation today, there are dramatic signs of improvement. Racist rhetoric sadly still exists, but it is increasingly a bug instead of a feature of political talk. Most politicians avoid the type of overt demonization and biological determinism so prevalent in the past, and those who speak this way are roundly condemned (though never quite silenced). A more highly educated population is also more likely to find this talk distasteful. As poverty rates across the world decrease and education rates increase, we can only hope that one hundred years from now, people will have made the same level of progress.

The geography of ethnicity began as a sprinkling of culturally distinct people in some urban neighborhoods. These have come to form interconnections between far-flung places, tying together members of the same cultural group from the homeland to all the different communities where they settle. Long and infrequent trips home by sailing ships and steamers have been replaced by regular visits by jet airplane. More dramatic has been the impact of communications, which now allow people a virtual presence to nearly every place on earth—keeping the community close by, even if it is six thousand miles away. The future will only see more of these advances, and the result is that emigrants will never have to really leave their country; their homeland is just a click away.

To be sure, political strife, poverty, and violence still restrict some people from interacting with one another. A horribly repressive regime like North Korea can try to completely shut off the taps of communication. But these attempts do not usually succeed; information seeps out, in even the most hermetic society. The future likely belongs to greater openness and interaction. The increasing flows of social connection, political support, economic investment, and cultural comfort—all harnessed to ever-more sophisticated technologies—will affect ethnicity in every possible way, and globalize the experience of many individual ethnic groups.

The nature of ethnicity within the city, the importance of segregation and clustering, ethnicity's effects on the landscape, and the ramifications, both good and bad, of this geography—these will all be contingent on individual and broader circumstances. We can expect that the variety of spatial forms discussed throughout this book will continue, and that the geography of ethnicity will have real-time consequences into the future. If there is any larger change to discern going forward, it is that transnationalism, increased spatial mobility, and the exacerbation of global inequality will stretch the geography of ethnicity. Of course, residential placement enforced by discrimination, social distance, and political conflict will remain as a cause for true segregation into the future. But it makes sense to envision a future where clustering is significant mostly at larger scales, like counties, where mobile people still command the threshold population needed to maintain institutions. The possibility of wholly ethnic towns or suburbs remains in this scenario, but the need for fine-grained clustering of a small ethnic neighborhood will diminish and be less evident.

While possibly less spatially concentrated into the future, ethnicity is not going anywhere, and will likely play an even bigger role within the cities of the future. As to what this means for these cities, some form of adaptation will be required. The majority group can try to squelch minority groups through persecution, but this can only last so long before the pressure boils over. A country may try to limit the diversity of cities by restricting migration, but this goes against the hunger of people to find their best lives, no matter where it takes them. Newcomers may seek assimilation, but this can become more difficult as ethnics can now call on a continuous stream of cultural and economic reinforcements that keep their culture alive and maintain the essence of the group. Those ethno-national, anti-immigrant movements that have boiled over in recent years appear as more of a rearguard reaction to these powerful trends. A future where ethnic diversity thrives—augmented by multiculturalist policies that vary in practice—still seems an increasingly probable outcome in most places in the world.

References

Abbott, C. W. 2006. Nigerians in North America: New frontiers, old associations. In *The new African diaspora in North America*, edited by K. Konadu-Agyemang, B. K. Takyi, and J. A. Arthur, 141–65. Lanham, MD: Lexington Books.

Abrahamson, M. 2005. *Urban enclaves*. New York: Macmillan.

Abu-Lughod, J. L. 1987. The Islamic city: Historic myth, Islamic essence, and contemporary relevance. *International Journal of Middle East Studies* 19(2): 155–76.

———. 2007. *Race, space, and riots in Chicago, New York, and Los Angeles*. New York: Oxford University Press.

Adachi, N. 2006. Constructing Japanese Brazilian identity: From agrarian migrants to urban white-collar workers. In *Japanese diasporas: Unsung pasts, conflicting presents and uncertain futures*, edited by N. Adachi, 102–20. New York: Routledge.

Adams, J. K. 2006. Going Deutsch: Heritage tourism and identity in German Texas. PhD diss., University of Texas at Austin.

Adams, P. C., and R. Ghose. 2003. India.com: The construction of a space between. *Progress in Human Geography* 27(4): 414–37.

Adams, R. 1966. *The evolution of urban society: Early Mesopotamia and pre-Hispanic Mexico*. Chicago: Aldine Publishers.

Agyei-Mensah, S., and G. Owusu. 2010. Segregated by neighbourhoods? A portrait of ethnic diversity in the neighbourhoods of the Accra Metropolitan Area, Ghana. *Population, Space and Place* 16(6): 499–516.

Airriess, C. A., ed. 2015. *Contemporary ethnic geographies in America*, 2nd edition. Lanham, MD: Rowman & Littlefield.

Ajulu, R. 2002. Politicised ethnicity, competitive politics and conflict in Kenya: A historical perspective. *African Studies* 61(2): 251–68.

Alba, R. D. 1985. The twilight of ethnicity among Americans of European ancestry: The case of Italians. *Ethnic and Racial Studies* 8(1): 134–58.

Alba, R. D., J. R. Logan, and K. Crowder. 1997. White ethnic neighborhoods and assimilation: The greater New York region, 1980–1990. *Social Forces* 75(3): 883–912.

Alba, R. D., and V. Nee. 2014. Assimilation. In *An introduction to immigrant incorporation studies: European perspectives*, edited by J. Rath, 53–70. Amsterdam: Amsterdam University Press.

Alberts, H. 2006. Geographic boundaries of the Cuban enclave economy in Miami. In *Landscapes of the ethnic economy*, edited by D. Kaplan and W. Li, 35–48. Lanham, MD: Rowman & Littlefield.

Aldrich, H., J. Cater, T. Jones, D. McEvoy, and P. Velleman 1985. Ethnic residential concentration and the protected market hypothesis. *Soci.al Forces* 63(4): 996–1009.

Allen, J. P., and E. Turner. 1989. The most ethnically diverse urban places in the United States. *Urban Geography* 10(6): 523–39.

———. 1997. *The ethnic quilt: Population diversity in Southern California*. Northridge: Center for Geographical Studies, California State University, Northridge.

Anas, A. 2006. Ethnic segregation and ghettos. In *A companion to urban economics*, edited by R. Arnott and D. McMillen, 94–122. Malden, MA: Blackwell Publishing.

Anderson, K. J. 1987. The idea of Chinatown: The power of place and institutional practice in the making of a racial category. *Annals of the Association of American Geographers* 77(4): 580–98.

Andersson, E. K., J. Östh, and B. Malmberg. 2010. Ethnic segregation and performance inequality in the Swedish school system: A regional perspective. *Environment and Planning A* 42(11): 2674–86.

Andersson, L., M. Hammarstedt, and E. Neuman. 2012. Residential mobility, tipping behaviour, and ethnic segregation: Evidence from Sweden. Working Paper, Linnaeus School of Business and Economics.

Arreola, D. D. 1995. Urban ethnic landscape identity. *Geographical Review* 85(4): 518–34.

Ashworth, G. 2011. Public pasts in plural societies: Models for management in the postsecular city. In *Postsecular cities: Space, theory and practice*, edited by J. Beaumont and C. Baker, 168–83. London: Bloomsbury.

Asmal, K. 2000. Truth, reconciliation and justice: The South African experience in perspective. *Modern Law Review* 63: 1–24.

Aubet, M. E. 2001. *The Phoenicians and the West: Politics, colonies and trade*. Cambridge: Cambridge University Press.

Bailey, B. 2007. Multilingual forms of talk and identity work. In *Handbook of multilingualism and multilingual communication*, edited by P. Auer and W. Li, 341–69. Berlin: Walter de Gruyter.

Bailey, T., and R. Waldinger. 1991. Primary, secondary, and enclave labor markets: A training systems approach. *American Sociological Review* 56(4): 432–45.

Balsdon, J. P. V. D. 1979. *Romans and aliens*. London: Duckworth.

Banting, K., and W. Kymlicka, eds. 2006. *Multiculturalism and the welfare state: Recognition and redistribution in contemporary democracies*. New York: Oxford University Press.

Barber, B. 1995. *Jihad vs. McWorld*. New York: Random House.

Barkan, E. R. 2006. Immigration, incorporation, assimilation, and the limits of transnationalism: Introduction. *Journal of American Ethnic History* 25(2/3): 7–32.

Barrett, G. A., and D. McEvoy. 2006. The evolution of Manchester's curry mile: From suburban shopping street to ethnic destination. In *Landscapes of the ethnic economy*, edited by D. Kaplan and W. Li, 193–207. Lanham, MD: Rowman & Littlefield.

Barros, V., and J. Marillier. 2010. A La Goutte-d'Or, La polemique ne prend pas. *Liberation*, 22 December. http://www.liberation.fr/societe/2010/12/22/a-la -goutte-d-or-la-polemique-ne-prend-pas_702350.

Barth, F., ed. 1969. *Ethnic groups and boundaries: The social organization of culture difference*. Boston: Little, Brown and Company.

Baser, B., and A. Swain. 2009. Diaspora design versus homeland realities: Case study of Armenian diaspora. *Caucasian Review of International Affairs* 3(1): 45–62.

Bekker, S., and A. Leildé. 2003. Is multiculturalism a workable policy in South Africa? *International Journal of Multicultural Societies* 5(2): 121–36.

Bell, S., S. Alves, E. S. de Oliveira, and A. Zuin. 2010. Migration and land use change in Europe: A review. Living Reviews in Landscape Research, 41–49.

Berry, B. J. L., and P. H. Rees. 1969. The factorial ecology of Calcutta. *American Journal of Sociology* 74(5): 445–91.

Berry, K. A., and M. L. Henderson. 2002. *Geographical identities of ethnic America: Race, space, and place*. Reno: University of Nevada Press.

Bhabha, H. 1994. *The location of culture*. New York: Routledge.

Bhardwaj, S. M., and N. M. Rao. 1990. Asian Indians in the United States: A geographic appraisal. In *South Asians overseas: Migration and ethnicity*, edited by C. Clarke, C. Peach, and S. Vertovec, 197–217. Cambridge: Cambridge University Press.

Bickford-Smith, V., E. van Heyningen, and N. Worden. 1999. *Cape Town in the twentieth century: An illustrated social history*. Claremont, South Africa: David Philip Publishers.

Blum, A. 2002. Resistance to identity categorization in France. In *Census and identity: The politics of race, ethnicity, and language in national censuses*, edited by D. Kertzer and D. Arel, 121–47. Cambridge: Cambridge University Press.

Boal, F. W. 1969. Territoriality on the Shankill-Falls Divide, Belfast. *Irish Geography* 6(1): 30–50.

———. 1976. Ethnic residential segregation. In *Social areas in cities: Spatial processes and form*, edited by D. Herbert and R. J. Johnston, 41–79. Chicago: University of Chicago Press.

Bogardus, E. S. 1925. Measuring social distance. *Journal of Applied Sociology* 9(2): 299–308.

Bollens, S. A. 2002. Urban planning and intergroup conflict: Confronting a fractured public interest. *Journal of the American Planning Association* 68(1): 22–42.

———. 2012. *Cities and soul in divided societies*. New York: Routledge.

Bolt, G., R. Van Kempen, and M. Van Ham. 2008. Minority ethnic groups in the Dutch housing market: Spatial segregation, relocation dynamics and housing policy. *Urban Studies* 45(7): 1359–84.

Bonacich, E. 1973. A theory of middleman minorities. *American Sociological Review* 38(5): 583–94.

Borman, K. M., T. McNulty, D. Michael, D. Eitle, R. Lee, L. Johnson, D. Cobb-Roberts, S. Dorn, and B. Shircliffe. 2004. Accountability in a postdesegregation era:

The continuing significance of racial segregation in Florida's schools. *American Educational Research Journal* 41(3): 605–31.

Bose, N. 1965. Calcutta: A premature metropolis. *Scientific American* 213(3): 90–102.

Boswell, T. D., and J. R. Curtis. 1984. *The Cuban-American experience: Culture, images and perspectives*. Totowa, NJ: Rowman & Allanheld Publishers.

Bourgeois, D., and Y. Bourgeois. 2005. Territory, institutions and national identity: The case of Acadians in Greater Moncton, Canada. *Urban Studies* 42(7): 1123–38.

Bramadat, P. A. 2001. Shows, selves, and solidarity: Ethnic identity and cultural spectacles in Canada. *Canadian Ethnic Studies* 33(3): 78.

Breton, R. 1964. Institutional completeness of ethnic communities and the personal relations of immigrants. *American Journal of Sociology* 70(2): 193–205.

———. 1988. From ethnic to civic nationalism: English Canada and Quebec. *Ethnic and Racial Studies* 11(1): 85–102.

Brickell, K., and A. Datta, eds. 2011. *Translocal geographies*. Burlington, VT: Ashgate Publishing.

Brinkerhoff, J. M. 2009. *Digital diasporas: Identity and transnational engagement*. Cambridge: Cambridge University Press.

Brodkin, K. 1998. *How Jews became white folks and what that says about race in America*. New Brunswick, NJ: Rutgers University Press.

Brooks, D. 2003. People like us: We all pay lip service to the melting pot, but we really prefer the congealing pot. *Atlantic Monthly* 29(2): 29–33.

Brown, K. 1983. Race, class and culture: Towards a theorization of the "choice/constraint" concept. In *Social interaction and ethnic segregation*, edited by P. Jackson, 185–203. London: Academic Press.

Brown, L., and S.-Y. Chung. 2006. Spatial segregation, segregation indices and the geographical perspective. *Population, Space and Place* 12: 125–43.

Browning, R. P., D. R. Marshall, and D. H. Tabb. 1984. *Protest is not enough: The struggle of blacks and Hispanics for equality in urban politics*. Berkeley: University of California Press.

———. 1990. *Racial politics in American cities*. New York: Longman Publishing Group.

Brubaker, R. 1992. *Citizenship and nationhood in France and Germany*. Cambridge, MA: Harvard University Press.

———. 2001. The return of assimilation? Changing perspectives on immigration and its sequels in France, Germany, and the United States. *Ethnic and Racial Studies* 24(4): 531–48.

Brush, J. E. 1962. *The morphology of Indian cities*.

Bulmer, M. 1984. *The Chicago school of sociology*. Chicago: University of Chicago Press.

Burton, J. F., M. Farrell, F. Lord, and R. Lord. 2002. *Confinement and ethnicity: An overview of World War II Japanese American relocation sites*. Seattle: University of Washington Press.

Buttimer, A. 1980. Social space and the planning of residential areas. In *The human experience of space and place*, edited by A. Buttimer and D. Seamon, 21–54. Abingdon, UK: Routledge.

Calame, J., and E. Charlesworth. 2009. *Divided cities*. Philadelphia: University of Pennsylvania Press.

Calimani, R. 1987. *The ghetto of Venice: A history*. New York: M. Evans and Company.

Cameron, C., D. Epstein, and S. O'Halloran. 1996. Do majority-minority districts maximize substantive black representation in Congress? *American Political Science Review* 90(4): 794–812.

Campbell, J. 2006. *Middle passages: African American journeys to Africa, 1787–2005*. New York: Penguin Press.

Carlá, A. 2007. Living apart in the same room: Analysis of the management of linguistic diversity in Bolzano. *Ethnopolitics* 6(2): 285–313.

Cartier, C. 2003. Diaspora and social restructuring in postcolonial Malaysia. In *The Chinese diaspora: Space, place, mobility, and identity*, edited by L. Ma and C. Cartier, 69–96. Lanham, MD: Rowman & Littlefield.

Castañeda, E. 2012. Place of stigma: Ghettos, barrios, and banlieues. In *The Ghetto: Contemporary Global Issues and Controversies*, edited by R. Hutchison and B. Haynes, 159–90. Boulder, CO: Westview Press.

Castles, S. 2006. Guestworkers in Europe: A resurrection? *International Migration Review* 40(4): 741–66.

Central Intelligence Agency. 2017. *The world factbook*. https://www.cia.gov/library/publications/the-world-factbook/.

Chabrol, M. 2011. De nouvelles formes de gentrification? Dynamiques residentielles et commerciales a Chateau-Rouge (Paris). PhD diss., Université de Poitiers.

Chacko, E. 2003. Ethiopian ethos and the making of ethnic places in the Washington metropolitan area. *Journal of Cultural Geography* 20(2): 21–42.

Chaney, J. 2010. The formation of a Hispanic enclave in Nashville, Tennessee. *Southeastern Geographer* 50(1): 17–38.

Chang, T. C. 2000. Singapore's Little India: A tourist attraction as a contested landscape. *Urban Studies* 37(2): 343–66.

Christopher, A. J. 2001. Urban segregation in post-apartheid South Africa. *Urban Studies* 38(3): 449–66.

Clark, W. A. V. 1991. Residential preferences and neighborhood racial segregation: A test of the Schelling segregation model. *Demography* 28(1): 1–19.

Clarke, C., and C. Peach. 1990. *South Asians overseas: Migration and ethnicity*. Cambridge: Cambridge University Press.

Clay, G. 1980. *Close-up: How to read the American city*. Chicago: University of Chicago Press.

Cochran, D. C. 1995. Ethnic diversity and democratic stability: The case of Irish Americans. *Political Science Quarterly* 110(4): 587–604.

Cohen, R. 1997. *Global diasporas: An introduction*. Seattle: University of Washington Press.

Cole, S. 2005. Capitalism and freedom: Manumissions and the slave market in Louisiana, 1725–1820. *Journal of Economic History* 65(4): 1008–27.

Conforti, Y. 2010. East and west in Jewish nationalism: Conflicting types in the Zionist vision? *Nations and Nationalism* 16(2): 201–19.

Connor, W. 1978. A nation is a nation, is a state, is an ethnic group, is a . . . *Ethnic and Racial Studies* 1(4): 379–88.

————. 1986. The impact of homelands upon diasporas. In *Modern diasporas in international politics*, edited by G. Sheffer, 16–46. New York: St. Martin's Press.

————. 1993. Beyond reason: The nature of the ethnonational bond. *Ethnic and Racial Studies* 16(3): 373–89.

Conversi, D. 2004. Can nationalism studies and ethnic/racial studies be brought together? *Journal of Ethnic and Migration Studies* 30(4): 815–29.

Conzen, M. 1993. Culture regions, homelands, and ethnic archipelagos in the United States: Methodological considerations. *Journal of Cultural Geography* 13(2): 13–29.

Cooper, H. L. F., J. E. Brady, S. R. Friedman, B. Tempalski, K. Gostnell, and P. L. Flom. 2008. Estimating the prevalence of injection drug use among black and white adults in large U.S. metropolitan areas over time (1992–2002): Estimation methods and prevalence trends. *Journal of Urban Health* 85(6): 826–56.

Cristaldi, F. 2002. Multiethnic Rome: Toward residential segregation? *GeoJournal* 58(2/3): 81–90.

Cronon, W. 1983. *Changes in the land: Indians, colonists and the ecology of New England*. New York: Macmillan.

Curtin, P. D. 1984. *Cross-cultural trade in world history*. Cambridge: Cambridge University Press.

Curtis, J. 2016. Transcribing from the mind to the map: Tracing the evolution of a concept. *Geographical Review* 106(3): 338–59.

Cybriwsky, R. A. 1978. Social aspects of neighborhood change. *Annals of the Association of American Geographers* 68(1): 17–33.

Davis, D. B. 2006. *Inhuman bondage: The rise and fall of slavery in the New World*. New York: Oxford Press.

Dawson, D. 1991. Panem and cicenses? A critical analysis of ethnic and multicultural festivals. *Journal of Applied Recreation Research* 16(1): 35–52.

Dear, M., and A. Burridge. 2005. Cultural integration and hybridization at the United States–Mexico borderlands. *Cahiers de géographie du Québec* 49(138): 301–18.

Deliège, R. 1999. *The Untouchables of India*. London: Bloomsbury Publishing.

De Souza Briggs, X. 2004. Civilization in color: the multicultural city in three millennia. *City & Community* 3(4): 311–42.

Devadoss, C. A. 2014. Expressions of Tamil identity: A fluid framework of sound and visuals. Master's thesis, Kent State University.

De Vos, G. A., and H. Wagatsuma. 2006. Cultural identity and minority status in Japan. In *Ethnic identity: Problems and prospects for the twenty-first century*, edited by L. Ross, G. De Vos, and T. Tsuda, 119–56. Lanham, MD: AltaMira Press.

Donoghue, J. D. 1957. An Eta community in Japan: The social persistence of outcaste groups. *American Anthropologist* 59(6): 1000–17.

Doomernik, J. 2003. Integration policies towards immigrants and their descendants in the Netherlands. In *The integration of immigrants in European societies: National differences and trends of convergence*, edited by F. Heckmann and D. Schnapper, 165–84. Berlin: Lucius & Lucius.

Douzet, F. 2009. Revisiting black electoral success: Oakland (CA), 40 years later. *Journal of Urban Affairs* 31(3): 243–67.

Douzet, F., and J. Robine. 2015. Les jeunes des banlieues: Neighborhood effects on the immigrant youth experience in France. *Journal of Cultural Geography* 32(1): 40–53.

Driedger, L. 1979. Maintenance of urban ethnic boundaries: The French in St. Boniface. *Sociological Quarterly* 20(1): 89–108.

———. 1999. Immigrant/ethnic/racial segregation: Canadian big three and prairie metropolitan comparison. *Canadian Journal of Sociology* 24(4): 485–510.

Du Bois, W. E. B. (1908) 1980. A reply to Stone. *American Journal of Sociology* 13: 834–38. Reprinted in T. F. Pettigrew, *The sociology of race relations*. New York: Free Press.

Dufoix, S. 2008. Diaspora and nationalism. In *Nations and nationalism: A global historical overview*, edited by G. Herb and D. Kaplan, 1364–78. Santa Barbara: ABC-Clio.

Duncan, O. D., and B. Duncan. 1955. A methodological analysis of segregation indexes. *American Sociological Review* 20(2): 210–17.

Dupont, V. 2004. Socio-spatial differentiation and residential segregation in Delhi: A question of scale? *Geoforum* 35(2): 157–75.

Dürr, E. 2003. Contested urban space. In *Urban ethnic encounters: The spatial consequences*, edited by A. Erdentug and F. Colombijn, 209–25. London: Routledge.

Dutt, A. K., G. D'Sa, and C. B. Monroe. 1989. Factorial ecology of Calcutta (1981) revisited. *GeoJournal* 18(2): 151–62.

Dutt, A. K., and G. M. Pomeroy. 1993. Cities of South Asia. In *Cities of the World*, edited by S. Brunn and J. Williams, 325–70. New York: HarperCollins.

Eade, J., and P. Ruspini. 2014. Multicultural models. In *An introduction to immigrant incorporation studies: European perspectives*, edited by J. Rath, 71–89. Amsterdam: Amsterdam University Press.

Eckert, J., and S. Shetty. 2011. Food systems, planning and quantifying access: Using GIS to plan for food retail. *Applied Geography* 31(4): 1216–23.

Ehrkamp, P. 2005. Placing identities: Transnational practices and local attachments of Turkish immigrants in Germany. *Journal of Ethnic and Migration Studies* 31(2): 345–64.

Elkins, S. 1963. *Slavery: A problem in American intellectual and institutional life*. New York: University Library.

Ellen, I. G., and M. A. Turner. 1997. Does neighborhood matter? Assessing recent evidence. *Housing Policy Debate* 8(4): 833–66.

Eller, J. D., and R. M. Coughlan. 1993. The poverty of primordialism: The demystification of ethnic attachments. *Ethnic and Racial Studies* 16(2): 183–202.

Elsheshtawy, Y. 2008. Transitory sites: Mapping Dubai's "forgotten" urban spaces. *International Journal of Urban and Regional Research* 32(4): 968–88.

Eriksen, T. H. 1993. A future-oriented, non-ethnic nationalism? Mauritius as an exemplary case. *Ethnos* 58(3/4): 197–221.

———. 1997. Ethnicity, race, and nation. In *The Ethnicity Reader: Nationalism, Multiculturalism, and Migration*, edited by M. Guibernau and J. Rex, 33–42. Cambridge, MA: Polity Press.

Esman, M. J. 2009. *Diasporas in the Contemporary World*. Cambridge, MA: Polity Press.

Espiritu, Y. 1992. *Asian American panethnicity: Bridging institutions and identities.* Philadelphia: Temple University Press.

Etzioni, A. 2011. Citizenship in a communitarian perspective. *Ethnicities* 11(3): 336–49.

Falah, G. 1996. Living together apart: Residential segregation in mixed Arab-Jewish cities in Israel. *Urban Studies* 33(6): 823–57.

Fargues, P. 2011. Immigration without inclusion: Non-nationals in nation-building in the Gulf States. *Asian and Pacific Migration Journal* 20(3/4): 273–92.

Farley, R., and W. H. Frey. 1994. Changes in the segregation of whites from blacks during the 1980s: Small steps toward a more integrated society. *American Sociological Review* 59(1): 23–45.

Fenton, S. 2003. *Ethnicity.* Cambridge: Cambridge University Press.

Fieldhouse, E., and D. Cutts. 2008. Diversity, density, and turnout: The effect of neighbourhood ethno-religious composition on voter turnout in Britain. *Political Geography* 27(5): 530–48.

Fielding, A. 2004. Class and space: Social segregation in Japanese cities. *Transactions of the Institute of British Geographers* 29(1): 64–84.

Fincher, R., K. Iveson, H. Leitner, and V. Preston. 2014. Planning in the multicultural city: Celebrating diversity or reinforcing difference? *Progress in Planning* 92: 1–55.

Firman, T. 2004. New town development in Jakarta metropolitan region: A perspective of spatial segregation. *Habitat International* 28(3): 349–68.

Fischer, C. S. 1975. Toward a subcultural theory of urbanism. *American Journal of Sociology* 80(6): 1319–41.

Fong, T. 1994. *The first suburban Chinatown: The remaking of Monterey Park, California.* Philadelphia: Temple University Press.

Fowler, C. S. 2015. Segregation as a multiscalar phenomenon and its implications for neighborhood-scale research: The case of South Seattle, 1990–2010. *Urban Geography* 37(1): 1–25.

Frazier, J. W., and E. Tettey-Fio, eds. 2006. *Race, ethnicity, and place in a changing America.* Binghamton, NY: Global Academic Publishing.

Freedman, A. 2000. *Political participation and ethnic minorities: Chinese overseas in Malaysia, Indonesia, and the United States.* New York: Routledge.

Friedman, T. 2005. *The world is flat: A brief history of the twenty-first century.* New York: Farrar, Straus and Giroux.

Friedrichs, C. R. 1981. The Swiss and German city-states. In *The city-state in five cultures*, edited by C. Thomas and R. Griffeth, 109–42. Santa Barbara: ABC-CLIO.

Fukuyama, F. 1989. The end of history? *The National Interest* 16: 3–18.

Gans, H. J. 1979. Symbolic ethnicity: The future of ethnic groups and cultures in America. *Ethnic and Racial Studies* 2(1): 1–20.

———. 1982. *Urban villagers.* New York: Simon and Schuster.

Geertz, C. 1973. *The interpretation of cultures: Selected essays.* New York: Basic Books.

Genberg, D. 2002. Borders and boundaries in post-war Beirut. In *Urban ethnic encounters: The spatial consequences*, edited by A. Erdentug and F. Colombijn, 81–96. London: Routledge.

Getis, A., and J. K. Ord. 1992. The analysis of spatial association by use of distance statistics. *Geographical Analysis* 24(3): 189–206.

Girouard, M. 1985. *Cities and people: A social and architectural history.* New Haven, CT: Yale University Press.

Gitelman, Z. 1998. The decline of the diaspora Jewish nation: Boundaries, content, and Jewish identity. *Jewish Social Studies* 4(2): 112–32.

Glazer, N., and D. P. Moynihan. 1963. *Beyond the melting pot: The Negroes, Puerto Ricans, Jews, Italians and Irish of New York City.* Cambridge, MA: MIT Press and Harvard University Press.

Glazer, N., and D. P. Moynihan, eds. 1975. *Ethnicity: Theory and experience.* Cambridge, MA: Harvard University Press.

Glick-Schiller, N., L. Basch, and C. Blanc-Szanton. 1992. Towards a definition of transnationalism. *Annals of the New York Academy of Sciences* 645(1): ix–xiv.

Godfrey, B. J. 1991. Modernizing the Brazilian city. *Geographical Review* 81(1): 18–34.

Goldfarb, M. 2009. *Emancipation: How liberating Europe's Jews from the ghetto led to revolution and renaissance.* New York: Simon and Schuster.

Goldstein, S. 1969. Socioeconomic differentials among religious groups in the United States. *American Journal of Sociology* 74(6): 612–31.

Goodstein, L. 2010. Across nation, mosque projects meet opposition. *New York Times,* 8 August, A1.

Gordon, C., M. Purciel-Hill, N. Ghai, L. Kaufman, R. Graham, and G. Van Wye. 2011. Measuring food deserts in New York City's low-income neighborhoods. *Health & Place* 17(2): 696–700.

Gordon, M. 1964. *Assimilation in American life: The role of race, religion, and national origins.* New York: Oxford University Press.

Gould, S. J. 1996. *The mismeasure of man.* New York: W. W. Norton & Company.

Grady, S. C. 2006. Racial disparities in low birthweight and the contribution of residential segregation: A multilevel analysis. *Social Science & Medicine* 63(12): 3013–29.

Greeley, A. M. 1974. *Ethnicity in the United States: A preliminary reconnaissance.* New York: Wiley.

Green, E. D. 2006. Redefining ethnicity. 47th Annual International Studies Association Convention, San Diego, CA, 22 March. http://research.allacademic.com/meta/p_mla_apa_research_citation/0/9/7/9/3/p97937_index.html.

Greenberg, J. 2010. Report on Roma education today: From slavery to segregation and beyond. *Columbia Law Review* 110(4): 919–1001.

Greiner, C., and P. Sakdapolrak. 2013. Translocality: Concepts, applications and emerging research perspectives. *Geography Compass* 7(5): 373–84.

Griffeth, R. 1981. The Hausa city-states from 1450 to 1804. In *The city-state in five cultures,* edited by C. Thomas and R. Griffeth, 143–80. Santa Barbara: ABC-CLIO.

Grofe, M. 2005. Anthropological Currents: The Construction of Maya Identity. *Current Anthropology* 46(1): 1–2.

Grosby, S. 1995. Territoriality: The transcendental, primordial feature of modern societies. *Nations and Nationalism* 1(2): 143–62.

Hackworth, J., and J. Rekers. 2005. Ethnic packaging and gentrification: The case of four neighborhoods in Toronto. *Urban Affairs Review* 41(2): 211–36.

Halter, M. 2007. *Shopping for identity: The marketing of ethnicity.* New York: Schocken Books.

Hane, Mi. 1982. *Peasants, rebels, and outcastes: The underside of modern Japan*. New York: Pantheon Books.

Hardwick, S. W. 2010. Inscribing ethnicity on the land. In *The making of the American landscape*, edited by M. Conzen, 229–52. New York: Routledge.

Hartshorne, R. (1939) 1949. *The nature of geography: A critical survey of current thought in the light of the past*. Reprinted in *Annals of the Association of American Geographers* 29(3/4): 171–658.

Hechter, M. 1986. Rational choice theory and the study of race and ethnic relations. In *Theories of race and ethnic relations*, edited by J. Rex and D. Mason, 264–79. Cambridge: Cambridge University Press.

Heckmann, F. 2003. From ethnic nation to universalistic immigrant integration: Germany. In *The integration of immigrants in European societies: National differences and trends of convergence*, edited by F. Heckmann and D. Schnapper, 45–78. Berlin: Lucius & Lucius.

Hegre, H., J. R. Oneal, and B. Russett. 2010. Trade does promote peace: New simultaneous estimates of the reciprocal effects of trade and conflict. *Journal of Peace Research* 47(6): 763–74.

Heller, M. 1985. Ethnic relations and language use in Montreal. In *Language of Inequality*, edited by N. Wolfson and J. Manes, 75–90. Berlin: Mouton Publishers.

Herb, G. H., and D. H. Kaplan, eds. 1999. *Nested identities: Nationalism, territory, and scale*. Lanham, MD: Rowman and Littlefield.

———. 2008. *Nations and nationalism: A global historical overview*. Santa Barbara: ABC-Clio.

Herberg, E. N. 1989. *Ethnic groups in Canada: Adaptations and transitions*. Scarborough, ON: Nelson Canada.

Herberg, W. 1983. *Protestant—Catholic—Jew: An essay in American religious sociology*. Chicago: University of Chicago Press.

Hero, R. E., and C. Tolbert. 2007. Voter turnout and other forms of participation in context. In *Racial diversity and social capital*, edited by R. Hero, 99–130. New York: Cambridge University Press.

Hester, J. T. 2002. Repackaging difference: The Korean "Theming" of a shopping street in Osaka, Japan. In *Urban ethnic encounters: The spatial consequences*, edited by A. Erdentug and F. Colombijn, 177–91. London: Routledge.

Hickman, P. 2013. "Third places" and social interaction in deprived neighbourhoods in Great Britain. *Journal of Housing and the Built Environment* 28(2): 221–36.

Hillier, A. E. 2003. Redlining and the home owners' loan corporation. *Journal of Urban History* 29(4): 394–420.

Hiro, D. 1975. *The untouchables of India*. London: Minority Rights Group.

Hirsch, A. R. 2009. *Making the second ghetto: Race and housing in Chicago, 1940–1960*. Chicago: University of Chicago Press.

Hoelscher, S. D., and R. C. Ostergren. 1993. Old European homelands in the American middle west. *Journal of Cultural Geography* 13(2): 87–106.

Holloway, S. R., M. Ellis, R. Wright, and M. Hudson. 2005. Partnering "out" and fitting in: Residential segregation and the neighbourhood contexts of mixed-race households. *Population, Space and Place* 11(4): 299–324.

Honig, E. 1992. *Creating Chinese ethnicity: Subei people in Shanghai, 1850–1980*. New Haven, CT: Yale University Press.

Hope, V. 2000. Status and identity in the Roman world. In *Experiencing Rome: Culture, identity and power in the Roman Empire*, edited by J. Huskinson, 125–52. London: Routledge.

Horne, G. 2009. *W. E. B. Du Bois: A biography*. Santa Barbara: Greenwood Pub Group.

Horowitz, D. 2000. *Ethnic groups in conflict*. Berkeley: University of California Press.

Hou, J., and A. Tanner. 2002. Constructed identities and contested space in Seattle's Chinatown-International District. *CELA 2002 Conference Proceedings*. Council of Educators in Landscape Architecture Conference, Syracuse, New York, 25–27 September.

Hourani, Albert. (1991) 2013. *A history of the Arab peoples*. Revised edition. London: Faber & Faber.

Howe, I. 1976. *World of our fathers: The journey of the Eastern European Jews to America and the life they found and made*. New York: Simon and Schuster.

Howell-Moroney, M. 2005. The geography of opportunity and unemployment: An integrated model of residential segregation and spatial mismatch. *Journal of Urban Affairs* 27(4): 353–77.

Hume, S. E. 2008. Ethnic and national identities of Africans in the United States. *Geographical Review* 98(4): 496–512.

Huntington, S. P. 1997. *The clash of civilizations and the remaking of world order*. New York: Simon and Schuster.

Hutchison, R., and B. Haynes, eds. 2012. *The ghetto: Contemporary global issues and controversies*. Boulder, CO: Westview Press.

Hutnyk, J. 2005. Hybridity. *Ethnic and Racial Studies* 28(1): 79–102.

Iceland, J., D. Weinberg, and E. Steinmetz. 2002. *Racial and ethnic residential segregation in the United States: 1980–2000*. Washington, DC: U.S. Census Bureau.

Inglehart, R. F., and P. Norris. 2016. Trump, Brexit, and the rise of populism: Economic have-nots and cultural backlash. Harvard Kennedy School Faculty Research Working Paper Series, August.

Ip, D. 2005. Contesting Chinatown: Place-making and the emergence of "ethnoburbia" in Brisbane, Australia. *GeoJournal* 64(1): 63–74.

Isajiw, W. W. 1974. Definitions of ethnicity. *Ethnicity* 1(2): 111–24.

Jackson, H. 2016. The long-form census is back, it's online—and this time, it's mandatory. *CNC News*, 2 May. http://www.cbc.ca/news/politics/mandatory-census-mail-out-1.3557511.

Jackson, K. T. 1985. *Crabgrass frontier: The suburbanization of the United States*. New York: Oxford University Press.

Jenkins, L. 2008. India. In *Nations and nationalism: A global historical overview*, edited by G. Herb and D. Kaplan, 1201–12. Santa Barbara: ABC-CLIO.

Jenkins, R. 1994. Rethinking ethnicity: Identity, categorization and power. *Ethnic and Racial Studies* 17(2): 197–223.

Johansson, O., and M. Cornebise. 2010. Place branding goes to the neighbourhood: The case of pseudo-Swedish Andersonville. *Geografiska Annaler: Series B, Human Geography* 92(3): 187–204.

Johnston, R., M. Poulsen, and J. Forrest. 2009. Research note—measuring ethnic residential segregation: Putting some more geography in. *Urban Geography* 30(1): 91–109.

———. 2010. Moving on from indices, refocusing on mix: On measuring and understanding ethnic patterns of residential segregation. *Journal of Ethnic and Migration Studies* 36(4): 697–706.

———. 2015. Increasing diversity within increasing diversity: The changing ethnic composition of London's neighbourhoods, 2001–2011. *Population, Space and Place* 21(1): 38–53.

Jones-Correa, M. 2009. Immigrant contexts and ethnic violence in Europe and the United States. Paper presented at the conference Together or separate: Spatial concentration and immigrant incorporation in the United States, France, and Great Britain. University of Paris 8, Paris.

Kain, J. F. 1968. Housing segregation, Negro employment, and metropolitan decentralization. *The Quarterly Journal of Economics* 82(2): 175–97.

K'Akumu, O. A., and W. Olima. 2007. The dynamics and implications of residential segregation in Nairobi. *Habitat International* 31(1): 87–99.

Kallen, E. 1982. Multiculturalism: Ideology, policy and reality. *Journal of Canadian Studies* 17(1): 51–63.

Kalra, V., R. Kaur, and J. Hutnyk. 2005. *Diaspora and Hybridity*. Thousand Oaks, CA: Sage Publishing.

Kantowicz, E. R. 1995. The ethnic church. In *Ethnic Chicago: A multicultural portrait*, edited by M. Holli and P. Jones, 346–77. Grand Rapids, MI: William B. Eerdmans.

Kaplan, D. H. 1990. "Maîtres chez nous": The evolution of French-Canadian spatial identity. *American Review of Canadian Studies* 19(4): 407–28.

———. 1992. Nationalism at a micro-scale: Educational segregation in Montreal. *Political Geography* 11(3): 259–82.

———. 1997. The creation of an ethnic economy: Indochinese business expansion in Saint Paul. *Economic Geography* 73(2): 214–33.

———. 1998. The spatial structure of urban ethnic economies. *Urban Geography* 19(6): 489–501.

———. 2001. The uneven distribution of employment opportunities: Neighborhood and race in Cleveland, Ohio. *Journal of Urban Affairs* 21(2): 189–212.

Kaplan, D. H., and S. Holloway. 1998. *Segregation in cities*. Washington, DC: Association of American Geographers.

Kaplan, D. H., S. Holloway, and J. Wheeler. 2014. *Urban geography*. New York: Wiley Global Education.

Kaplan, D. H., and W. Li. 2006. *Landscapes of the ethnic economy*. Lanham, MD: Rowman & Littlefield.

Kaplan, D. H., and G. G. Sommers. 2009. An analysis of the relationship between housing foreclosures, lending practices, and neighborhood ecology: Evidence from a distressed county. *Professional Geographer* 61(1): 101–20.

Kasarda, J. D. 1989. Urban industrial transition and the underclass. *The Annals of the American Academy of Political and Social Science* 501(1): 26–47.

———. 1990. Structural factors affecting the location and timing of urban underclass growth. *Urban Geography* 11(3): 234–64.

Kasinitz, P. 2004. Race, assimilation and "Second Generations": Past and present. In *Not just black and white*, edited by N. Foner and G. Frederickson, 278–98. New York: Russell Sage Foundation.

Katz, N. 2000. *Who are the Jews of India?* Berkeley: University of California Press.

Kaufmann, E. 2016. Assimilation and the immigration debate: Shifting people's attitudes. *Fabian Essays*, 26 September. http://www.fabians.org.uk/assimilation -and-the-immigration-debate/.

Kedourie, E. 1993. *Nationalism.* 4th ed. Cambridge, MA: Blackwell Publishing.

Kertzer, D. I., and D. Arel, eds. 2002. *Census and identity: The politics of race, ethnicity, and language in national censuses.* Cambridge: Cambridge University Press.

Kim, N. H.-J. 2015. The retreat of multiculturalism? Explaining the South Korean exception. *American Behavioral Scientist* 59(6): 727–46.

King, C. 1998. Introduction: Nationalism, transnationalism, and postcommunism. In *Nations abroad: Diaspora politics and international relations in the former Soviet Union,* edited by C. King, 1–26. Boulder, CO: Westview Press.

Koopmans, R. 2013. Multiculturalism and immigration: A contested field in cross-national comparison. *Annual Review of Sociology* 39: 147–69.

Kosambi, M., and J. E. Brush. 1988. Three colonial port cities in India. *Geographical Review* 78(1): 32–47.

Kotlowitz, A. 1991. *There are no children here: The story of two boys growing up in the other America.* New York: Anchor.

Kovacs, D. 1998. Relativism and pluralism in ancient Greece. *Boston University Journal of Education* 180(3): 1–20.

Kozol, J. (1991) 2012. *Savage inequalities: Children in America's schools.* New York: Broadway Books.

Kraay, H. 2001. *Race, state, and armed forces in independence-era Brazil: Bahia, 1790s– 1840s.* Palo Alto, CA: Stanford University Press.

Kristiansen, S., and A. Ryen. 2002. Enacting their business environments: Asian entrepreneurs in East Africa. *African and Asian Studies* 1(3): 165–86.

Kugelmass, J., and A. Orla-Bukowska. 1998. "If you build it they will come": Re-creating an historic Jewish district in post-Communist Kraków. *City & Society* 10(1): 315–53.

Kusek, W. A. 2014. The construction and development of diasporic networks by recent Polish migrants to London, UK. PhD diss., Kent State University.

Kuusisto-Arponen, A. 2002. Urban borderlands and the politics of place in Northern Ireland. In *Boundaries and place: European borderlands in geographical context,* edited by D. Kaplan and J. Häkli, 159–77. Lanham, MD: Rowman and Littlefield.

Kwate, N. 2008. Fried chicken and fresh apples: Racial segregation as a fundamental cause of fast food density in black neighborhoods. *Health & Place* 14(1): 32–44.

Kymlicka, W. 2012. *Multiculturalism: Success, failure, and the future.* Washington, DC: Transatlantic Council on Migration, Migration Policy Institute.

Lacoste, Y. 2006. *Géopolitique: La longue histoire d'aujourd'hui.* Paris: Larousse.

Lai, D. C. 1990. The visual character of Chinatowns (vision, culture and landscape). *Places* 7(1): 29–31.

Lal, B. V. 2003. Heartbreak islands: Reflections on Fiji in transition. *Asia Pacific Viewpoint* 44(3): 335–50.

Law, K.-V., and K.-M. Lee. 2012. The myth of multiculturalism in "Asia's world city": Incomprehensive policies for ethnic minorities in Hong Kong. *Journal of Asian Public Policy* 5(1): 117–34.

Lawrence, C. 2007. *Blood and oranges: Immigrant labor and European markets in rural Greece*. New York: Berghahn Books.

———. 2010. "Τ'ωρα είμαστε όλοι ρατσιστές": εργασία και ανισότητα στην αγροτική Ελλάδα ["We are all racists now": Labor and inequality in rural Greece]. Πανελλήνια Γεωγραφικά Συνέδρια, Συλλογή Πρακτικών, 3, 351–57.

Leisch, H. 2002a. Perception and use of space by ethnic Chinese in Jakarta. In *Urban ethnic encounters: The spatial consequences*, edited by A. Erdentug and F. Colombijn, 99–108. London: Routledge.

———. 2002b. Gated communities in Indonesia. *Cities* 19(5): 341–50.

Lesińska, M. 2014. The European backlash against immigration and multiculturalism. *Journal of Sociology* 50(1): 37–50.

Le Vine, V. T. 1997. Conceptualizing "ethnicity" and "ethnic conflict": A controversy revisited. *Studies in Comparative International Development* 32(2): 45–75.

Levitt, P., and D. Lamba-Nieves. 2010. It's not just about the economy stupid: Social remittances revisited. *Migration Information Source*, 21 May. Migration Policy Institute. http://www.migrationpolicy.org/article/its-not-just-about -economy-stupid-social-remittances-revisited.

Ley, D. 2004. Transnational spaces and everyday lives. *Transactions of the Institute of British Geographers* 29(2): 151–64.

———. 2008. The immigrant church as an urban service hub. *Urban Studies* 45(10): 2057–74.

———. 2010. *Millionaire migrants: Trans-Pacific life lines*. Malden, MA: Wiley-Blackwell.

Li, W. 1998. Anatomy of a new ethnic settlement: The Chinese ethnoburb in Los Angeles. *Urban Studies* 35(3): 479–501.

Li, W., G. Dymski, M. Chee, H. Ahn, C. Aldana, and Y. Zhou. 2006. How ethnic banks matter: Banking and community/economic development in Los Angeles. In *Landscapes of the Ethnic Economy*, edited by D. Kaplan and W. Li, 113–34. Lanham, MD: Rowman & Littlefield.

Lieberson, S. 1980. *A piece of the pie: Blacks and white immigrants since 1880*. Berkeley: University of California Press.

Light, I., and S. Karageorgis. 1994. The ethnic economy. In *The handbook of economic sociology*, edited by N. Smelser and R. Swedberg, 647–71. Princeton, NJ: Princeton University Press.

Lin, J. 1998. *Reconstructing Chinatown: Ethnic enclave, global change*. Minneapolis: University of Minnesota Press.

Lleras, C. 2008. Race, racial concentration, and the dynamics of educational inequality across urban and suburban schools. *American Educational Research Journal* 45(4): 886–912.

Lo, L. 2006. Changing geography of Toronto's Chinese ethnic economy. In *Landscapes of the ethnic economy*, edited by D. Kaplan and W. Li, 83–96. Lanham, MD: Rowman & Littlefield.

———. 2009. The role of ethnicity in the geography of consumption. *Urban Geography* 30(4): 391–415.

Logan, J. R., W. Zhang, and R. Alba. 2002. Immigrant enclaves and ethnic communities in New York and Los Angeles. *American Sociological Review* 67(2): 299–322.

Lynch, K. 1960. *The image of the city*. Cambridge, MA: MIT Press.

Malheiros, J. 2002. Ethni-cities: Residential patterns in the Northern European and Mediterranean metropolises—implications for policy design. *International Journal of Population Geography* 8(2): 107–34.

Malik, K. 2015. The failure of multiculturalism. *Foreign Affairs* 94(2): 21–32.

Malmberg, B., E. Andersson, and J. Östh. 2013. Segregation and urban unrest in Sweden. *Urban Geography* 34(7): 1031–1046.

Maly, M. 2000. The neighborhood diversity index: A complementary measure of racial residential settlement. *Journal of Urban Affairs* 22(1): 37–47.

Mann, Jatinder. 2012. The introduction of multiculturalism in Canada and Australia, 1960s–1970s. *Nations and Nationalism* 18(3): 483–503.

Marcuse, P. 1997. The enclave, the citadel, and the ghetto: What has changed in the post-Fordist U.S. city. *Urban Affairs Review* 33(2): 228–64.

Maré, D. C., R. Pinkerton, J. Poot, and A. Coleman. 2012. Residential sorting across Auckland neighbourhoods. *New Zealand Population Review* 38, 23–54.

Markman, S. D. 1978. The gridiron town plan and the caste system in colonial Central America. In *Urbanization in the Americas from its beginnings to the present*, edited by R. Schaedel, J. Hardoy, and N. Kinzer, 471–89. The Hague: Mouton Publishers.

Marston, S. A. 1988. Neighborhood and politics: Irish ethnicity in nineteenth century Lowell, Massachusetts. *Annals of the Association of American Geographers* 78(3): 414–32.

Martin, G. J., and P. James. 1993. *All possible worlds: A history of geographical ideas.* 3rd ed. New York: Wiley.

Martin, P. 2002. Germany: Managing migration in the 21st century. Working Paper CIIP-1.

Martiniello, M. 2009. Immigrants and their offspring in Europe as political subjects. In *Bringing outsiders in: Transatlantic perspectives on immigrant political incorporation*, edited by J. Hochschild and J. Mollenkopf, 33–47. Ithaca, NY: Cornell University Press.

Massey, D. 1991. A global sense of place. *Marxism Today* 38: 24–29.

Massey, D., and N. Denton. 1988. The dimensions of residential segregation. *Social Forces* 67(2): 281–315.

———. 1993. *American apartheid: Segregation and the making of the underclass.* Cambridge, MA: Harvard University Press.

Massey, D. S., and M. J. Fischer. 2000. How segregation concentrates poverty. *Ethnic and Racial Studies* 23(4): 670–91.

Massey, D. S., A. B. Gross, and M. L. Eggers. 1991. Segregation, the concentration of poverty, and the life chances of individuals. *Social Science Research* 20(4): 397–420.

Mazumdar, S., S. Mazumdar, F. Docuyanan, and C. McLaughlin. 2000. Creating a sense of place: The Vietnamese-Americans and Little Saigon. *Journal of Environmental Psychology* 20(4): 319–33.

McCloud, D. G. 1995. *Southeast Asia: Tradition and modernity in the contemporary world.* Boulder, CO: Westview Press.

McConnell, D. L., and C. E. Hurst. 2006. No "Rip Van Winkles" here: Amish education since *Wisconsin v. Yoder. Anthropology and Education Quarterly* 37(3): 236–54.

McGee, T. G. 1967. *The Southeast Asian city: A social geography of the primate cities of Southeast Asia.* New York: Praeger.

McGruder, K. 2015. *Race and real estate: Conflict and cooperation in Harlem, 1890–1920.* New York: Columbia University Press.

McKee, J. O. 2000. *Ethnicity in contemporary America: A geographical appraisal.* Lanham, MD: Rowman & Littlefield.

McPeake, J. 2000. Owner occupier residential search in a divided city. In *Ethnicity and housing: Accommodation differences,* edited by F. Boal, 198–216. Brookfield, VT: Ashgate.

Meer, N., P. Mouritsen, D. Faas, and N. de Witte. 2015. Examining "postmulticultural" and civic turns in the Netherlands, Britain, Germany, and Denmark. *American Behavioral Scientist* 59(6): 702–26.

Meinig, D. W. 1964. The Mormon culture region: Strategies and patterns in the geography of the American West, 1847–1964. *Annals of the Association of American Geographers* 55(2): 191–220.

———. 1986. *The shaping of America. Vol. 1: Atlantic America, 1492–1800.* New Haven, CT: Yale University Press.

Menkhoff, T. 2009. Chinese philanthropy in Southeast Asia: Between continuity and change. *Social Space* 2(1): 62–67.

Menocal, M. R. 2002. *"The ornament of the world": How Muslims, Jews and Christians created a culture of tolerance in medieval Spain.* Boston: Little, Brown.

Mickelson, R. A. 2001. Subverting Swann: First- and second-generation segregation in the Charlotte-Mecklenburg schools. *American Educational Research Journal* 38(2): 215–52.

Min, P. G. 1993. Korean immigrants in Los Angeles. In *Immigration and entrepreneurship: Culture, capital, and ethnic networks,* edited by I. Light and P. Bhachu, 185–204. New Brunswick, NJ: Transaction Publishers.

Missiou, M. 2010. The enduring battle of good vs. evil in comic books. In *creating monstrosity, discovering humanity,* edited by E. Nelson, 281–90. Oxford: Interdisciplinary Press.

Mitchell, K. 1997. Different diasporas and the hype of hybridity. *Environment and Planning D: Society and Space* 15(5): 533–53.

Monkkonen, P. 2010. *Measuring residential segregation in urban Mexico: Levels and patterns.* Institute of Urban & Regional Development.

Morning, A. 2008. Ethnic classification in global perspective: A cross-national survey of the 2000 census round. *Population Research and Policy Review* 27(2): 239–72.

———. 2012. Multiraciality and census classification in global perspective. In *International perspectives on racial and ethnic mixedness and mixing,* edited by R. Edwards, S. Ali, C. Caballero, and M. Song, 10–22. New York: Routledge.

Morrill, R. L. 1965. The negro ghetto: Problems and alternatives. *Geographical Review* 55(3): 339–61.

———. 1991. On the measure of geographic segregation. *Geography Research Forum* 11(1): 25–36.

Mueller, C. 2006. Integrating Turkish communities: A German dilemma. *Population Research and Policy Review* 25(5/6): 419–41.

Mugaddam, A. R. H. 2006. Language maintenance and shift in Sudan: The case of migrant ethnic groups in Khartoum. *International Journal of the Sociology of Language* 181: 123–36.

Murdie, R. A., and L. E. Borgegard. 1998. Immigration, spatial segregation and housing segmentation of immigrants in metropolitan Stockholm, 1960–95. *Urban Studies* 35(10): 1869–88.

Murdie, R. A., and C. Teixeira. 2000. The city as social space. *Canadian cities in transition: The twenty-first century*, edited by T. Bunting and P. Filion, 198–223. Toronto: Oxford University Press.

Murphy, A. B. 2002. Brussels: division in unity or unity in division? *Political Geography* 21(5): 695–700.

Murphy-Shigematsu, S. 2000. Identities of multiethnic people in Japan. In *Japan and global migration: Foreign workers and the advent of a multicultural society*, edited by M. Douglass and G. Roberts, 196–216. Honolulu: University of Hawaii Press.

Musterd, S., and N. Smakman. 2000. Integration of Caribbean immigrants in a welfare state city: Surinamese and Antilleans in Amsterdam. *International Journal of Population Geography* 6(4): 303–20.

Myrdal, G. 1944. *An American dilemma, volume 1: The Negro problem and modern democracy*. New Brunswick, NJ: Transaction Publishers.

Nagar, R. 1997. Communal places and the politics of multiple identities: The case of Tanzanian Asians. *Ecumene-London* 4: 3–26.

Nagel, J. 1994. Constructing ethnicity: Creating and recreating ethnic identity and culture. *Social Problems* 41(1): 152–76.

Neary, I. 2009. Burakumin in contemporary Japan. In *Japan's minorities: The illusion of homogeneity*, edited by M. Weiner, 59–83. London: Routledge.

Negro Motorist Green Book. 1949. New York: Vicot H. Green & Co.

Nelson, R., L. Winling, R. Marciano, N. Connolly, et al. 2017. Mapping inequality. In *American Panorama*, edited by Robert K. Nelson and Edward L. Ayers, n.p. https://dsl.richmond.edu/panorama/redlining/#loc=11/41.9442/-87.5792&opacity=0.8&city=chicago-il.

Nightingale, C. H. 2012. *Segregation: A global history of divided cities*. Chicago: University of Chicago Press.

Nirenberg, D. 1996. *Communities of violence: Persecution of minorities in the Middle Ages*. Princeton, NJ: Princeton University Press.

Novak, M. 1972. *The rise of the unmeltable ethnics: Politics and culture in the seventies*. New York: Macmillan.

Numrich, P. D. 1997. Recent immigrant religions in a restructuring metropolis: New religious landscapes in Chicago. *Journal of Cultural Geography* 17(1): 55–76.

Oberle, A. 2006. Latino business landscapes and the Hispanic ethnic economy. In *Landscapes of the ethnic economy*, edited by D. Kaplan and W. Li, 149–63. Lanham, MD: Rowman & Littlefield.

Odoom, H. S. 2012. Ethnic markets in the American retail landscape: African markets in Columbus, Cleveland, Cincinnati, and Akron, Ohio. PhD diss., Kent State University.

Ogden, P. 1989. International migration in the nineteenth and twentieth centuries. In *Migrants in modern France*, edited by P. Ogden and P. White, 34–59. London: Unwin Hyman.

Olwig, K. F. 1993. Defining the national in the transnational: Cultural identity in the Afro-Caribbean diaspora. *Ethnos* 58(3/4): 361–76.

Omi, M. A. 2001. The changing meaning of race. In *America becoming: Racial trends and their consequences, volume 1*, edited by N. Smelser, W. J. Wilson, and F. Mitchell, 243–63. Washington, DC: National Academies Press.

Ongley, P., and D. Pearson. 1995. Post-1945 international migration: New Zealand, Australia and Canada compared. *International Migration Review* 29(3): 765–93.

Orfield, G., and E. Frankenberg. 2014. Increasingly segregated and unequal schools as courts reverse policy. *Educational Administration Quarterly* 50(5): 718–34.

Orfield, G., and C. Lee. 2005. *Why segregation matters: Poverty and educational inequality*. Cambridge, MA: Civil Rights Project, Harvard University.

Osofsky, G. 1971. *Harlem: The making of a ghetto: Negro New York, 1890–1930*. New York: HarperCollins College.

Owens, A. 2016. Inequality in children's contexts: Income segregation of households with and without children. *American Sociological Review* 81(3): 549–74.

Pan, L. 1994. *Sons of the Yellow Emperor: A history of the Chinese diaspora*. New York: Kodansha International.

Panggabean, S., and B. Smith. 2011. Explaining Anti-Chinese Riots in Late 20th Century Indonesia. *World Development* 39(2): 231–42.

Papadopoulos, A. G. 2012. Transnational immigration in rural Greece: Analysing the different mobilities of Albanian immigrants. In *Translocal ruralism: Mobility and connectivity in European rural spaces*, edited by C. Hedberg and R. do Carma, 163–83. Dordrecht: Springer Netherlands.

Papastergiadis, N. 2013. *The turbulence of migration: Globalization, deterritorialization and hybridity*. Hoboken, NJ: John Wiley and Sons.

Peach, C. 1983. Ethnic intermarriage as a reflection of ethnic residential mixing. *Journal of Biosocial Science* 15(S8): 189–205.

———. 1996. Good segregation, bad segregation. *Planning perspectives* 11(4): 379–98.

———. 2007. Sleepwalking into segregation? The British debate over segregation. Berlin, Germany: WZB, Social Science Research Center, Discussion Paper SP IV 2007-602. http://bibliothek.wz-berlin.de/pdf/2007/iv07-602.pdf.

Perry, M., L. Kong, and S. Yeoh. 1997. *Singapore: A developmental city state*. New York: Wiley.

Phillips, D. 2006. Parallel lives? Challenging discourses of British Muslim self-segregation. *Environment and Planning D* 24(1): 25–40.

———. 2008. The problem with segregation: Exploring the racialisation of space in northern Pennine towns. In *New geographies of race and racism*, edited by C. Dwyer and C. Bressey, 187–92. New York: Routledge.

Piana, G. 1927. Foreign groups in Rome during the first centuries of the Empire. *Harvard Theological Review* 20(4): 183–403.

Pineo, P. C. 1977. The social standing of ethnic and racial groupings. *Canadian Review of Sociology/Revue canadienne de sociologie* 14(2): 147–57.

Porter, J. 1965. *The vertical mosaic*. Toronto: University of Toronto Press.

Portes, A. 1998. Social capital: Its origins and applications in modern sociology. *Annual Review of Sociology* 24: 1–24.

———. 2003. Conclusion: Theoretical convergences and empirical evidence in the study of immigrant transnationalism. *International Migration Review* 37(3): 874–92.

Portes, A., and R. Rumbaut. 2001. *Legacies: The story of the immigrant second generation*. Berkeley: University of California Press.

Portes, A., and A. Stepick. 1993. *City on the edge: The transformation of Miami*. Berkeley: University of California Press.

Portes, A., and M. Zhou. 1992. Gaining the upper hand: Economic mobility among immigrant and domestic minorities. *Ethnic and Racial Studies* 15(4): 491–522.

———. 1993. The new second generation: Segmented assimilation and its variants. *Annals of the American Academy of Political and Social Science* 530(1): 74–96.

Pounds, N. J. 1990. *An historical geography of Europe*. Cambridge: Cambridge University Press.

Prins, B., and S. Saharso. 2010. From toleration to repression: The Dutch backlash against multiculturalism. In *The multiculturalist backlash: European discourses, policies and practices*, edited by S. Vertovec and S. Wessendorf, 92–110. London: Routledge.

Putnam, R. D. 2007. *E pluribus unum*: Diversity and community in the twenty-first century: The 2006 Johan Skytte Prize Lecture. *Scandinavian Political Studies* 30(2): 137–74.

Qadeer, M. 2014. Viewpoint: The multicultural city. *Canadian Journal of Urban Research* 23(1S): 116–26.

———. 2016. *Multicultural cities: Toronto, New York, and Los Angeles*. Toronto: University of Toronto Press.

Rapoport, M. 2011. Creating place, creating community: The intangible boundaries of the Jewish "Eruv." *Environment and Planning D* 29(5): 891–904.

Reardon, S. F., S. Matthews, D. O'Sullivan, B. Lee, G. Firebaugh, C. Farrell, and K. Bischoff. 2008. The geographic scale of metropolitan racial segregation. *Demography* 45(3): 489–514.

Richards, M. 1996. Constructing the nationalist state: Self-sufficiency and regeneration in the early Franco years. In *Nationalism and the nation in the Iberian peninsula*, edited by A. Smith and C. Mar-Molinero, 149–67. London: Bloomsbury.

Robine, J. 2011. *Les ghettos de la nation: Ségrégation, délinquance, identités, Islam*. Paris, Vendémiaire.

Robinson, V. 1984. Asians in Britain: A study in encapsulation and marginality. In *Geography and ethnic pluralism*, edited by C. Clarke, D. Ley, and C. Peach, 231–57. London: Unwin Hyman.

Roediger, D. R. 2005. *Working toward whiteness: How America's immigrants became white: The strange journey from Ellis Island to the suburbs*. New York: Basic Books.

Rose, H. 1969. The origin and pattern of development of urban black social areas. *Journal of Geography* 68(6): 326–32.

Rowland, R. H. 1986. Geographical patterns of the Jewish population in the pale of settlement of late nineteenth century Russia. *Jewish Social Studies* 48(3/4): 207–34.

Royce, A. P. 1982. *Ethnic identity: Strategies of diversity*. Bloomington: Indiana University Press.

Rydgren, J., and P. Ruth. 2013. Contextual explanations of radical right-wing support in Sweden: Socioeconomic marginalization, group threat, and the halo effect. *Ethnic and Racial Studies* 36(4): 711–28.

Safran, W. 1991. Diasporas in modern societies: Myths of homeland and return. *Diaspora: A Journal of Transnational Studies* 1(1): 83–99.

———. 2005. The Jewish diaspora in a comparative and theoretical perspective. *Israel Studies* 10(1): 36–60.

Said, E. 1978. *Orientalism*. New York: Vintage.

Sampson, R. J. 2012. *Great American city: Chicago and the enduring neighborhood effect*. Chicago: University of Chicago Press.

Sauvadet, T., 2004. Jeunes de la cité et contrôle du territoire: Le cas d'une cité de la banlieue parisienne [Youth of the city and territorial control: The case of a city in the Parisian suburbs]. *Hérodote* 113: 113–33.

Schelling, T. C. 1971. Dynamic models of segregation. *Journal of Mathematical Sociology* 1(2): 143–86.

Schlichting, K., P. Tuckel, and R. Maisel. 1998. Racial segregation and voter turnout in urban America. *American Politics Research* 26(2): 218–36.

Schnapper, D. 2003. French immigration and integration policy: A complex combination. In *The integration of immigrants in European societies: National differences and trends of convergence*, edited by F. Heckmann and D. Schnapper, 15–44. Berlin: Lucius & Lucius.

Schönwälder, K. 2010. Integration policy and pluralism in a self-conscious country of immigration. In *The multiculturalism backlash: European discourses, policies and practices*, edited by S. Vertovec and S. Wessendorf, 152–69. Abingdon, UK: Routledge.

Seiler, C. 2006. So that we as a race might have something authentic to travel by: African American automobility and cold-war liberalism. *American Quarterly* 58(4): 1091–1117.

Sen, A. 2006. Chili and liberty: The uses and abuses of multiculturalism. *The New Republic*, 27 February, 27.

Shaw, H. J., 2006. Food deserts: Towards the development of a classification. *Geografiska Annaler: Series B, Human Geography* 88(2): 231–47.

Sheffer, G. 1986. *Modern diasporas in international politics*. New York: St. Martin's.

Sheth, A. 2010. Little India, next exit: Ethnic destinations in the city. *Ethnography* 11(1): 69–88.

Shevky, E., and W. Bell. 1955. *Social area analysis: Theory, illustrative application, and computational procedures*. Stanford, CA: Stanford University Press.

Shevky, E., and M. Williams. 1949. *The social areas of Los Angeles: Analysis and typology*. Berkeley: University of California Press.

Shlay, A. B., and G. Rosen. 2010. Making place: The shifting green line and the development of "Greater" metropolitan Jerusalem. *City & Community* 9(4): 358–89.

Siddle, R. 2009. The Ainu. In *Japan's minorities: The illusion of homogeneity*, edited by M. Weiner, 21–39. London: Routledge.

Sim, D. 2016. Paris: Roma people evicted from Petite Ceinture camp along disused railway line in France. *International Business Times*, 3 February. http://www.ibtimes.co.uk/paris-roma-people-evicted-petite-ceinture-camp-along-disused-railway-line-france-1541657.

Simon, P. 2010. The mosaic pattern: Cohabitation between ethnic groups in Belleville, Paris. In *Selected studies in international migration and immigrant incorporation*, edited by N. Martiniello and J. Rath, 339–54. Amsterdam: Amsterdam University Press.

Simon, P., and V. Piché. 2012. Accounting for ethnic and racial diversity: The challenge of enumeration. *Ethnic and Racial Studies* 35(8): 1357–65.

Sit, V. F. S. 1995. *Beijing: The nature and planning of a Chinese capital city*. New York: Wiley.

———. 2010. *Chinese city and urbanism: Evolution and development*. Singapore: World Scientific Publishing.

Sjoberg, G. 1960. *The preindustrial city: Past and present*. New York: Free Press.

Skop, E. 2012. *The immigration and settlement of Asian Indians in Phoenix, Arizona, 1965–2011: Ethnic pride vs. racial discrimination in the suburbs*. Lewiston, NY: Edwin Mellen Press.

Smedley, A. 1997. Origins of "race." *Anthropology News* 38(8): 52.

Smiley, S. 2009. The city of three colors: Segregation in colonial Dar es Salaam, 1891–1961. *Historical Geography* 37: 178–96.

———. 2010. Expatriate everyday life in Dar es Salaam, Tanzania: Colonial origins and contemporary legacies. *Social & Cultural Geography* 11(4): 327–42.

Smith, A. D. 1986. *The ethnic origins of nations*. Oxford: Basil Blackwell.

———. 1991. *National identity*. Reno: University of Nevada Press.

Smith, J. M. 2006. Spatial and identity transformations of the Japanese American ethnic economy in globalizing Los Angeles. In *Landscapes of the ethnic economy*, edited by D. Kaplan and W. Li, 177–92. Lanham, MD: Rowman & Littlefield.

Stepan, N. 1982. *Idea of race in science: Great Britain, 1800–1960*. London: MacMillan Press.

Stone, J. 2003. Max Weber on race, ethnicity, and nationalism. In *Race and ethnicity, comparative and theoretical approaches*, edited by J. Stone and D. Rutledge, 28–42. Oxford: Blackwell.

Sumption, M. 2012. Visas for entrepreneurs: How countries are seeking out immigrant job creators. *Migration Information Source*, 13 June. Migration Policy Institute. www.migrationpolicy.org/article/visas-entrepreneurs-how-countries-are-seeking-out-immigrant-job-creators.

Taeuber, K. E., and A. F. Taeuber. 1969. *Negroes in cities: Residential segregation and neighborhood change*. Cambridge, MA: Atheneum.

Takenaka, A. 1999. Transnational community and its ethnic consequences: The return migration and the transformation of ethnicity of Japanese Peruvians. *American Behavioral Scientist* 42(9): 1459–74.

Tasan-Kok, T., R. van Kempen, M. Raco, and G. Bolt. 2013. *Towards hyper-diversified European cities: A critical literature review*. Utrecht: Utrecht University, Faculty of Geosciences.

Tatla, D. S. 2005. *The Sikh diaspora: The search for statehood*. New York: Routledge.

Taub, A. 2016. "White nationalism," explained. *New York Times*, 21 November. https://www.nytimes.com/2016/11/22/world/americas/white-nationalism-explained.html?_r=0.

Teixeira, C. 2006. Residential segregation and ethnic economies in a multicultural city: The Little Portugal of Toronto. In *Landscapes of the ethnic economy*, edited by D. Kaplan and W. Li, 49–65. Lanham, MD: Rowman & Littlefield.

———. 2007. Residential experiences and the culture of suburbanization: A case study of Portuguese homebuyers in Mississauga. *Housing Studies* 22(4): 495–521.

Teixeira, C., A. Kobayashi, and W. Li, eds. 2012. *Immigrant geographies of North American cities*. New York: Oxford University Press.

Teixeira, C., and R. A. Murdie. 1997. The role of ethnic real estate agents in the residential relocation process: A case study of Portuguese homebuyers in suburban Toronto. *Urban Geography* 18(6): 497–520.

Thomas, C. 1981. The Greek polis. In *The city-state in five cultures*, edited by C. Thomas and R. Griffeth, 109–42. Santa Barbara: ABC-CLIO.

Tillman, B. F., and C. F. Emmett. 1999. Spatial succession of sacred space in Chicago. *Journal of Cultural Geography* 18(2): 79–108.

Tölölyan, K. 1991. The nation-state and its others: In lieu of a preface. *Diaspora: A Journal of Transnational Studies* 1(1): 3–7.

———. 1996. Rethinking diaspora(s): Stateless power in the transnational moment. *Diaspora: A Journal of Transnational Studies* 5(1): 3–36.

———. 2000. Elites and institutions in the Armenian transnation. *Diaspora: A Journal of Transnational Studies* 9(1): 107–36.

Tönnies, F. 1957. *Community and society*. Mineola, NY: Courier Dover Publications.

Traub, J. 2016. The party that wants to make Poland great again. *New York Times Magazine*, 2 November. https://mobile.nytimes.com/2016/11/06/magazine/the-party-that-wants-to-make-poland-great-again.html.

Trenin, D. 2016. Revival of the Russian military: How Moscow reloaded. *Foreign Affairs* 95: 23.

Tsuda, T. G. 2006. When minorities migrate: The racialization of Japanese Brazilians in Brazil and Japan. In *Ethnic identity: Problems and prospects for the twenty-first century*, edited by L. Romanucci-Ross, G. de Vos, and T. Tsuda, 208–32. Lanham, MD: AltaMira Press.

———. 2008. Japanese-Brazilian ethnic return migration and the making of Japan's newest immigrant minority. In *Japan's minorities: The illusion of homogeneity*, edited by M. Weiner, 206–26. London: Routledge.

Tuan, Y. F. 1974. *Topophilia*. Englewood Cliffs, NJ: Prentice-Hall.

Turton, D. 2006. *Ethnic federalism: The Ethiopian experience in comparative perspective*. Athens: Ohio University Press.

Twaddle, M. 1990. East African Asians through a hundred years. In *South Asians overseas: Migration and ethnicity*, edited by C. Clarke, C. Peach, and S. Vertovec, 149–66. Cambridge: Cambridge University Press.

Uberoi, V. 2008. Do policies of multiculturalism change national identities? *Political Quarterly* 79(3): 404–17.

Uitermark, J., U. Rossi, and H. Van Houtum. 2005. Reinventing multiculturalism: Urban citizenship and the negotiation of ethnic diversity in Amsterdam. *International Journal of Urban and Regional Research* 29(3): 622–40.

United Nations Department of Economic and Social Affairs. 2014. *International Migration 2013: Migrants by Origin and Destination*. Population Facts no. 2013/3. https://esa.un.org/unmigration/documents/PF_South-South_migration_2013.pdf.

Vallejo, J. 2015. Leveling the playing field: Patterns of ethnic philanthropy among Los Angeles' middle-and upper-class Latino entrepreneurs. *Ethnic and Racial Studies* 38(1): 125–40.

Vance, J. E. 1990. *The continuing city: Urban morphology in Western civilization.* Baltimore: Johns Hopkins University Press.

Van Hear, N. 1998. *New diasporas: The mass exodus, dispersal, and regrouping of migrant communities.* London: UCL Press.

Van Kempen, R., and J. Van Weesep. 1998. Ethnic residential patterns in Dutch cities: Backgrounds, shifts and consequences. *Urban Studies* 35(10): 1813–33.

Vecoli, R. J. 1983. The formation of Chicago's "Little Italies." *Journal of American Ethnic History* 2(2): 5–20.

Vertovec, S. 1996. Multiculturalism, culturalism and public incorporation. *Ethnic and Racial Studies* 19(1): 49–69.

———. 1999. Conceiving and researching transnationalism. *Ethnic and Racial Studies* 22(2): 447–62.

———. 2004. Cheap calls: The social glue of migrant transnationalism. *Global Networks* 4(2): 219–24.

Veyne, P., ed. 1987. *A history of private life, vol. 1: From pagan Rome to Byzantium,* trans. Arthur Goldhammer. Cambridge, MA: Belknap Press.

Vidal de la Blache, P. 1913. Des caracteres distinctifs de la geographie. *Anales de geographie* 22: 289–99.

Vieten, U., and S. Poynting. 2016. Contemporary far-right racist populism in Europe. *Journal of Intercultural Studies* 37(6): 533–40.

Vincent, P., and B. Warf. 2002. Eruvim: Talmudic places in a postmodern world. *Transactions of the Institute of British Geographers* 27(1): 30–51.

Wacquant, L. 2011. A Janus-faced institution of ethnoracial closure: A sociological specification of the ghetto. In *The ghetto: Contemporary global issues and controversies,* edited by R. Hutchison and B. Haynes, 1–32. Boulder, CO: Westview Press.

Wade, R. C. 1964. *Slavery in the cities: The South, 1820–1860.* New York: Oxford University Press.

Walcott, S. forthcoming. Nested identities: Complexities of Chinese connections. In *Scaling identities: Nationalism and territory,* edited by G. Herb and D. Kaplan. Lanham, MD: Rowman & Littlefield.

Waldinger, R., and D. Fitzgerald. 2004. Transnationalism in question. *American Journal of Sociology* 109(5): 1177–95.

Walks, R. A., and L. Bourne. 2006. Ghettos in Canada's cities? Racial segregation, ethnic enclaves, and poverty concentration in Canadian urban areas. *Canadian Geographer/Le Géographe Canadien* 50(3): 273–97.

Wang, L. 1991. Roots and changing identity of the Chinese in the United States. *Daedalus* 120(2): 181–206.

Wang, Q. 2009. How does geography matter in the ethnic labor market segmentation process? A case study of Chinese immigrants in the San Francisco CMSA. *Annals of the Association of American Geographers* 100(1): 182–201.

Ward, D. 1971. *Cities and immigrants: A geography of change in nineteenth-century America.* New York: Oxford University Press.

Weber, Eugen. 1976. *Peasants into Frenchmen: The modernization of rural France, 1870–1914.* Palo Alto, CA: Stanford University Press.

Weber, R. E. 2000. Race-based districting: Does it help or hinder legislative representation? *Political Geography* 19(2): 213–47.

Weeks, J. R., A. Hill, A. Getis, and D. Stow. 2006. Ethnic residential patterns as predictors of intra-urban child mortality inequality in Accra, Ghana. *Urban Geography* 27(6): 526–48.

Weightman, B. A. 2002. *Dragons and tigers: A geography of South, East, and Southeast Asia.* New York: Wiley.

Weiner, M., and D. Chapman. 2009. Zainichi Koreans in history and memory. In *Japan's minorities: The illusion of homogeneity,* edited by M. Weiner, 1–20. London: Routledge.

Wen, M., D. Lauderdale, and N. Kandula. 2009. Ethnic neighborhoods in multi-ethnic America, 1990–2000: Resurgent ethnicity in the ethnoburbs? *Social Forces* 88(1): 425–60.

Werbner, P. 2010. Complex diasporas. In *Diasporas: Concepts, intersections, identities,* edited by K. Knott and S. McLoughlin, 74–78. London: Zed Books.

Western, J. 1981. *Outcast Cape Town.* Berkeley: University of California Press.

White, M. J. 1986. Segregation and diversity measures in population distributions. *Population Index* 52(2): 198–221.

White, M. J., A. H. Kim, and J. E. Glick. 2005. Mapping social distance: Ethnic residential segregation in a multiethnic metro. *Sociological Methods & Research* 34(2): 173–203.

Wiese, A. 2004. *Places of their own: African American suburbanization in the twentieth century.* Chicago: University of Chicago Press.

Wilson, K. L., and W. A. Martin. 1982. Ethnic enclaves: A comparison of the Cuban and black economies in Miami. *American Journal of Sociology* 88(1): 135–60.

Wilson, W. J. 1987. *The truly disadvantaged: The inner city, the underclass, and public policy.* Chicago: University of Chicago Press.

———. 1997. *When work disappears: The world of the new urban poor.* New York: Vintage.

Wirth, L. 1927. The ghetto. *American Journal of Sociology* 33(1): 57–71.

Wong, D. W. S. 2003. Implementing spatial segregation measures in GIS. *Computers, Environment and Urban Systems* 27(1): 53–71.

Wood, J. 1997. Vietnamese American place making in northern Virginia. *Geographical Review* 87(1): 58–72.

Woodhouse, K. D. 2005. Latvian placemaking in three North American cities. Master's thesis, Kent State University.

Wright, R., and M. Ellis. 2000. Race, region and the territorial politics of immigration in the U.S. *International Journal of Population Geography* 6(3): 197–211.

Yamanaka, K. 1996. Return migration of Japanese-Brazilians to Japan: The Nikkei-jin as ethnic minority and political construct. *Diaspora: A Journal of Transnational Studies* 5(1): 65–97.

Yang, L., and G. Wall. 2008. Ethnic tourism and entrepreneurship: Xishuangbanna, Yunnan, China. *Tourism Geographies* 10(4): 522–44.

Yazdiha, H. 2010. Conceptualizing hybridity: Deconstructing boundaries through the hybrid. *Formations* 1(1): 31–38.

Zapata-Barrero, R., and R. Gropas. 2012. Active immigrants in multicultural contexts: Democratic challenges in Europe. In *European multiculturalisms: Cultural, religious and ethnic challenges,* edited by A. Triandafyllidou, T. Modood, and N. Meer, 167–91. Edinburgh: Edinburgh University Press.

Zeitz, J. 2015. When America hated Catholics. *Politico Magazine*, 23 September. http://www.politico.com/magazine/story/2015/09/when-america-hated -catholics-213177.

Zelinsky, W. 1990. Seeing beyond the dominant culture (vision, culture and land- scape). *Places* 7(1): 32–35.

———. 1992. *The cultural geography of the United States*. New York: Pearson College Division.

———. 2001. *The enigma of ethnicity: Another American dilemma*. Iowa City: Univer- sity of Iowa Press,

Zelinsky, W., and B. A. Lee. 1998. Heterolocalism: An alternative model of the sociospatial behaviour of immigrant ethnic communities. *International Journal of Population Geography* 4(4): 281–98.

Zhou, M. (1992) 2010. *Chinatown: The socioeconomic potential of an urban enclave*. Philadelphia: Temple University Press.

Index

Note: Page references for figures and the table are italicized.

About the Author

David Kaplan is a professor of geography at Kent State University, where he has taught since 1995. He has written some 60 peer-reviewed articles and chapters, and is co-author or co-editor of *Segregation in Cities, Nested Identities, Boundaries and Place, Human Geography, Urban Geography, Landscapes of the Ethnic Economy, Perthes World Atlas,* and the four-volume *Nations and Nationalism: A Global Historical Overview.* Dr. Kaplan's research interests include nationalism, borderlands, ethnic and racial segregation, urban and regional development, housing finance, and sustainable transportation. He has directly supervised over 40 graduate students, and teaches courses on many different aspects of human geography. He edits the *Geographical Review* and *National Identities.*